END OF AN ERA

END OF
AN ERA

*HOW CHINA'S AUTHORITARIAN
REVIVAL IS UNDERMINING
ITS RISE*

CARL MINZNER

OXFORD
UNIVERSITY PRESS

OXFORD

UNIVERSITY PRESS

Oxford University Press is a department of the University of Oxford. It furthers the University's objective of excellence in research, scholarship, and education by publishing worldwide. Oxford is a registered trade mark of Oxford University Press in the UK and certain other countries.

Published in the United States of America by Oxford University Press
198 Madison Avenue, New York, NY 10016, United States of America.

© Oxford University Press 2018

First issued as an Oxford University Press paperback, 2020

CIP data is on file at the Library of Congress
ISBN 978-0-19-067208-9 (hardcover); ISBN 978-0-19-005634-6 (paperback)

To my mother, Pamela Burgy Minzner, who made it all possible.

TABLE OF CONTENTS

ACKNOWLEDGMENTS

Writing a book takes a long time. In my case, it has extended well over a decade. Many of the general ideas for this manuscript originated while serving as senior counsel to the Congressional-Executive Commission on China from 2003 to 2006, monitoring and writing on a range of Chinese rule-of-law and human rights developments along with an outstanding team of coworkers and research assistants (many of whom have gone on to fascinating China-related careers of their own). Others were developed between 2006 and 2007, as a fellow at the Council on Foreign Relations. But as so happens to academics facing the tenure process, this project lay inchoate for a number of years as I began my teaching career and found myself confronting incentives for producing much more narrowly specialized academic articles.

I owe a deep debt of gratitude to the National Committee on United States–China Relations for providing me with a much-needed morale boost to restart this work, through including me in their Public Intellectuals Program from 2011 to 2013. Aimed at encouraging mid-career academics to communicate with the general public, the program played a crucial role in prompting me to try to write for a broader audience. It also served an invaluable role of helping to break down the artificial disciplinary barriers that divide China scholars, introducing me to a much wider range of experts, ranging from Taylor Fravel (foreign policy), Victor Shih (politics and finance), and Karrie Kossel (politics and religion). Many valuable conversations were had around baijiu-soaked dinners (and lunches) throughout coal-mining districts of Guizhou along with Jay Carter, Michael Chang, Martin Dimitrov, Yinan He, Joanna Lewis, Anthony Spires, Elanah Uretsky, and the National Committee's indefatigable Jan Berris (master at the art of discreetly disposing of alcohol in nearby potted plants). Such scholars (and others like them) are a wonderful exception to the increasingly narrow focus of much academic work on China today as mentioned in the preface.

This book draws on nearly two decades of conversations with a range of Chinese citizens and activists outside the Party-state, officials inside it, and academics with a foot in both worlds. It is they—not outsiders—who will shape the direction that their country will take. More than anyone, they are deeply aware of the dangerous shifts that are beginning to take place within China. They see how the system is beginning to slide. In part, this work represents an effort to synthesize and reflect back their views as to what is happening. But precisely because I am no longer certain that it is safe, I have generally avoided listing their names. Over the past fifteen years, an increasingly repressive atmosphere has swept through one field after another—state organs, the bar, media, civil society. Institutions of higher education, Chinese and foreign alike, are now being targeted as well. As China's reform era ends, many will come under increasing pressure—both from Beijing's security forces and from rabid nationalists trafficking in anti-foreign sentiment.

This work could not have been completed without the outstanding aid of a team of research assistants—Mathias Rabinovitch, Jennifer Whitman, Jason Zhang, and Laura Chao—who helped cite-check every single footnote. Alissa Black-Dorward and Gail McDonald of Fordham's law school library provided excellent assistance in tracking down sources and helping to obtain permissions for charts and photos. Jon Berkeley, Mary Gallagher, Aaron Halegua, Brian O'Hagan, and David Parkins graciously provided permission to use crucial images and charts. Thanks are also due to the two designers who worked so hard on encapsulating the visceral sense of this manuscript in the cover art, both to Robert Yasharian for his work on initial drafts, and to Brian Moore for generating the final product. Fordham Law School and Fordham University provided essential financial support, allowing me to work on this project both over the summers and during a sabbatical.

I also owe special thanks to those people who helped organize events at which early-stage versions of different chapters were presented—including Jay Carter (St. Joseph's University), Debbie Denno (Fordham Law School), Ira Belkin and Jerome Cohen (NYU Law School), Mark Frazier (New School), Benjamin Liebman (Columbia Law School), Margaret Lewis (Seton Hall Law School), Victor Shih (University of San Diego/Association of Asian Studies panel), William Woolridge and Robbie Barnett (Modern China Seminar at Columbia University), Benjamin van Roij and Jeffrey Wasserstrom (University of California at Irvine), and Ezra Vogel (Harvard)—and all the commentators at those events who provided suggestions and comments. Editors and staff at the *Journal of Democracy* provided excellent assistance in editing and publishing two earlier articles that comprise key sections of Chapters 1 and 5, while the editors and staff of the China Quarterly did the same for a co-authored article I wrote with Wang Yuhua and that has been incorporated into Chapter 3. Similar thanks are owed to the editors and staff at the *American Journal of Comparative Law, Asia Policy, East Asian Forum at Australian National University, Fordham International Law Journal, Jamestown Foundation's China Brief, New York Times/International Herald Tribune, Los Angeles Times, University of Pennsylvania Journal of International Law,* and the *Stanford Journal of International Law,* all of whom helped edit and publish prior articles of mine that in some form fed into various chapters in the manuscript. Paul Bostick, Sam Crane, Keith Hand, Loren Frank, Richard Minzner, Marissa Molé, Ana Nathe, Kevin Slaten, Carsten Vala, Alex Wang, Madeline Zelin, and two anonymous reviewers also read assorted chapters and provided valuable suggestions with regard to both content and readability. I am also deeply appreciative to a much broader range of experts and laypersons for graciously sharing their insights on developments in China and elsewhere over the years, but whom space prevents from thanking individually.

I would also like to express particular gratitude to Peter Bernstein and Lily Oei for their help in assisting me to navigate the process of going about thinking through how to publish my first book, and to

Cheryl Merritt and the copyediting and artwork teams at Newgen for their work on the manuscript. Naturally, this entire project would have been impossible without the efforts of many people at Oxford University Press (OUP), including Leslie Johnson (editing), Jonathan Kroberger and Jenny Lee (publicity) and Kim Craven (marketing), and particularly David McBride, Claire Sibley, and Kathleen Weaver, who capably guided this entire project to fruition.

Last, I would like to thank my family for their support through the long years of researching and writing.

CHINA — Administrative Divisions

Source: Central Intelligence Agency, *The World Factbook* (2011)

PREFACE

———◆———

Hopes ran high in early-twentieth-century China. A new world was dawning. The fall of the Qing dynasty in 1912 marked an abrupt break with two millennia of autocratic imperial rule. Modern industry and commerce were sweeping inland from the coast, reworking the economic sinews of the country in their wake. That same year, newspapers boasted of the opening of new high-speed trains linking Beijing to the booming commercial center of Shanghai, reducing transit time from an interminable five days to the then breathtakingly rapid time of a mere forty hours.[1]

Intellectuals drank deeply of these changes. They dreamed of reviving a nation laid low by decades of imperial torpor and foreign exploitation. Law was central to their goals. Some traveled overseas to study at schools in Japan or the West. Others threw themselves into translating foreign statutes. Foreigners, too, were drawn into the whirlpool of reform efforts. From 1913 to 1914, Frank Goodnow, a prominent American administrative law expert (and first head of the American Political Science Association), served as legal adviser to President Yuan Shikai, assisting in drafting the first constitution for the new Chinese republic. Such efforts expanded in the 1920s. Newly established law schools trained thousands of judges and legal personnel in new codes adopted by Nationalist authorities. Learned scholars penned vibrant essays on the need to adopt federalism to resolve pressing governance problems facing China.[2]

But this idealism soon foundered. As Yuan steadily became more dictatorial, Goodnow lost faith in his mission. And after Yuan's abortive 1915 effort to proclaim himself emperor, one of America's earliest experiments with Chinese legal reform rapidly faded into a forgotten historical footnote. The 1920s and 1930s saw trained Nationalist legal personnel and institutions blown to the four winds as internal tensions devolved into civil war. Dense scholarly works on Chinese law gradually yellowed into unread tomes gathering dust on musty, half-forgotten library shelves.

I didn't want to write such a book.

Many will find this work surprising. After all, I am a law professor. My prior work has focused on China's legal institutions. And yet, this book is not—primarily at least—about law. Why?

Times have changed. There was an era when one could believe that law would play a crucial role in China's evolution. In the 1980s, China's leaders embraced legal reform as a key part of their efforts to transition away from the political chaos of the Maoist era toward a more institutionalized model of governance. This was the birth of the reform era—an era of political stability, rapid economic growth, and relative ideological openness to the outside world. Even after China's rulers eliminated fundamental political reform as an option following their brutal suppression of student protestors in 1989, many in China still saw legal reform as offering hope for gradual transformation. Sure, one-Party rule would continue. But the exercise of power could be rationalized and made orderly. Social conflict could be steered into alternative channels. Steadily, the harsh edges of the political system might be sanded smooth.

Unfortunately, these doors are being shut. Law is becoming less and less relevant to China's future.

This is not without precedent. Precisely this problem—how to build stable institutions of governance for a new era—has regularly frustrated Chinese leaders over the past century and a half. Last-ditch efforts by late-nineteenth-century imperial Qing officials at legal and institutional reform were stymied first by a conservative counter-reaction, then rapidly overtaken by events as decaying dynastic power crumbled in the face of spreading unrest. Tentative efforts during the 1950s to build stable Party and state mechanisms of governance to run the newly established People's Republic of China collapsed in the face of Mao Zedong's distrust of institutionalized constraints on the exercise of power, his fear of political rivals, and his preference for ruling through populist street movements and black-box political machinations.

Naturally, this has consequences. When prospects for gradual reform are stifled, pressure for revolutionary change rises. The early twentieth century saw moderate voices of the late Qing dynasty, such as constitutional monarchist Liang Qichao, give way to strident nationalists seeking to overthrow the regime. The 1960s witnessed hardened Communist cadres intent on maintaining top-down control through formal Party and legal institutions outmaneuvered by political opponents and student radicals willing to raze these structures to the ground to promote their own rise to power. State and society alike began to slide uncontrollably. Remote risks once barely visible on the horizon rapidly loomed into view as inescapable endgames.

Now this cycle is repeating itself yet again. Increasingly, it appears likely that China will see a hard landing of its political system.

This book has several aims. First, it seeks to explain what is taking place in China.

Many are in denial. They cling to a linear, short-term, ahistorical view of China. For them, China changed fundamentally with the birth of the reform era in 1978. China has since been on a one-way track toward a better future. Sure, they admit that there are problems. Beijing's pollution is bad. Xi Jinping is more repressive than his immediate predecessors. Economic troubles are more serious. But their faith remains unshaken. China is experiencing but transitory turbulence accompanying its takeoff, its inexorable rise to "shake the world"—or whatever the current catchphrase of the day might be. After all, Beijing's leaders are technocratic supermen, with a track record of steering China through decades of growth that leave rulers of other nations gasping with envy. And whatever is happening today, it clearly doesn't—yet—compare to the bad old days of the Maoist era. So why worry? If anything, they argue, shouldn't the concern be reversed—that China is *too* successful? That it has founded a model authoritarian rule that could endure—or even be exported abroad? That, as President Donald Trump has phrased it, "China [is] beating us like a punching bag daily?"[3]

This view still holds wide sway among many American elites and the public at large. As a result, one crucial goal of this book is to demonstrate that we really are witnessing something new: the end of China's reform era. In the late 1970s and early 1980s, China transitioned out of the Maoist era (1949–1976). Decades of elite political instability, stagnant economic growth, and radical ideological fervor were left behind. In their place: relatively stable and more institutionalized Party rule, supercharged economic growth, and an openness to the outside world—the trifecta of factors that characterized the decades-long reform era in China that followed.

These are now ending. In part, China is simply following the track of other East Asian countries. China's economy is exiting its own period of rapid growth. Its population is also rapidly aging. But there is a deeper reason underlying the end of China's reform era. Precisely because of their unyielding commitment to one-Party rule, China's leaders have steadily undermined all their own tentative efforts at political institutionalization. In the absence of this—the very glue that bound the reform-era consensus together—things are beginning to give way. Historical processes and political practices thought long buried are thrusting themselves, zombie-like, to the surface once again. China's one-Party system is beginning to cannibalize itself.

Second, this book seeks to explain the complex interplay between state and society that has developed in China during the reform era.

Why is this important? America has a serious genetic disorder when it comes to understanding societies undergoing political transitions. We tend to look at them as *tabulae rasae*—blank slates capable of being inscribed at will. Locate the appropriate George Washington–like figure. Refer to a few basic principles of representative government. Presto—instant democracy. American obsession with our own creation myth is one major reason for this. We look at our own past and see a handful of inspired Founders coming together to create a sacred constitutional text. Blindly overlooked: the five hundred years of yet earlier British state-society relations responsible for evolving the framework upon which the entire project is based. Americans regularly misunderstand political transitions in the rest of the world as a result.

Authoritarian regimes undergoing turbulent change—whether the Soviet Union (1991), Iraq (2003), or Egypt (2011)—are viewed initially through rose-colored glasses. Television anchors rush to file breathless reports in front of cheering crowds—the seeds of democracy are flowering yet again! When liberal dreams run aground, against renewed authoritarian rule (as in Russia) or spreading ethnic and religious turmoil (as in Syria), Americans are left saddened and confused. It wasn't supposed to work out this way.

But of course, in all these countries—just as in the United States itself—what emerges in the aftermath of political transitions is deeply marked by the social forces that developed in the decades *prior* to the dramatic front-page headlines. In Egypt, for example, both the role of the Muslim Brotherhood in replacing the Mubarak regime, as well as that of the army in restoring military rule, were but the logical outgrowth of a specific state-society relationship stretching well back into the twentieth century.

China is no different. The three decades of the reform era—from 1978 to the early 2000s—have deeply marked state and society alike. They have set into motion a series of political, economic, and ideological trends that are beginning to spin faster and faster as China's reform era unwinds. This book is an effort to set the stage, so that outsiders can fully appreciate the underlying dynamics for what is about to take place.

Third, this book attempts to think through various possibilities as to what might happen in China, and how outsiders might respond. It tries to avoid sweeping assertions or definitive timetables. But it raises various hypothetical scenarios, as a way to focus attention on the underlying dynamics that might unfold.

A few disclaimers are in order. Some will misunderstand this work. When I discuss legal and governance problems facing the United States with my American students, no one thinks I have an ulterior political motive. No one labels me as pro- or anti-American. This isn't true when one writes on China. Many in the United States insist on looking through any discussion of China for confirmation of their own biases as to the superiority of the American political system. Others have exactly the opposite reaction. They feel any discussion of negative trends abroad requires an immediate reply in the form of "But what about the problems here in America of [wealth gap/excessive individ-ualism/fill-in-the-issue-of-the-day]?" In China, the situation is flipped around. State media has a regrettable tendency to indiscriminately label any and all positive praise of the Party-state as reflecting the views of a true "friend of China," while discussions of its failings warrant condem-nation as groundless "anti-China" sentiment.

Of course, this makes zero sense. No one labels weather forecasters as pro- or anti-hurricane. Rather, they are expected to try to discern important trends and patterns. If I were an American political expert, I would undoubtedly analyze how decades of rising income inequal-ity, worsening social polarization, and spreading political dysfunction in America are contributing to the erosion of U.S. liberal democratic institutions. Not because I am pro- or anti-American, but because those are some of the most pressing issues facing us today. But I am a China specialist. So this is a book about China. And if I talk about social and political problems facing China, it certainly isn't because I want to see bad things happen to it. I have a lot of friends there. I very much hope they can avoid the storm clouds I see gathering. But I do no one any favors in drawing my blinds and pretending all is fine.

This work also seeks to respond to a deep problem in American academia—one particularly facing those of us who work on China.

Few outsiders realize how narrowly focused we have become. Back in the mid-twentieth century, American scholars looked at big ques-tions related to China. Scholars such as Jonathan Spence examined the broad sweep of dynasties. Figures like John Fairbank sought to interpret post-1949 political trends in the People's Republic of China in light of Nationalist or imperial history. Such efforts have fallen out of favor. In part, this reflects a trend in U.S. academia toward ever-greater discipli-nary specialization. But China's reform era has also seen an explosion of information sources permitting us to delve into much more detail on specific topics. Historians can burrow into once-unavailable archives to examine how, for example, the porcelain industry evolved in specific counties during the late Qing dynasty. Political scientists can run large-N data regressions to compare disability benefits programs in China with those in Brazil or Italy. This has advantages. It brings a degree of precision to our understanding of China. But it also has serious costs. As a leading expert on Chinese politics has argued:

> [A] danger exists that the field of Chinese politics is being hollowed out because . . . there are many islands of highly specialized research with few bridges between them. . . . At a time when China's economic growth and prominence in world affairs have generated remarkable interest inside and outside the academy, few scholars are willing to take a stab at . . . addressing . . . large questions.[4]

This concern is far from simply academic. Crucial issues in China are coming to a boil. Meanwhile, the very experts who are best equipped to try to explain these to their fellow citizens are locked in what one of America's top international relations scholars has termed "a cult of irrelevance . . . devot[ing] vast amounts of time to researching topics that are of interest only to a handful of their fellow scholars."[5] As China experiences some of the most wrenching transitions in history, do we really want to walk off the field entirely? Leave public opinion to be informed solely by pundits willing to reduce 1.4 billion people to single-sentence sound bites? To politicians mouthing inane assertions?

This leads into one further comment regarding the writing style, endnotes, and target audience for this work. (This is directed toward my academic colleagues. If my nonspecialist readers sense a degree of defensiveness in the following, you're dead-on). My prior writing consists of dense academic tomes heavily footnoted to things such as Gansu provincial regulations on citizen petitioning—precisely the kinds of topics of interest only to a handful of other specialists following the narrow details of Chinese judicial reform policies or cadre evaluation systems. This book is different. It is intended to be accessible to the public at large. So it is written in a different style—because the developments discussed here will extend far beyond the world of China specialists.

Last, this book in no way pretends to be the final word. The best I can do is to try to synthesize my own (few) areas of knowledge with the research of others to describe what I see taking place in China today. One of my earnest hopes in writing this book is that experts

in economics, history, politics, and religion far more qualified than
I—both inside and outside China—will take it as an opportunity to
respond and offer their own criticism and commentary.[6] If I succeed in
that, then I will have accomplished what the classical Chinese expression refers to as *pao zhuan yin yu*—placing out a brick, and receiving
jade (of high value) in return.

Carl Minzner
New York, July 3, 2017

END OF AN ERA

Introduction

RISING AMID THE JAGGED cliffs of the Yangtze River, the Three Gorges Dam is a visible embodiment of China's rise. Enormous turbines hum as they generate electricity to power the nation's rapid growth. Massive dam walls hold back the waters of the world's third longest river, reducing the risk of seasonal flooding to downstream cities such as Shanghai.

As with so much else in China today, statistics astound. Completed in 2009, the total electrical capacity is eleven times that of the Hoover Dam. It could power all of Pakistan.[1] Filling the reservoir behind the dam created an enormous 400 mile–long man-made lake snaking its way back toward the steamy Sichuan highlands. The two-decade-long construction process required one of the most sweeping resettlement operations in human history outside of wartime. As ancient cobble-stoned villages slowly disappeared beneath the surging floodwaters, some 1.4 million rural residents were uprooted and evacuated to new townships built from scratch.

Upstream lies the neon-lit metropolis of Chongqing, the vibrant economic core of southwestern China. There, the newly constructed Three Gorges museum situates the dam's construction in a national narrative detailing China's rise. Expansive first-floor exhibits proudly remind well-heeled tour groups how generations of twentieth-century Chinese rulers—Sun Yat-Sen, Chiang Kai-shek, and Mao Zedong himself—dreamed of taming the Yangtze. Now, China's current leadership has realized that ambition.

Yet earlier historical allegories are invoked as well. For thousands of years, successive Chinese dynasties sank vast quantities of peasant labor and imperial treasure into maintaining the impressively thick dams, levees, and dikes that shore up the banks of the Yellow River—China's other major river—and protect the surrounding farmland. Success in controlling the rivers brought bountiful harvests, satisfied citizens, and overflowing tax coffers. Unsurprisingly, Chinese legends of national origin feature semi-mythic figures such as Yu the Great, famed for taming the rivers crossing the Chinese heartland and enabling the expansion of agriculture. The message is clear. If millennia of emperors derived legitimacy from success in mastering the rivers of northern China, the Communist Party has replicated (if not surpassed) their deeds in the south.

Water and rivers. Dams and irrigation. These are not merely engineering questions. They are metaphors for Chinese governance and society at large. Chinese philosophers have frequently invoked the concept of water to represent the people, their desires, and their demands. Confucius himself cautioned that "the ruler is the boat, the people the water. The water can support the boat, it can also sink it. The ruler should consider this, and realize the risks."[2]

Generations of Chinese rulers have heeded these words. They lavished resources on maintaining the physical dams and levees holding back the rushing waters of the Yellow River. And they developed highly evolved institutions of governance to similarly channel, check, and control the turbulent eddies of Chinese society. Bureaucratic rule allows central leaders to effectively steer a continent-wide empire to an extent unimagined elsewhere in the world. State-owned monopolies draw emerging business elites into a tight embrace. Authoritarian censorship and ideological controls limit the spread of alternative voices. Imperial China may have given birth to these practices. But they have been perfected under China's post-1949 "red dynasty."

However, these efforts have latent weaknesses. Take the physical rivers first. The Yellow River is heavily laden with silt. Plunge your hands in the water, and you can feel the fine-grained yellow-brown soil of the northeast Asian plains flow across your palms. Regular silt deposits raise the riverbed year after year. Generations of villagers and emperors alike steadily increased the height of the surrounding levees to prevent the river from flooding over its banks. Over hundreds of years, this tug-of-war between man and nature has gradually raised the level of the river far above that of the surrounding plains. Visitors from New Orleans find the results visually similar, if yet more striking, to their hometown vistas of the Mississippi River. In downstream reaches, one can experience the unusual sight of standing at ground level and looking *up* at the Yellow River stately flowing dozens of feet above your head.

Naturally, this is not stable. Natural disasters can break dams and levees. Corrupt officials may divert funds used to maintain them. Catastrophic floods result. In both 1887 and 1931, a combination of these factors led to two of the largest disasters in human history. Billions of tons of pent-up water rapidly eroded the man-made barriers, exploding across eastern China in violent torrents that carved new paths to the sea. Estimated death tolls: 2 and 4 million, respectively. Human culpability can be even more direct. In 1938, retreating Nationalist Chinese troops deliberately breached the Yellow River dikes to slow advancing Japanese forces, killing hundreds of thousands of their own citizens in the process.

Nor are such concerns merely historical. After decades spent vaunting the technical prowess behind the Three Gorges Dam project, the Chinese State Council obliquely acknowledged in 2011 that "urgent problems must be resolved regarding . . . ecological protection and geological disaster prevention."[3] Chinese scientists have concluded that since authorities began filling the reservoir in 2003, the massive increase in water pressure on the earth's crust has generated a dramatic upsurge in local earthquake and landslide activity. No consensus yet exists as to the risk this poses to the dam itself. But in the worst-case scenario of a catastrophic structural failure, the entire population of the Yangtze floodplain—some 75 million in total—would be in peril.

Parallel concerns exist with regard to the Chinese state. As with the levees along the Yellow River, it looks impressive from the outside. But the apparently solid construction of China's Party-state masks internal weakness. Official controls are themselves undermining the stability of the system, exacerbating sharp socioeconomic divides, weakening state governance, fueling social unrest, and intensifying ideological polarization.

We have not been accustomed to thinking in these terms. Decades of rapid economic expansion and firm state control during China's post-1978 reform era created comfortable narratives that outsiders could fall back on to "explain" China. Corporate investors could reel off stories of meritocratic Party rule and expanding opportunities for all Chinese citizens. Human rights organizations could inveigh against the Party's iron hand and extol liberal activists who spoke the language of rights and democracy. But these simple paradigms overlook a deeper interplay between Chinese state and society—one that is now fast eroding the fundamentals on which these narratives are based.

Take China's high-speed rail network, for example. Launched over a decade ago, construction moved into high gear in 2008 as part of a massive state stimulus in response to the global financial crisis. It is the source of justifiable national pride. Over twelve thousand miles of track now weld together China's major urban areas. Speedy trains zip along at 186 miles per hour, reducing the countryside to a rapidly shifting blur of green and brown. One can now travel from Beijing to Guangzhou—equivalent to the distance from New York to southern Florida—in a mere eight hours. Foreign visitors riding the rails for the first time invariably sigh in admiration, particularly Americans distressed with the sad state of public transportation in their own country.

Despite its bright exterior, high-speed rail is a textbook illustration of how Chinese politics have fed major social and economic problems. Authorities have poured hundreds of billions of dollars into rail construction. But as Evan Osnos has noted, given China's unreformed political institutions, this has created "an ecosystem almost perfectly hospitable to corruption—opaque, unsupervised, and overflowing with cash."[4] When Railway Minister Liu Zhijun fell from power in 2011, state media revealed the staggering corruption associated with his reign—18 mistresses, 350 apartments, and over a hundred million dollars in cash alone.[5]

Not all of these massive infrastructure investments make economic sense. True, they have propped up Chinese growth statistics, even as other national economies slowed dramatically. But they have also contributed to dangerously swelling government debt burdens (the railroad ministry requiring a central bailout).[6] And benefits have been artificially steered to a narrow segment of the public—state-owned monopolies awash in cash, established urban residents whose apartment values have skyrocketed. Left behind: the rural farmers who receive limited compensation for their lands seized for construction purposes, and blue-collar workers deprived of the slower, less expensive trains they had previously relied on to travel home for the Chinese New Year's festival.[7]

Such social grievances are flowing into China's frozen political institutions. To be sure, life today is dramatically different from that in the Maoist era. State control has receded. Ordinary citizens enjoy significant freedoms. Hundreds of millions of migrants circulate throughout the country in search of a better life. The wealthy can indulge on an epic scale—buying everything from Prada handbags to luxury apartments in residential districts that replicate entire European cities (right down to a 350-foot scale model of the Eiffel Tower).[8] But such changes have not disturbed the core of China's authoritarian one-Party political system. Citizens have few channels to influence major political decisions that affect their lives. And they have limited legal ones to challenge the petty abuses of local authorities.

Citizen activism is being driven into the streets as a result. In May 2013, when authorities announced the construction of a chemical plant outside the southwestern city of Kunming, thousands of students and residents launched a coordinated series of confrontations with police stretching over weeks.[9] Similar protests and petitions by Chinese citizens—regarding everything from local tax exactions to illegal land seizures to police abuses—have risen steadily in size and number since the early 1990s. Sometimes, these spiral into violence. In 2008, the drowning of a teenage girl in the southern town of Weng'an sparked rumors regarding the involvement of local officials in her death. Family grievances fused with latent social discontent among local residents regarding the seizure of their lands by local authorities for hydroelectric and mining projects. Protests broke out. Police responded. Six days after her death, both the county government offices and the police headquarters were burned down amid a mass riot involving tens of thousands of people.[10]

Nor is the slide toward extreme behavior limited to collective protests. China is experiencing a rash of individual actions as well. Take several examples from one four-month period. A wheelchair-bound man detonates a bomb in the Beijing airport to call attention to his decade-long legal struggle with police.[11] A failed job-seeker knifes China's second wealthiest man.[12] A disgruntled petitioner ignites a fire on a public bus in Xiamen, killing forty-seven people.[13] Faced with such developments, Chinese public security officials themselves have asserted that "the foundation of social order is relatively fragile," and bemoan the inability of state authorities to effectively resolve citizen grievances.[14]

Dramatic social shifts have created pressure for ideological change. The political slogans mouthed by state television anchors are now empty anachronisms. Since the late 1990s, capitalists have been welcomed into the Communist Party. Top leaders and their relatives are integral parts of complex family networks controlling billions of dollars of assets. In such a world, Mao's socialist vision no longer makes coherent sense. Halcyon days filled with revolutionary ardor exist only in the fading memories of an older generation and the relentlessly cheery propaganda pumped out by state media. Elsewhere, there is a pervasive sense that China has lost its moral compass amid the frenetic economic development of the past thirty years. In 2011, after a two-year-old toddler was hit by two trucks and left dying in an alley, security cameras captured no fewer than eighteen people passing by without helping her, some pausing to examine her still-moving body before moving on. Release of the video on Chinese social media prompted an anguished burst of national self-reflection expressed in millions of online comments: "Some people with no beliefs and a twisted value system can do terrible, unimaginable things"; "Farewell, and do not be born in China in your next life."[15] Six years later, the same story played itself out—yet again—after surveillance cameras recorded a pedestrian in central China being hit repeatedly by oncoming traffic, as dozens of gawking bystanders passed within feet of her prone body without lifting a finger.[16]

Many seek something deeper. Newly wealthy elites look for meaning in a world where almost anything—and anyone—can be bought. Rural migrants lost among the anonymity of Chinese cities search for a sense of belonging. Christian house churches, Buddhist lay congregations, and other beliefs have flourished as a result. Even Party authorities are flirting with alternatives. China's top Party leader, Xi Jinping, has called for rehabilitating China's "traditional faiths" as means of addressing the moral breakdown in society.[17] Since 2008, state authorities have allowed Tzu Chi, one of the largest Buddhist civil society organizations in Taiwan, to operate openly in mainland China, recruiting volunteers and caring for the suffering. And when officials unveiled the newly renovated national history museum in 2011, they prominently located a 31-ton statue of Confucius in front, mere steps away from the symbolic heart of state power—Tiananmen Square and Mao's mausoleum.

Surging citizen spirituality coexists uneasily with China's authoritarian political system. Party leaders remain suspicious of religious beliefs and organizations that might challenge their control. They try to channel believers into state-run mosques, temples, and churches run by "patriotic religious associations." Alternative underground madrasas and house churches organized by religious activists exist in a shifting gray zone of uncertainty—ears perpetually cocked for the knock at the door announcing a police crackdown. Such suppression has perverse effects. It supports the emergence of more evangelical and charismatic groups, driving them into confrontations with authorities. Falun Gong, a Buddhist spiritual offshoot, recruited millions of elderly *qigong* practitioners during its explosive growth in the early 1990s. Following peaceful protests at central Party headquarters seeking better treatment, the movement was brutally suppressed by Chinese authorities in 1999. It has since morphed into a worldwide multimedia conglomerate of newspapers, cable stations, and performance troupes (circulating from Tokyo to Paris, and from Chattanooga to Ogden) with a consistent political demand: the downfall of the Communist Party.

State efforts to forge a new ideological foundation are also generating fierce crosswinds. Attempts to repackage Party rule under the banner of Confucianism have outraged many leftist intellectuals who view this as a repudiation of Mao's ideals. Bitter online criticism flowed following the decision to place Confucius' statue in the center of Beijing. When, under the cover of night, it was suddenly removed to the rear of the museum, neo-Maoist websites erupted with glee: "The witch doctor who has been poisoning people for thousands of years with his slave-master spiritual narcotic has finally been kicked out of Tiananmen Square!"[18]

Party leaders also face pressure from the right. Liberal intellectuals took speeches made by China's new leaders in 2012 regarding the importance of the constitution to mean that real institutional reform might be in the offing. They began to push against China's political controls. After heavy-handed state censorship resulted in a crackdown on one of China's most respected independent-leaning publications in January 2013, hundreds converged on its headquarters to show their support. Authorities quickly reasserted ideological orthodoxy. Dire warnings about Western constitutionalism issued forth in the state media. And Maoist rhetoric that had gone into remission for decades began to flourish once again.

Mounting socioeconomic problems, worsening governance difficulties, rising social unrest, and increasing ideological polarization—these are the key challenges facing China today, analyzed in depth in Chapters 2–4.

Chapter 1 first provides the overall framework for understanding these trends. It sketches the broad history of China's post-1978 reform era. And it outlines how this era—defined by rapid economic growth, partially institutionalized Party rule, and relative ideological openness—has steadily unwound.

Back in the late 1970s, after Mao's death, Chinese leaders examined the tortured legacy he had left them. In 1949, the wily old revolutionary had successfully realized the nationalist dream of unifying China after decades of brutal civil war and foreign aggression. But the state-run economy and radical ideological campaigns he implemented in the wake of victory led to mass famine in the Great Leap Forward (1958–1960) and severe political turmoil during the Cultural Revolution (1966–1976).

Under Deng Xiaoping, Chinese leaders charted a new course. After 1978, they loosened their grip on the economy and society. Collective farms were disbanded; private businesses legalized. Economic liberalization resulted in an explosion of bottom-up entrepreneurship. Rural incomes surged. Hundreds of millions were lifted out of poverty. Controls over the private lives of citizens weakened as the state-owned economy eroded. The decision to travel (or marry) no longer required seeking a permission slip from your boss in the state-run company. Finding a job increasingly became a test of your skills rather than your political connections; obtaining an apartment, a question of your financial resources. New forms of art and culture flourished. In the late 1980s, Chinese authorities even began to experiment with limited political reforms aimed at separating Party and government functions.

The dramatic events of 1989–1991 ended any flirtation with serious political reform. Faced with the Tiananmen Square protests, the fall of Communism in Eastern Europe, and the collapse of the Soviet Union, Chinese leaders closed ranks. Their conclusion: never here. True, Party leaders have since experimented with a range of institutional innovations (village elections, judicial reforms) to address pressing governance problems facing China. But in a regular one-step-forward, one-step-back dance, each of these reforms has been systematically neutered when they have begun to bump up against core principles of one-Party control. And in the absence of deep political reform, China went sideways in the following two decades.

This may seem hard to believe. Compared with the early 1990s, the Beijing and Shanghai skylines are unrecognizable (because of both skyscrapers and smog). Successive waves of restructuring and privatization have led to the collapse of many state-run companies. New private technology firms such as Baidu and Alibaba have risen. Chinese businessmen now shuttle between African capitals closing major investment deals. Their children flock to college campuses throughout America and Europe. Given this, how can one possibly describe the years following 1990—perhaps the most dramatic in Chinese history ever—as a story of stagnation?

But such trends obscure a deeper reality. Beginning in the early 1990s, earlier economic reforms were thrown in reverse.[19] Chinese leaders began to pursue a policy of state-led capitalism—privileging large state-run monopolies at the expense of private firms. The benefits of China's dramatic economic growth increasingly began to accrue to a narrower and narrower slice of the population—established urban residents, state employees, and the ultra-rich. Rural incomes stagnated. Income inequality widened. In the late 1990s, central authorities pulled off the hat trick of redefining the Communist Party as also representing the interests of capitalist entrepreneurs, rendering the fusion of economic and political power a tenet of ideological orthodoxy. This has led to eye-popping contradictions for the vanguard of the proletariat. In 2012, when Party authorities assembled to select their next generation of leaders, some 160 of China's 1,000 wealthiest people were seated in either the Party Congress or national legislature.[20] Their total collective family net worth—some $221 billion—was roughly twenty times greater than the total worth of the top 660 officials of all three branches of the U.S. government.[21]

Politically, China underwent a similar deformation. In large part, this was the inevitable result of Beijing's adamant refusal to contemplate substantive political reform. Unwilling to allow courts or legislatures to mature as independent institutions, central authorities have been regularly forced back on relying on Party institutions to "coordinate" responses to a wider and wider swath of citizen grievances and protests. The power and responsibilities of the domestic security apparatus steadily expanded. By 2010, this dynamic had enabled national Party political-legal committee chairman Zhou Yongkang to establish his own quasi-independent fiefdom within the domestic security apparatus, with a budget reportedly exceeding that of the military.[22] The current iteration of these efforts: vast investments in big data and facial recognition technology to build a nationwide social credit monitoring system by 2020 allowing Beijing to keep tabs on jaywalkers, insolvent debtors, and political dissidents alike.

This is the reality of China today. Faced with a rising tide of social and economic pressures, Chinese authorities are raising, strengthening, and improving the levees they rely on to keep the waters of a turbulent society in check. And as a result, since the early 2000s, China has experienced a steady unwinding of the political, economic, and ideological givens of the reform era, a trajectory that has only gathered speed since 2012.

On both sides of the Pacific, pessimism has risen regarding the stability of China's governance model. In the United States, the early 2000s witnessed a proliferation of works such as *China's Trapped Transition* (2006) and *China: A Fragile Superpower* (2008), exploring the internal contradictions at the heart of the Chinese state. Such concerns went into temporary remission following the 2008 financial crisis. Economic turmoil wracked Western nations, while China emerged relatively unscathed. Foreign observers such as Thomas Friedman extolled the wisdom of Beijing's policies. Books such as *When China Rules the World* (2009) became bestsellers at airport stores around the world. China's diplomatic corps and state media shifted into overdrive. The superiority of Chinese state practices became a regular talking point in official conferences. Now, fears are mounting yet again. Since 2010, financial analysts have increasingly recognized that China's continued economic growth of the past few years has been bought at the price of an unsustainable credit expansion, and that the nation faces an imminent and potentially dramatic slowdown in economic growth. Politically, the fierce infighting among top Chinese leaders both before and after the 2012 leadership transition surprised many. Discussions of "resilient authoritarianism" emphasizing the extent to which Chinese Party authorities successfully charted a new course after the collapse of the Soviet Union (including stable norms of internal succession among leaders) have become tinged with increasing notes of unease.[23] Deepening worries over the direction of China's domestic politics have thrown dark shadows over Beijing's efforts to present itself as a world leader, one capable of filling the void left by the twin 2016 shocks of Brexit and the U.S. election of Donald Trump as president.

Such concerns are not limited to foreigners. Liberal Chinese intellectuals and government insiders alike now regularly refer to the ten years of the Hu Jintao administration (2002–2012) as a "lost decade," during which the economic fruits of blazing economic growth were frittered away in the extension of state monopolies and the growth of a "stability-maintenance" regime directed at suppressing domestic discontent, rather than undertaking needed economic and political reforms.[24] Increasingly, citizens with the means to do so are voting with their feet (and their bank accounts). By 2014, some two-thirds of Chinese millionaires had emigrated or were planning to do.[25] This is positive news for American real estate agents and college admissions officers suddenly deluged with inquiries from wealthy Chinese customers seeking to move their money and children overseas, perhaps, but a worrying sign of emerging cracks within the system.

The 2012 leadership transition brought a burst of new hope. China's new general Party secretary, Xi Jinping, delivered his first press conferences in a casual, plain-spoken manner that differed dramatically from the wooden performances and political slogans of his predecessor. Other moves followed. He abolished the much-criticized system of labor camps. He jailed former security czar Zhou Yongkang (who had stepped down in 2012) for life on corruption charges—breaking with long-standing norms exempting top leaders from investigation. And he announced broad economic reforms in which the market was to be the "decisive factor." Such moves seized the imagination of foreigners and Chinese alike. In 2013, the *New York Times* columnist Nicholas Kristof predicted, "Xi Jinping will spearhead a resurgence of economic reform, and probably some political easing as well. Mao's body will be hauled out of Tiananmen Square on his watch, and Liu Xiaobo, the Nobel Peace Prize–winning writer, will be released from prison."[26]

Might China, then, follow in the path of South Korea or Taiwan in the 1970s and 1980s? Dramatic economic growth and social change. A steady lowering of political controls allowing building social tensions to flow into new channels. Last, the growth of these institutions into an increasingly stable and open system of government.

Recent years have disabused these early hopes. Xi has proved to be just as implacably committed to maintaining existing one-Party controls as his predecessors. Social media has been subjected to a sweeping crackdown; liberal activists jailed. Liu Xiaobo did indeed walk out of prison in 2017, but only after belatedly being diagnosed with terminal liver cancer by prison authorities, and dying three weeks later. What initially seemed a more accessible public demeanor has turned out to be an aggressive campaign to consolidate Xi's personal power. In the process, reform-era political and ideological norms have steadily been broken, one after another. The spotlight of Party propaganda has been increasingly trained on his populist appeals to the masses, while a nationwide anti-corruption campaign has allowed him to purge rivals from the bureaucracy and replace them with his own. Within just a few short years, Xi has emerged as the most powerful Chinese leader in recent decades.[27] Yet substantive political reform lies nowhere on the horizon. Unsurprisingly, many have registered disillusionment. In January 2014, Kristof tweeted that Xi was an "utter disappointment so far," while Chinese intellectuals initially enthralled by the new regime are disturbed to see it evolving in a more and more authoritarian direction.[28] When Xi proclaimed at the 19th Party Congress in 2017 that China had entered a "new era," he was both confirming that the post-1978 reform era was over ... and that his own had begun.

More generally, China today differs from other late-twentieth-century authoritarian regimes in crucial ways, as outlined in Chapter 5. Although repressive, in the decades leading up to their political transitions, both Taiwan and South Korea had a range of semi-institutionalized political channels into which popular discontent could flow. Backed by independent labor unions and churches, public-interest lawyers emerged as opposition activists. They formed political movements, then parties (if periodically jailed for doing so). They participated in semi-competitive elections. And crucially—they helped channel building waves of social discontent toward reforming existing political institutions, rather than seeking to overthrow them. But this is not the dynamic in China today. Beijing's grip on formal political participation is tighter than Seoul or Taipei ever exercised. And Chinese authorities have systematically blocked all attempts at organizing independent social networks of any real size outside their controls, whether in real life or online.

On the one hand, this is the Party's greatest strength. There is no organized political opposition—no independent labor unions, no Muslim Brotherhood—with which it must contend. Beijing crushes (or co-opts) all who try. This has been one of the keys to the apparent stability of Party control. But ironically, it is also the Party's—and China's—greatest weakness. Outside the Party's own political levees, China has few institutions to funnel citizen discontent toward gradual reform. Irate petitioners hardened by years of persecution, nationalist bloggers venting their spleens against perceived enemies, underground secret societies rooted in centuries-old traditions—these China has in spades. But moderate voices and independent civil society organizations committed to gradual institutional reform—these China sorely lacks. Indeed, what limited space exists for them has steadily degraded. Public-interest lawyers once lionized by the press for representing the rights of the disadvantaged have had their licenses revoked, their organizations shuttered. Many have been arrested. At his trial in 2014, one of the most well-known, Xu Zhiyong, made an impassioned plea:

One hundred years on, where China wants to go is still the most crucial question the Chinese nation faces. As vested interests consolidate, the economy slows down, and accumulated social injustice leads to concentrated outbursts, China has once again arrived at an historical crossroads. . . . To a large extent, what we see happening around us today is re-enactment of the tragedy of the late Qing [dynasty] reforms, and for that reason I am deeply concerned about the future of the Chinese nation. When hopes of reform are dashed, people will rise up and seek revolution. The privileged and powerful have long transferred their children and wealth overseas; they couldn't care less of the misfortune and suffering of the disempowered, nor do they care about China's future.[29]

China is indeed at a crucial point in history. Existing political and economic institutions face a rising tide of new pressures. One can still hold out the remote hope that China might someday walk the road of gradual reform. Political institutions could open. Popular pressures could find their institutional outlets. Xu (and others like him) might leave prison to play the historical role of a Mandela or Gandhi in facilitating a stable political transition.

But there are other, darker possibilities, discussed in Chapter 6. Continued state controls might leave Chinese society atomized and fragmented. Beijing might retain firm control, steadily remodeling their one-Party regime into an updated twenty-first-century version of the personalized authoritarian-bureaucratic model familiar to centuries of imperial dynasties (and adopted by modern-day Russia under Putin). Or increased repression could radicalize citizen activists. Popular discontent could be forced underground, where it fuses with brewing nationalism. In such a universe, activists such as Xu might model themselves after a very different progressive lawyer who suffered under state repression: Lenin. Rather than the road of reform, they might find themselves driven toward that of revolution.

Alternatively, a black swan event—war with Japan, a banking crisis—could result in a disorderly implosion of the existing regime. China's future then might resemble that of some of more unfortunate Mideast states in the wake of the 2011 Arab Spring, or its own past (following the 1911 collapse of the Qing dynasty)—torn in the throes of decades-long struggles between a myriad of contending factions.

Modern art markets. Investment patterns in Africa. The balance of power in Asia. China's economic rise has indeed altered the globe. Many have asserted that Napoleon's prediction that "when China wakes, it will shake the world" has come true.

But what if this has just been the first act? What if the true drama still lies ahead? What will happen when the surging tensions lapping against China's frozen political facade finally surface?

I

Overview: The End of China's Reform Era

AUTHORITARIANISM IS ON THE rise worldwide. Amid economic malaise and stagnation, far-right parties are making inroads in European politics. Populist strongmen have risen to power via the ballot box in countries ranging from Turkey to Philippines to India. Nor are Western democracies immune from these trends, as witnessed by the stunning upset victory of political outsider Donald Trump in the 2016 American presidential election.[1]

In this era of democratic decline, American foreign policy makers are looking afresh at authoritarian states. Their fingers burned after Iraq and Afghanistan, U.S. officials have backed away from the democracy promotion agenda identified with prior administrations. Authoritarian regimes in Cuba, Iran, and Burma were once scorned by Washington elites. Under the Obama administration, they became targets of careful diplomatic outreach. Iron-fisted autocrats and demagogues such as Russia's Vladimir Putin or the Philippines' Rodrigo Duterte were once pariahs among Western leaders. Under Trump, they have been singled out for praise.

A new tone has entered academia as well. During the 1990s, experts spoke confidently about a "third wave" of democratization. Now they characterize the decade since 2005 as one of "democratic recession" and "authoritarian resurgence."[2] Even Francis Fukuyama, who famously argued in 1989 that the future would witness the inevitable rise of liberal democratic models worldwide, has altered course. Struck by a plethora of unsuccessful democratic transitions—in Russia, Africa, and the Middle East—he now cautions readers to focus less on the high-minded goal of building liberal democracy, and more on constructing the basic machinery of rule by an efficient state.[3]

Given this, one can understand why China might seem attractive today. Compared with the steadily escalating turmoil in the Middle East and the slow-moving train wreck of Russia and Ukraine, China appears a relative haven. No revolution. No civil war. For roughly three decades, economic growth averaged 10 percent a year. On the surface, China seems the very incarnation of the efficient state machine—a model for other aspiring authoritarians to follow. But a closer look at China's reform era reveals a different truth. China's heady accomplishments have been grounded in a set of norms and policies—political, economic, and ideological—adopted in the last quarter of the twentieth century. These are now unraveling.

Since 1989, Beijing has firmly adhered to one core principle: uphold the rule of the Chinese Communist Party (CCP) at all costs. Naturally, this has led Chinese leaders to take political liberalization off the table. But it has also led them to undermine the very governance reforms that have been key to the resilience shown by China's authoritarian regime. Put simply, in the narrow pursuit of maintaining political power, CCP leaders have eroded the late-twentieth-century bedrock on which China's success has been built. Rather than serving as the poster child for successful authoritarian governance, China is actually an example of the perils of failing to undertake political reform.

THE BIRTH OF REFORM

In the late 1970s, few would have deemed China a successful authoritarian model. It was poor, isolated, and unstable. Socialist planning had rendered it an economic basket case, with a per capita income lower than that of Afghanistan, India, or Zaire. Decades of political radicalism under Mao Zedong had left China in disarray. Mao's preference for ruling as supreme leader ("the great helmsman") through mass movements destabilized state and society alike. During the chaos of the Cultural Revolution (1966–1976), bureaucratic and legal institutions collapsed entirely. Ideologically, China closed itself off. Western capitalist and Soviet revisionist practices were decried; religion and tradition ruthlessly suppressed in the name of socialist modernization. Universities shut their doors. Intellectuals were packed off to do hard labor in remote rural areas. Nor was the political elite above the fray. Individual leaders and their families regularly rose and fell with the shifting winds of court politics. Serving as Mao's heir apparent was positively hazardous to one's health. The first two ended up dead, while his wife, who had tried to usurp power in his waning years, was arrested after Mao's own death in 1976.

Deng Xiaoping's rise to power in 1978 marked a dramatic shift. The searing experience of the Cultural Revolution convinced him and other leaders of the need for deep change. They stabilized elite politics. Unlike Mao, Deng never exercised one-man rule. In part, this was because CCP elders elevated other respected figures, particularly Chen Yun, to the top ranks as a check on Deng. But Deng's own preferences also played a role. He eschewed Mao's cult of personality, opting instead for a low-key management style marked by a search for consensus among top leaders.

Under Deng, Party governance was regularized. Mass movements faded. There was less stress on ideology, and more on results. In his famous words, "It does not matter if a cat is black or white, so long as it catches mice." Merit-based systems were established to recruit and promote new officials. Orderly retirement procedures were adopted to clear out the elderly. China thus avoided the fate of the Soviet Union in the 1980s, where leadership ranks resembled a slowly decaying geriatric ward. Political purges, once so fierce, grew rarer and milder. Although Deng's first two hand-picked successors were forced to resign following outbreaks of student unrest during the late 1980s, neither was physically harmed, nor were their families targeted.

The rest of the Chinese bureaucracy swung back toward institutionalized governance as well. No longer were the rules of the game supposed to shift with each new leader.[4] Legal reform became a hallmark of the post-Mao era. Authorities issued hundreds of new statutes and regulations, constructing a comprehensive framework of criminal, civil, and commercial law. They reopened law schools. Thousands of new graduates began to flow into the courts and other government legal bureaus that rose from the ashes of the Maoist era.

Economically, the 1980s saw dramatic improvements in standards of living. Collectivized agriculture unraveled. Market incentives were introduced. Rural incomes soared, lifting hundreds of millions out of crushing poverty. The urban-rural gap narrowed. As Yasheng Huang points out, "Chinese capitalism—*in the 1980s*—was also a poor man's affair."[5] Financial liberalization led to expanded credit in the countryside. Rural entrepreneurship boomed as township and village enterprises grew.

Socially, China gradually opened up. Authorities backed away from the pervasive ideology that had characterized the Maoist era. The Party no longer had any deep interest in controlling citizens' internal beliefs, just their public actions. Churches, mosques, and temples reopened. So did colleges and universities. Official controls over the lives of citizens eroded. As ration coupons and state employment gave way to market forces, people became less dependent on bureaucrats. When greener pastures beckoned in the next county or province, many began to simply pick up and leave. And as China turned outward, foreign students, businesspeople, and ideas began to flow in.

By the late 1980s, such trends had culminated in an unusually open atmosphere. Relaxed religious policies had generated improved relations between the state and minority ethnic groups such as the Muslim Uighurs and Buddhist Tibetans, including a series of talks between representatives of Beijing and the Dalai Lama. Intellectuals gathered in Beijing salons to debate liberal reform. In these years, even state television could air controversial programs such as *River Elegy* (1988), which critiqued traditional Chinese culture and urged greater exposure to the outside world as a means to modernize China.

Chinese authorities themselves began to experiment with yet deeper reform. Controls over the media were relaxed. And in 1987, under reform-minded CCP general secretary Zhao Ziyang, they edged tentatively toward separating the Party from the organs of government—the furthest steps toward meaningful political reform that China has seen to date.

CONSTRAINED REFORM

Then came Tiananmen. After a period of seeming indecision, the Party-state came crashing down on the 1989 student democracy movement with savage repression. Reform experiments were cut short. Party elders sacked Zhao, purged reformists from the bureaucracy, and reinstated tight controls over the media and government. Horrified by the fate that began to overtake the communist regimes of Central and Eastern Europe just a few months after the Tiananmen Square crackdown of June 1989, the CCP chiefs set their faces implacably against fundamental political reform.

With an existential crisis looming, Deng Xiaoping moved carefully. Viewing the politics of leadership succession as a major driver of the Soviet collapse, Deng eased the older generation of CCP leaders into retirement. He crowned his own political heir, Jiang Zemin (1989), and anointed Hu Jintao as Jiang's eventual successor. Combined with increasingly regularized promotion and retirement standards, this brought an unusual degree of stability to the Party bureaucracy for roughly two decades, lasting even beyond Deng's death in 1997.

Party authorities took other preventive measures as well. In 1991, they established an embryonic new bureaucracy to coordinate responses to social unrest and nip incipient protests in the bud.[6] That same year, they launched a nationalistic "patriotic education" campaign in schools and the media.[7] Beginning in the 1990s, movies and films focused on atrocities that Japan had committed in China during the 1930s and 1940s steadily migrated to the center of the state-run entertainment industry. "Patriotic education" also spread to Tibet, which had experienced its own unrest in 1988. Party authorities sent cadres into Buddhist monasteries to press monks to publicly renounce the Dalai Lama.

Although fundamental political change was out, limited institutional reforms were not. Central authorities desired better channels to cope with the mounting conflicts brought by rapid social change. Administratively, they sought new ways to monitor their local agents. Giving citizens limited powers—to challenge local officials in court, offer opinions through legislative channels, or choose village officials through grassroots elections—looked like a solution. The 1990s saw law and litigation become a new state mantra. Authorities professionalized the judiciary and privatized the bar. In 1997, "rule according to law" became a core CCP slogan, enshrined in the constitution two years later.[8]

Deng remained convinced that economic development was the key to modernizing China and avoiding the USSR's fate. Overcoming resistance within the CCP, he reinvigorated market reforms in 1992. Labor markets were liberalized. State-run systems for allocating jobs and housing gradually dissolved. By the late 1990s, this culminated in the full privatization of urban housing in China. As the economy boomed, college graduates were left to their own skill, luck, or connections to make their careers and fortunes. Instead of going to work in state-owned enterprises, many sought jobs in the now-recognized private sector, including the growing numbers of foreign firms seeking to do business in China. Party leaders stood ready to welcome the newly wealthy with open arms. By 2002, they had managed to turn communist orthodoxy on its head—redefining Party tenets to accept self-made billionaires into the CCP itself. Money and power thus fused into "red capitalism."[9]

In the 1990s, China was increasingly open to the outside world. Students flocked to learn English in preparation for overseas study. Joining the World Trade Organization in 2001 meant China, after decades of isolation, became rapidly intertwined with networks of global commerce. "Linking up with the outside world" (*yu guoji jie-gui*) and adapting Chinese practices to mesh with international norms became national obsessions. Globalization was a source of national pride and state legitimacy.

Such sentiments infused a broader range of state policies. China spent vast sums on a crash expansion of higher education in the late 1990s, seeking to create universities of global repute equal to Harvard or Oxford. Numerically, at least, the effects were dramatic. From 1998 to 2000, the number of entering college students *doubled* to 2 million, resulting in overflowing classrooms and dormitories. The surging tide of students fed another trend—the explosion of the Internet, which began to spread rapidly in the late 1990s. Growing numbers of students began using loosely controlled college online chat rooms to discuss a wide range of topics.

Offline, the 1990s saw a boom in civil society organizations. Some groups were religious; others worked for causes such as women's rights, poverty alleviation, and the like. As Beijing steadily backed away providing services under a socialist economic model, it left many health and development tasks to citizens. Voluntary organizations naturally sprang up to fill the void. Overseas influences played a role too. International events such as the 1995 UN World Conference on Women in Beijing helped to raise the stature of Chinese domestic organizations, while overseas Chinese in Southeast Asia, Christian churches, and international NGOs such as the Ford Foundation provided crucial financial assistance.

The Party-state remained wary. When activists used civil society channels to organize politically (such as the China Democracy Party in 1998), the regime crushed them. In 1999, Falun Gong members leveraged new online tools to help them stage a surprise demonstration at CCP headquarters in Beijing, during which they peacefully appealed for official recognition of their spiritual movement. After a brief tactical pause, authorities responded by expanding the "stability maintenance" organs set up in 1991 and turning them against Falun Gong in a brutal eradication campaign.

By the turn of the millennium, Chinese leaders appeared to have surmounted the crises of the early 1990s. As Andrew Nathan noted in 2003, they had seemingly managed to institutionalize single-party political rule, fusing it with market capitalism and global trade networks to create a "resilient authoritarian" regime that would carry forward into the twenty-first century.

REFORM STAGNATES

Beneath the surface, however, the reforms of the 1990s were creating new challenges for the regime. By the early twenty-first century, economic shifts had given birth to a new range of institutional forces. Increasing commercialization meant that media outlets such as the *Southern Weekend* group were no longer simple extensions of the CCP propaganda apparatus. Now, they had to compete for readers and advertising. A generation of crusading and muckraking journalists arose. They began to test the limits of censorship, reporting aggressively on corruption and abuses of power by local officials throughout China. The burgeoning Internet supercharged these efforts as more and more citizens took to new media channels to voice complaints. Legal reforms led some judges and bureaucrats to suggest that it was time to give China's written constitution real weight. Outside the circles of government, meanwhile, there emerged a cadre of public-interest lawyers—figures such as Teng Biao and Xu Zhiyong—who were skilled at wielding media pressure and legal rhetoric to press for deeper institutional reforms.

In 2003, these trends reached their high-water mark. The beating death in police custody of Sun Zhigang, a young college graduate and internal migrant to booming Guangzhou (Canton), triggered an explosion of outrage both online and offline. Liberal legal activists quickly emerged as opinion leaders, articulating legal and constitutional deficiencies with the case. Faced with overwhelming social pressure, Beijing annulled the nationwide detention system under which Sun had been held.

China's leaders began to take a hard look at their society. They saw similarities with conditions in the Eastern European and Central Asian countries where "color revolutions" toppled authoritarian regimes during the first half of the 2000s. Thus began a steadily escalating crackdown aimed at reasserting official control where it had slipped. The Party's leaders turned against many of its own late-twentieth-century legal reforms. Within the courts, new political campaigns reminded judges of the supremacy of CCP rule over the constitution and laws. Pressure on public lawyers escalated. Regular police visits came first, followed by denial of law licenses, closure of organizations such as the Open Constitution Initiative (2009), and the arrests or lengthy disappearances of key activists.

Similar controls spread on the Internet as well. In 1987, the first email from China to Germany had read: "Across the Great Wall, we can reach every corner of the world." Two decades later, Beijing sought to prevent precisely that. State authorities steadily adapted their methods of censoring print and television to the online world, strengthening systems for blocking and filtering information to the point where they became known as the "Great Firewall of China." Rather than a total barrier, the Firewall aims to make certain information outside China so hard to access that most Chinese citizens will give up looking for it. Within China, it attempts induce self-censorship on the part of most users and Internet providers. Those who refuse to cooperate face strict sanctions. Such pressures led Google, which had entered China in 2005, to shutter their domestic Chinese search engine five years later. More-compliant domestic firms such as Baidu now dominate the mainland Chinese search market.

Tighter controls produced an especially dire turn in Xinjiang and Tibet. Since the 1990s, repressive policies in both regions had fueled rising popular resentment. After 2000, Beijing's development policies brought a tide of Han Chinese migrants to both areas, but limited benefits for locals. Festering tensions exploded into violence in Tibet in 2008 and Xinjiang a year later. Brutal ethnic riots wracked Urumqi, killing hundreds of residents, both Han and Uighurs alike. Authorities cracked down hard with mass arrests and extensive use of force.

By the early twenty-first century, economic reforms were filling China's cities with the emblems of modern success: skyscrapers and Starbucks. State investment was steered into massive infrastructure and urban-development programs. But in stark contrast to the 1980s, the benefits of such development now flowed disproportionately to a much narrower elite—state companies and foreign investors—rather than the populace at large. Credit policies increasingly disfavored rural entrepreneurs. Township and village enterprises that had helped rural China boom during the 1980s faltered. Many went bankrupt.

The impact of these changes rippled through all levels of society. In the early 1990s, the best and brightest of China's college graduates had sought their fortunes in the private sector. By the early 2000s, this had reversed. State employment offered more attractive possibilities for enriching oneself—if not through legitimate earnings, then through corruption. Applications to join the civil service surged through the century's early years.[10] Shifts occurred among the working poor as well. With fewer jobs to be had in the countryside, rural residents flowed to the cities in search of work. The migrant population, which had hovered between 60 and 70 million in the early 1990s, surged to 137 million in 2000, and over 200 million a decade after that.[11] In the cities, however, only established residents had access to urban social benefits—health, education, and pensions. New migrants went without. Trends such as these fueled dramatically accelerating income inequality; by 2008, it reached levels found in Latin America and sub-Saharan Africa.

Chinese authorities were acutely aware of these problems. In 2007, Premier Wen Jiabao warned that China's development path was "unstable, unbalanced, uncoordinated, and ultimately unsustainable." And under Hu Jintao, authorities took steps to improve the lot of the rural poor. Agricultural taxes were abolished, and rural health care expanded. Such measures helped to stem rising inequality but did little to address underlying imbalances, particularly the steadily expanding privileges of state-owned enterprises. After a bout of reform in the 1990s, a silent counter-revolution had occurred in which state-owned enterprises (SOEs) saw their financial and political privileges reconfirmed. By 2006, Beijing was openly promulgating policies to help state-owned "national champions" compete with the foreign firms that had arrived to do business in China during the reform period.

These economic shifts reflected a deeper political ossification. As Deng's generation of leaders with roots in the 1949 communist revolution passed from the stage, political power diffused among a broader elite. Jiang was weaker than Deng, and Hu was weaker than Jiang. Chinese politics increasingly resembled a feudal oligarchy. Top CCP figures controlled extensive networks of personal influence composed of loyal followers spread throughout middle- and lower-level posts. The fusion of money and power that had taken place since the 1990s meant that these networks sprawled across Party organs, SOEs, and private financial institutions. Such was the case with Zhou Yongkang, a Politburo Standing Committee member, and thus one of China's top nine leaders between 2007 and 2012. On paper, his official portfolio consisted of the massive security apparatus that had ballooned over the prior decade to deal with internal dissent. But his actual turf extended deep into the state energy sector and the Sichuan provincial administration as well. Such cliques defied the basic Leninist principle of centralized rule in a one-party state, facilitated rampant corruption, and stymied systematic reform by fostering nests of resistance to increasingly weak central leaders.

As China approached 2012, politics appeared frozen. With economic and institutional reform seemingly blocked by the twin forces of internal CCP politics and total resistance to political liberalization, China appeared to be locked in a "trapped transition."[12]

REFORM UNWINDS

Behind the scenes, however, things were beginning to break loose. The year 2012 marked the end of the clear line of political succession set by Deng back in the early 1990s. Factional struggles intensified over who would be elevated to positions of power. Opportunistic politicians sought to catapult themselves to higher office. In the southwestern metropolis of Chongqing, local CCP secretary Bo Xilai attempted to turbocharge his efforts to obtain a seat on the Politburo Standing Committee. Breaking with long-accepted political norms that emphasized low-key public personas for up-and-coming cadres, he aggressively cultivated a charismatic populist image during his tenure from 2007 to 2012. His signature tactics included mass rallies, a revival of Maoist "red" culture, and an intense campaign against "organized crime" that swept up criminal suspects, legitimate businessmen, and their lawyers alike.

Economically, China's decades-long boom was ending. After averaging a phenomenal 10 percent annual growth rate between 1979 and 2010, GDP growth slipped to 6.7 percent by 2016, and continued to sink in following years. In part, China was experiencing the same structural and demographic transitions that other developing East Asian economies such as South Korea and Taiwan had gone through. But Beijing's specific development choices exacerbated problems. Since the late 1990s, state-led investment spending on roads, airports, and housing had loomed large as drivers of economic growth. This reached manic proportions after the 2008 world financial crisis. Seeking to jump-start a slowing economy, Beijing launched a massive stimulus program that included building the world's most extensive high-speed rail network almost overnight. Such policies helped to prop up growth in the short term, but at the cost of soaring public debt, anemic domestic consumption, and a threefold overdependence on China's frothy real estate market to act simultaneously as an engine of growth, a source of local-government revenue (via land sales), and a place to invest private wealth. When the housing bubble partially deflated after a peak in 2011–2013, the pain made itself felt throughout the Chinese economy.

To avert a dramatic slowdown, central officials have repeatedly resorted to yet further rounds of stimulus spending in the years since. But like a junkie seeking to avoid withdrawal, Beijing has found each injection less and less effective. Meanwhile, the side effects have been progressively severe. Debt has surged rapidly, to 277 percent of GDP by the end of 2016. And one asset class after another—stocks, metals, bonds, real estate—have seen a regular boom-to-bust cycle, each larger than the last.

It was amid this mounting economic and political stress that Xi Jinping took power. Like Bo, he was a "princeling" with an impeccable revolutionary pedigree. Born in 1953, his father had served with Mao. Xi had emerged as a compromise candidate acceptable to the competing factions identified with Hu and Jiang. Yet once Xi had ensconced himself in China's triad of top offices (general secretary of the CCP, president of the People's Republic, and head of the Central Military Commission) in 2013, he quickly snapped the bonds of established patterns and norms and shook the political landscape.

Xi moved to solidify his position by taking down his rivals. First in line was Bo Xilai. Bo had fallen from grace when his wife was implicated in a sordid murder plot involving the 2011 death of a British businessman, after which Bo's police chief had fled to the U.S. consulate in Chengdu in early 2012. Xi quickly weeded out officials loyal to Bo and placed Bo himself on trial for corruption and abuse of power in 2013. Such a move was not entirely unprecedented. Similar investigations had been used in the 1990s and 2000s to fell individual Politburo members whom Jiang and Hu had regarded as threats during their respective ascents to power.

What followed, however, was new. In 2013, Xi moved against his next target—former security czar Zhou Yongkang, who had apparently dissented from the decision to purge Bo. In doing so, Xi broke with unwritten Party rules that exempted former and current Politburo Standing Committee members from prosecution. Xi's decision radically upended conventions that had existed since the beginning of the reform period. The targeting of family members (in this case, Zhou's sons) by investigators further intensified unease among members of the political elite. Wild rumors began to proliferate as to which other former leaders might be next.

Xi coupled his efforts to solidify control with a tough campaign against graft. Run under opaque rules by the secretive CCP disciplinary apparatus, it is the severest such campaign since the reform era began. Week after week, lists of officials sacked or placed under investigation flowed forth. Xi thus shattered 1990s-era norms that had tolerated both the fusion of money and politics and the unabashed displays of excess that resulted. Once self-confident cadres began to grow palpably afraid. Sales of Prada handbags and receipts of Macau gambling houses nosedived. China's ultra-rich have since busied themselves with efforts to move their assets and families abroad, while midlevel bureaucrats have hunkered down in fear that a wrong move will end their careers, or worse.

By 2014, rumors began swirling that retired top leaders such as Hu and Jiang had warned Xi to curb his efforts. If indeed they had urged him to avoid tangling with too many of the elite patronage networks, there is little evidence that he has heeded their message. On the contrary, 2015 saw the anticorruption campaign sweep across top military ranks, claiming a former Central Military Commission vice-chairman and dozens of generals. These tides have even begun to envelop Hu's and Jiang's own factional allies. For example, the 2016 overhaul of Hu's former stomping grounds, the Communist Youth League, and the subsequent sidelining of many of its alumni from positions of power, served to further strengthen Xi's hand in his efforts to elevate his own loyal aides and associates within the system. Elites who had thought themselves untouchable suddenly found themselves vulnerable. When Beijing moved against a range of the wealthiest tycoons in 2017, targets included the CEO of one of China's most politically connected financial firms, who was married to a granddaughter of Deng Xiaoping.

With both the bureaucracy and other top leaders cowed, Xi centralized his power. A plethora of new internal Party leadership groups has taken shape in the areas of foreign affairs, economic reform, and Internet security. Their shared feature is Xi Jinping at the apex. The domestic-security apparatus that Zhou Yongkang and his predecessors had assiduously built has been folded into a new national-security commission, chaired (unsurprisingly enough) by Xi. Such moves run contrary to internal CCP practices dating from the 1980s. Under these old customs, top Party officials had divided power among themselves, seeking elite stability through a rough balance of power. Xi has overturned this, stamping himself as the most powerful Chinese leader in decades. The 2017 19th Party Congress confirmed this, enshrining "Xi Jinping Thought" in the ideological pantheon of the Chinese Communist Party, vaulting him well above Jiang or Hu in importance, and approaching that of Mao. Nor is Xi's power limited to mere words on paper. Under him, China is currently engaged in the most sweeping reorganization of its military since 1949.[13]

During his rise, Xi has borrowed directly from the playbook of his fallen rival Bo Xilai. He has projected a populist image, aided by the star quality of his wife, a renowned folk singer. His confident, easy interactions with the public have formed a sharp contrast with those of his predecessor Hu Jintao, a wooden speaker given to stiff sloganeering. Nor is this merely show. Xi has tapped into a real vein of support among citizens who are disgusted by official graft and love seeing the rich and powerful being brought to their knees by a strong leader who knows how to get things done.

Xi has built on this sentiment. His image-building has begun to give off a whiff of a personality cult, with aromatic notes steadily strengthening over time. His public appearances have received a level of television coverage dwarfing that accorded to any other top official. Starting in 2014, he has begun delivering an annual personal address to the nation. Popular adulation for "Papa Xi"—a nickname that began online and has now drifted into the state press—has become a noticeable phenomenon. After Xi's surprise December 2013 visit to a Beijing dumpling restaurant to dine with ordinary customers, it became a pilgrimage site for tourists. By early 2015, art students at one Beijing college were sketching his portrait as part of their entrance examination. The 2015 edition of the annual Chinese New Year's gala on state television—the world's most-watched annual broadcast, with a viewership approaching 800 million—featured singers crooning "I give you my heart" while scenes of Xi visiting citizens and troops flashed behind them. This is a long way from the low-key style of collective leadership that had prevailed since the end of the Cultural Revolution in the 1970s.

Playing the populist card has gone hand in hand with reinforcing hardline policies launched under Hu Jintao. The crackdown on public-interest lawyers has tightened. Social media sites have been subjected to tighter controls. Even those used to a degree of immunity have found themselves targeted. Foreign businesses have been alarmed by stepped-up corruption probes into pharmaceutical companies, dawn raids by antimonopoly regulators on firms ranging from Microsoft to

Mercedes-Benz, and a steadily chilling atmosphere for foreign software companies seeking to do business in China. The draconian new foreign NGO law that entered into effect in 2017 has caused many overseas civil society organizations that have worked in China since the beginning of the reform era to consider pulling out entirely. Such policies are spreading. Central CCP organs are currently ramping up efforts to "rectify" higher education, slash imports of children's cartoon books (such as Peppa Pig), and redirect art and architecture back toward traditional Chinese forms.

These moves reflect a deeper shift. For decades, state ideology had remained in limbo—a matter of perfectly coiffed television anchors mouthing increasingly anachronistic Marxist slogans. Xi has deepened efforts to find a new basis for the legitimacy of single-party rule. This son of a Maoist revolutionary has pivoted back to the past, making a 2013 pilgrimage to the hometown of Confucius, extolling traditional Chinese culture, and embracing Qing dynasty reformers once derided as "feudal" or "reactionary." Under Xi's mantra of the "China Dream," a new ethnonationalist narrative has been taking shape. Slowly, China has begun to turn away from the late twentieth century and its policies of cultural openness. In schools, the role of English in the national college-entrance test has been deemphasized. On television, risqué knockoffs of Western dating programs have been eclipsed by game shows that test contestants on knowledge of Chinese characters, and shows featuring South Korean pop stars have been barred from broadcast.

For many, the new emphasis on China's own cultural roots has fed a welcome sense of national pride. But it has intensified tensions with those who do not fit the new state narrative. Christian churches in Zhejiang province, whose booming congregations had been tacitly tolerated for decades, have been hit by a sweeping official campaign to take down their crosses. Relations between the vast Han Chinese majority and ethnically distinct minority populations have worsened. In Tibet, continued state repression has produced a wave of self-immolations by more than a hundred young people. In Xinjiang, state suppression of Uighur identity and the Muslim religion have fueled radicalization and a rising wave of domestic terrorism. In Hong Kong, increasing mainland influence and Beijing's heavy-handed controls have stirred discontent among Cantonese-speaking citizens fearful over the fate of their distinctive cultural and political identity, resulting in the 2014 Occupy Central movement—the largest protests anywhere in China since 1989.[14]

THE COUNTER-REFORM ERA

Political stability, ideological openness, and rapid economic growth were the hallmarks of China's reform era. But they are ending. China is entering a new era—the counter-reform era.

This is not entirely bad. For some in China, it is creating space to address reform-era excesses, such as rampant ecological damage, stark social inequality, and a cultural heritage badly damaged in the rush to modernize. But there is also a dark side.

What kept China stable during the reform era can be summed up in a single phrase: partial political institutionalization. The last two decades of the twentieth century saw the rise of an increasingly steady set of norms in China to govern state and society alike:

- An increasingly norm-bound politics of elite succession;
- A depoliticization of the bureaucracy, marked by the decline of factional purges and the rise of meritocratic norms;
- Steady institutional differentiation, with top CCP leaders handling more clearly defined portfolios and SOEs responding to market pressures;
- The emergence of bottom-up "input" institutions—local elections, administrative-law channels, and a partly commercialized media airing popular grievances—that gave citizens a limited political voice and helped boost state legitimacy;
- New channels that helped give the rising new economic elite a sense of being invested in both China's future as well as in the existing Party-state;
- An ideological stance open enough to welcome a broad range of domestic social constituencies and foreign institutional innovations alike.[15]

These all are now unwinding. Some—such as semi-competitive local elections or assertive domestic media outlets—have quietly given way since the early 2000s in the face of renewed state controls. Since Xi's rise in 2012, other norms have been broken more dramatically.

The reasons for the unwinding are twofold. First, Beijing has systematically undercut its own bottom-up reforms. Over the past three decades, a regular pattern has developed. Individual leaders sponsor reforms to address latent governance problems. Doors open. Citizens start to use them to participate politically. Villagers begin to organize around semi-open elections. Public-interest lawyers explore new legal channels. Social media start to take shape as a forum for citizens to air grievances. At that point, central Party authorities get nervous. They see shades of 1989 and step in to put a lid on things. Reforms are smothered, activists detained. For precisely this reason, China has remained locked in a one-step forward, one-step-back dance since the 1990s, with the Party regularly deinstitutionalizing everything outside its own walls.

Naturally, this is a problem for Chinese society. It robs social activists of the gradual evolutionary path toward becoming a moderate, institutionalized political force. But it is a problem for the rulers too. Absent effective internal or external checks, authoritarian one-Party rule has fused (since the 1990s) with the fastest accumulation of wealth in human history to produce vested political and economic interests that are both highly corrupt and deeply resistant to change—the Chinese analogue of the K Street lobbyist–U.S. Congress nexus, but without even the shadow of elections, judicial oversight, or a free press as checks.

Now put yourself in Xi Jinping's shoes. You know that China faces deep economic and social challenges. You sense that the Party itself has gone badly astray. Yet you lack any external institutions to rectify it. Nor is there an alternative political force—such as the organized opposition movements that emerged despite authoritarian rule in Taiwan and South Korea—that you might employ as a counterweight. (Not that you would even remotely entertain that notion: the lessons of 1989 run too deep.) What would you do?

Here we come to the second reason for the shifts noted above. Xi appears to have concluded that his only path to a breakthrough requires him to tear up the existing rules—reversing many if not all of the partially institutionalized internal Party norms that Andrew Nathan noted back in 2003. Politicized anticorruption purges of rivals. Centralization of power in his own hands. Cultivation of a populist image. An ideological turn toward nationalism and cultural identity. These are not mere transitory policies. For Xi, they are absolutely fundamental shifts necessary to address the crisis he sees facing China.

He may be right. Optimists can point to his efforts at fiscal and economic reform. They can cite his efforts to strengthen Party disciplinary and legal systems as indications that he will build new political institutions on the ashes of the old.[16] Perhaps Xi does indeed belong to that rarest of all rare breeds—the benevolent authoritarian emperor who presides wisely over the remodeling of China, while ruthlessly crushing dissent in the process.

Moreover, there are still several key reform-era norms that have not yet been breached. The ideological redefinition of China remains embryonic. Marxist dialectics still figure in CCP speeches even as Confucian quotations proliferate. And Chinese state television, unlike its Russian counterpart, continues to promote interethnic harmony rather than rank appeals to majority-group chauvinism. Most importantly, Xi has drawn a clear line at social mobilization. For all of his invocation of Mao-era symbolism, there has been no sign that he intends to resort to mass movements.

But China is now steadily cannibalizing its own prior political institutionalization. Observers such as David Shambaugh, who once pointed to such institutionalization as a source of stability for the Party-state, are sharply revising downward their evaluations of the system's sustainability. [17] Others have begun to speculate openly whether reform-era policies limiting top Party leaders to ten years in office might be next to go, with Xi Jinping perhaps trying to extend his rule well beyond 2022.[18] Uncertainty hangs in the air. Chinese with the most to lose are diversifying against risk—placing their money in Vancouver real estate and their children in U.S. colleges, and seeking passports from one or another of the small Caribbean nations that offer citizenship for sale.

The events of 1989 did not resolve the core question of China's political future. Nor did they put it on hold indefinitely. Rather, they launched a cascading set of effects that have swept through China's politics, economy, and society in the years since. The resulting reverberations have now begun to dislodge core elements of the institutional consensus that has governed China for decades. A new future is slouching toward Beijing to be born.

2

Society and Economy: The Closing of the Chinese Dream

THE BIRTH OF THE reform era in China saw doors open up.

For intellectuals, the revival of college entrance exams meant a return of meritocratic channels to influence within the state bureaucracy that had been closed off during a decade of Maoist radicalism. For private entrepreneurs, the economic reforms of the 1980s opened paths to financial success. And for the rural masses, land reforms provided a route out of absolute poverty amid a relatively egalitarian society.

Forty years later, things are very different. China as a nation is richer. But social mobility has declined. Channels once open have closed down. As college graduates have exploded in number, their employment statistics have declined dramatically. Articles with titles such as "Graduate with Masters in Law Seeks Position as Cafeteria Worker" now proliferate in the press.[1]

Other paths have narrowed as well. Since the 1990s, the township and village enterprises established in the first wave of reform have foundered. Rural laborers have flooded into China's cities instead—a tidal wave now nearly 300 million strong.[2] But they find themselves a social underclass, barred from receiving benefits such as education, health, and pensions enjoyed by their established urban neighbors. Income disparities have surged. China has blown past levels of inequality seen in other developing Asian economies to approach those seen in strife-prone nations in Latin America and Africa and other highly unequal countries, such as the United States.

Understanding how this happened—how the initial dreams of the reform era unwound as an unreformed one-Party political system fused with late-twentieth-century go-go capitalism—is crucial to understanding China today. For as the Chinese expression goes: *shui luo shi chu.* When the water recedes, the rocks come out. In flush times, it is easy to float over all forms of hidden dangers. Only when things are hard does the true extent of problems come to light, and the jagged divide separating society's winners from the losers begin to break the surface.

THE IMPERIAL DREAM: MERITOCRATIC RISE THROUGH EDUCATION

For centuries, stories such as that of Fan Zhongyan (AD 989–1052) have helped craft the imperial version of the Chinese Dream: success through exams.[3]

His childhood was tragic—his father having died when he was but two years old, he was later abandoned by his mother. Impoverished, he sought refuge and education in a Buddhist temple. Tales of his austere work ethic are legion: studying late into the night, subsisting on morsels of cold porridge, and splashing cold water on his face to stay awake. When fatigue overcame him, he forsook the comforts of a bed in favor of resting at his desk, sleeping in his clothes to save time in the morning. His study and hard work paid off. After passing the notoriously difficult imperial civil service examination, he earned the highest degree of *jinshi* in 1015. His subsequent career saw a steady rise in the bureaucratic ranks—salt inspector, military prefect, culminating in the exalted position as imperial vice chancellor. Recounted by generations of parents at bedtime, and inscribed into literature and poetry, stories such as Fan's have nurtured deeply engrained beliefs throughout East Asia as well as among the Chinese diaspora regarding education as a means for upward mobility for even the poorest in society.

Reality is more complicated. Studies of the imperial bureaucracy reveal their ranks were disproportionately filled by members of wealthy southern families able to pay for decades of tutoring to prepare them for the exams.[4] But there is a kernel of truth to the stories. Success could alter lives overnight. And just as exceptional tales such as those of John D. Rockefeller or Steve Jobs feed the American Dream of becoming a self-made billionaire through hard work and persistence, so have those like Fan Zhongyan fueled the traditional Chinese Dream. Study hard, young man, and you too can become a county magistrate.

There is a deep sense that this is how things *should* work. Zhu Suli, former dean of Beijing University Law School, argues that it amounts to an unwritten Chinese constitutional pact between rulers and ruled.[5] Accept our rule, and your children will have an equal opportunity to serve in our ranks. Violated, it provokes a sense of injustice. When Mongol rulers of the Yuan dynasty (AD 1271–1368) annulled the imperial examinations, it produced deep resentment among the educated southern elite excluded from channels of power, contributing to an early fall of the regime.[6] Conversely, when central leaders respect this principle, it provides legitimacy. The Manchus who conquered China in 1644 were but a small, semi-nomadic, foreign tribe from beyond the Great Wall. Nonetheless, they successfully solidified their rule into the Qing dynasty (AD 1644–1911) by co-opting Han intellectuals through adopting the examination system and offering them paths to influence within the system.[7]

The Communist Party's rise to power in 1949 did not alter this dynamic. If anything, the first administration of the *gaokao* (national college entrance examination) in 1952 marked a re-establishment of the historical pact between Chinese state and society after decades of wartime chaos. Intellectuals embraced the opportunity to see their college-educated children rise up as cadres, while rural farmers could hold on to the faint hope that successful completion of a mass literacy program might at least result in a desk job in the village commune.

This is why the Cultural Revolution was such a traumatic event. Millions were violently persecuted in internecine political violence. But it is the closure of schools and the cancellation of the *gaokao* in 1966 that continues to evoke particular horror among educated Chinese. Even today, many still regard with disdain the *gongnongbing* (worker, peasant, solider) students admitted to what passed for higher education via "political recommendations" during the early 1970s.

In the fall of 1977, Deng Xiaoping's first step on his return to power was . . . the revival of the *gaokao*. The signal was unmistakable; the effect, electric. Normalcy was returning. For a decade's worth of intellectuals trapped in hard labor on rural communes, it was a heaven-sent opportunity to escape. Across China, they pulled out faded textbooks carefully hidden away for years. And by flickering candlelight, they began to prepare.

If you were one of the lucky few to enter college in 1978, you were part of a golden generation. Intense competition between 6 million applicants had produced an entering class of just 273,000. With a matriculation rate of just 4.7 percent, it was the lowest in modern Chinese history. As the cream of China's youth gathered in newly reopened classrooms, there was a sense of limitless possibilities. "It was a time full of dreams and hopes for the future," as one put it.[8] Even decades later, members of the class such as legal scholar He Weifang still remember the sense of awe they felt upon entering school libraries for the first time.[9] Plucked from rural obscurity, they stood poised to realize the millennia-old Chinese dream of both improving their own life status and helping to guide the nation to a better future.

And it was true. Those who emerged from China's colleges in the early 1980s found the world at their feet. Between decades of Maoist radicalism and Deng's efforts to reverse the Cultural Revolution, two entire generations had been swept away. Across all fields—art, government, science—there was a total void between the new graduates and their elderly Soviet-trained mentors. Advancement came quickly. Scholars who stayed on to teach in universities (such as Zhu and He) saw their careers ascend rapidly, as the expanding numbers of students generated a voracious need for new teachers. Similar trends took place in other spheres. Today, these early graduates disproportionately occupy the pinnacles of influence throughout China, including figures such as Li Keqiang (state premier) and Zhang Yimou (film director).

Of course, numbers of college graduates during the 1980s remained minuscule—a few hundred thousand in a nation of a billion. For the vast masses of Chinese citizens eagerly seeking education, a spectrum of vocational colleges, technical high schools, and short-term programs provided training. Needs were immense. In 1983, only 3 percent of judges, procurators, and justice bureau officials held the equivalent of a junior college degree in law or above. Over 54 percent had received less than a month of legal training.[10] And as the saying goes, in the land of the blind, the one-eyed man is king. In those early reform years, simply

getting *any* state educational certification offered the promise of changing one's life for the better.

That promise is now fraying.

Numerically, China's reform era saw a dramatic expansion in education. In the early 1980s, less than 70 percent of elementary school
graduates went on to junior high school, and only one-third of junior
high school students continued on to high school. Now, almost all students complete junior high school, while over 80 percent continue on
to high school.[11]

But higher education in China is seizing up in terms of its traditional
role of facilitating social mobility. On the one hand, state-led development plans have led to a dramatic devaluation in the worth of a college
degree in general. On the other, spreading socioeconomic inequalities
are combining to exclude poor, rural, and migrant children from those
key schools that still matter.

Take the latter point first. Just as with K–12 education, numbers of
rural students attending university increased steadily over the reform
era—rising from roughly 43 percent of entering college students in 1989
to 59 percent in 2012.[12] But elite institutions increasingly became the
exclusive preserve of wealthy urbanities. Peking University—China's
top school—is one example. In the 1980s, roughly 30 percent of the
entering class hailed from the countryside. Starting around 1990, however, those numbers began a steady decline. By 2010, they had fallen
to roughly 10 percent—when China's registered rural residents still
accounted for over two-thirds of the total population.[13] Other top
schools saw similar trends.[14]

What explains this?

One factor lies in the reform era itself. In the 1990s, Beijing began
to retreat from socialist policies of providing elementary and second-
ary school education as a public good. The share of such funding provided by the government dropped from 84 percent (1991) to 62 percent
(2004). Schools increasingly resorted to tuition and miscellaneous fees
to cover the difference.[15] These raised barriers faced by poor and rural
students, particularly at more elite institutions. Increasing privatization
of educational finance also facilitated proliferation of channels in K–12
schools—some legal, others not—to admit students whose exam scores

may not have reached required levels, but who came from wealthy or connected families.[16]

The effect was something very similar to that generated in the United States by a property tax–funded public school system, alumni preferences in college admissions, and declining state support for higher education—sharp social and economic divisions in access to education. By the early 2000s, the urban-rural divide had widened into a gaping chasm. Data from 2003 revealed that while some 64.9 percent of urban youth within the Beijing metropolitan area received any form of college education, only 14.6 percent of their rural counterparts did so. Even sharper divisions show up in relatively poorer inland regions. Corresponding statistics for Yunnan province, for example, reveal that only 28.7 percent of urban youth entered any college. The figure for rural youth: a mere 4.3 percent.[17]

A second reason for these divisions lies in the Maoist legacy of the *hukou* (household registration) system. Born in the 1950s as a tough system of population control and resource allocation, it separated citizens into caste-like categories. Rural peasants were bound to the land they farmed. Urban factory workers and state cadres were eligible for food rations, subsidized housing, old-age pensions, and other public services—all things denied to their rural counterparts. Tough barriers limited the ability of citizens to change their *hukou* registration (success at the *gaokao* being one crucial exception) and made status hereditary—parents passed on their own identification to their children.

Since the reform era, much about the *hukou* system has changed. Rationing has disappeared. Controls on physical movement have lifted. Hundreds of millions of rural migrants have flooded into China's cities as a result. But the tie to public services remains strong. Consequently, reform-era China experienced what observers have called "urbanization without 'citizen-ation'."[18] By 2010, China's *de facto* urban population totaled 666 million. But roughly 200 million of those—nearly a third—lacked urban *hukou*.[19] Faced with local regulations that impose strict conditions (such as the purchase of high-end housing) as a condition for obtaining urban *hukou*, blue-collar migrants find themselves an urban underclass, generally excluded local public services such as education for their children—many who are increasingly born in urban areas.

Rural migrants are left with few good options for their children's education. Bring their children with them to urban areas and send them to subpar private schools funded and run by migrants themselves.[20] Attempt to enroll them in urban public schools (sometimes forking out expensive fees to do so) and run the risk of being driven out by periodic enforcement campaigns aimed at limiting urban population growth, such as the one mounted by Beijing municipal authorities in 2014.[21] Or as is the case for 61 million children, or one out of five in China, leave them behind in rural areas with a single parent or elderly grandparents—and watch as family bonds, mental health, and school performance suffer under extended separations lasting a decade or more.[22] Naturally, such a choice also leaves deep emotional scars. Roughly half of such "left-behind" children suffer depression and anxiety, compared with 30 percent of their urban peers.[23]

For those children who manage to struggle through in the face of all of these challenges, the *hukou* system has yet one last cruel twist. Entrenched preferences favor registered urban residents of large metropolises. Consider Peking University again. In 2004, the annual quota for entering students was 1,748. Of those, some 308 spots were reserved for Beijing residents (some 80,000 applicants total), and 94 for those from Jiangsu province (400,000 applicants)—rendering the odds for a Beijing student to be admitted some thirty times greater than one from Jiangsu.[24] Nearly a decade later, the chasm had widened yet further, with Peking University taking some 408 students from Beijing (roughly 73,000 applicants), but only 57 from Jiangsu (out of 450,000 applicants).[25] Students with Beijing or Shanghai *hukou* whose parents have splashed out for expensive private tutors and vacations on the Rivera can consequently have dramatically *lower* scores on the *gaokao* than the corresponding rural (or migrant) student who has spent winters shivering in an unheated, dilapidated classroom and still enter an elite college, while the latter is denied entry.[26]

This lopsided lottery represents institutionalized discrimination in favor of registered urbanites—one systematically baked into the Chinese state. In the 1950s, this facilitated extraction of wealth from the countryside in favor of urban workers needed to carry out Mao's industrialization plans. With urbanization, that social division has now moved into China's cities themselves. Ironically, Chinese authorities have themselves fueled the rise of divisions even more severe than in highly unequal capitalist economies such as the United States. "Proletariat" and "bourgeoisie" are not abstract class labels—they are effectively stamped onto each individual's *hukou* registration. And in a reversal of Marxist logic, Communist authorities now stand on the side of the latter—discriminating against farmers and workers for the sake of middle class urbanites.

There is yet another problem facing Chinese higher education. The role of college itself as a springboard to a better future has declined. Worsening job prospects have seized popular attention. When in 2012, surveys revealed that starting salaries for 69 percent of Chinese college graduates were under 2000 *yuan* (US\$322) per month—a figure below the average wage for migrant laborers—newspaper headlines and social media posts exploded.[27] As late as the 1980s, university students had been officially ranked as state cadres upon entering college. How could their fortunes possibly have fallen so far?

This is tied to a third factor that has undermined the *gaokao*'s role in facilitating social mobility in China: a massive devaluation in the value of a college degree over the past two decades.

During the early reform era, only a limited number of students received admission to university. After the historic low of 1978, *gaokao* pass rates rose to around 25 percent by 1988, and increased only slightly—to 34 percent—by 1998.[28] As a rare commodity, a college degree was valuable, conferring social prestige, access to networks of successful and influential classmates, and a range of official benefits (urban *hukou*, state employment, and state-provided housing).

This ended decisively in the late 1990s, when Chinese authorities launched a crash expansion of higher education. This was partially a long-term effort to raise national educational levels, but it also represented a short-term stimulus effort aimed at increasing domestic demand in the wake of the 1997–1998 Asian financial crisis.[29] Total state expenditures on higher education increased sixfold between 1997 and 2005, doubling as a percentage of GDP.[30]

Opening the funding floodgates provoked a feeding frenzy among Chinese colleges, particularly since additional monies were disproportionately skewed toward schools designated as universities of "world repute" under programs run by the Ministry of Education. University presidents courted favor in the eyes of Beijing officials, seeking to be ranked more highly than rivals when it came time for state budget allocations. Colleges dramatically expanded their physical facilities. Expansive leafy new campuses sprouted like wildflowers in the remote outskirts of major urban areas—Changping district in Beijing, or Minhang district in Shanghai. Vocational training fell by the wayside as all schools began to gravitate toward one-size-fits-all models of university education. Politics and law institutes added mathematics, journalism, and foreign language programs. Local teacher training schools and colleges traditionally run by the postal and water resources bureaus all founded law programs, regardless of whether they had the appropriate resources.[31]

Numbers of students exploded. In just two years, between 1998 and 2000, the entering class of first-year college students *doubled* from 1 to 2 million. It has soared in the years since. In 2016, over 7 million students entered Chinese colleges to begin their studies.[32] Chart 2.1 illustrates this growth, depicting the total number of college graduates, per year.[33]

Now, one does not obtain that kind of growth without consequences. Injection of massive quantities of money into higher education almost overnight created ample opportunities for graft. University administrators took advantage of their positions to profit from sweetheart construction deals involved in building entire new campuses from scratch.

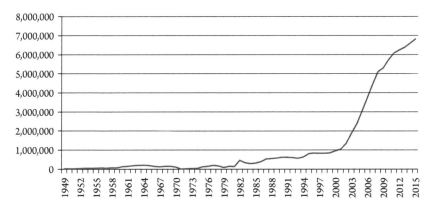

CHART 2.1 Number of New College Graduates in China
Source: National Bureau of Statistics, 2015

By 2009, nearly one in three institutions of higher education in Hubei province alone had been implicated in corruption scandals.[34]

Centrally mandated targets used by Beijing to generate rapid growth also produced a range of perverse effects. For example, to promote academic research, Chinese authorities linked financial and career incentives to numbers of published articles, issued patents, or scholarly citations produced by schools or individual professors. Such efforts did prompt a massive expansion in the volume of scholarly output. The percentage of articles in major international scientific journals published by Chinese researchers surged from near zero in 2001 to 9.5 percent in 2011, second only to the United States.[35] But this "Great Leap Forward" approach also fueled a massive cottage industry of fraud. Black markets developed, with fabricated papers and guarantees of placement in domestic Chinese journals trading for thousands of *yuan* apiece.[36] Nor is the effect limited to China. In December 2014, *Scientific American* revealed the existence of paper mills that, for a fee of some 93,000 RMB (US$15,000), would "sell" authorship of draft scholarly articles for submission to international journals, identifying some 100 published articles that it suspected "bore the hallmarks of fill-in-the-blanks science."[37] Many Chinese academics themselves are very negative about these trends. They perceive a significant decline in the quality of higher education since the late 1990s. "The system itself creates moral problems."[38] "We have forgotten what a university is."[39]

College graduates themselves also became collateral damage. Start with an educational system initially modeled along German lines, with many vocational schools and few university programs. Dramatically decrease *gaokao* selectivity (2015 acceptance rate: 74.3 percent). Increase the annual number of college graduates by 500 percent in less than a decade. What do you get? On one hand, a bubble of underemployed graduates. And on the other, a drought of skilled technicians and laborers. These are precisely the factors that have fueled an unemployment rate for Chinese college graduates (16.4 percent) almost *four* times higher than for those who had only completed elementary school (4.2 percent).[40] In turn, this has helped drive up salaries for blue-collar workers, while depressing those for recent college graduates. In 2000, fresh Chinese computer science graduates in Shenzhen could command salaries roughly ten times that of laborers lacking a high school degree. By 2013, the former received less than twice as much as their blue-collar counterparts.[41] Even more strikingly, salaries for many new college graduates are not simply remaining stagnant. They are actually falling. A 2017 survey found monthly wages for recent graduates had dropped 16 percent, marking the second year in a row that such a drop had occurred.[42]

Such shifts have been good for migrant workers, strengthening their bargaining positions with respect to employers, allowing them to demand higher salaries, and increasing their leverage to fight back against abusive working conditions.[43] And they are responsible for the beginnings of a fundamental change in attitudes toward higher education in China. As one blue-collar Shanghai elevator mechanic commented on possible paths for the eighteen-year-old high school daughter of his colleague, "Take the *gaokao* and go to college? Why—don't you know that's just a waste of time and money? She should just get a job!" [44] But these trends are a serious problem for millions of new graduates who expect that their newly minted educational credentials will allow them to improve their status.

So what do you do if you are an unemployed Chinese college graduate or at risk of becoming one? One answer: delay. This has been behind the massive expansion of master's programs in recent years—which allow students and school to kick the can down the road for another three years, but do not address the core institutional factors contributing to the glut of graduates.

Yet another option is exit. Increasingly, the Chinese Dream for those with the means involves getting your children out of China and into a U.S. college[45] (see Chart 2.2[46]). Unlike earlier waves of Chinese graduate students from the 1980s and 1990s, dependent on merit scholarships to attend, these are increasingly college (or even high school) students from well-heeled families paying full tuition, and representing a significant revenue stream for American schools. At the University of Washington, for example, over one out of seven members of the 2015 freshman class was an international student, primarily from mainland China, paying roughly $50,000 per year in tuition and fees.[47]

Higher education in China is increasingly becoming a luxury good— a status symbol divorced from its traditional role as an aspirational tool for social mobility.[48] Of course, this is not unique to China. Escalating

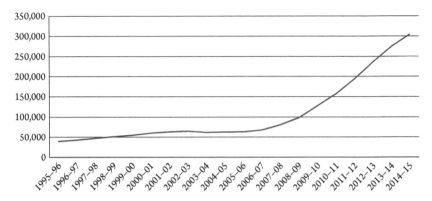

CHART 2.2 Number of Mainland Chinese Students in U.S. Colleges
Source: Internanational institute of Education, 2015

tuition, declining public funding, and rising student debt are producing parallel trends in the United States—a dramatic reduction in the financial accessibility of college to the public at large, and a corresponding decrease in its role as a steppingstone to a middle class lifestyle. But higher education has never been that central to the American Dream. John D. Rockefeller left high school. Bill Gates, Steve Jobs, and Mark Zuckerberg are college dropouts. If American universities continue their slide back toward the role that Harvard and Princeton historically occupied in the nineteenth century—expensive finishing schools for children of the wealthy to socialize and find mates, it might be an unfortunate tragedy, but it would not fundamentally challenge who Americans think they are.

This is not true in China. The annual June administration of the *gaokao* is one of the few truly national rites that bind society together, with police mobilized to reroute traffic, shutter noisy outdoor activities, and usher applicants to and from examination sites, while nervous parents mill around outside for hours in the sweltering heat to encourage (or console) their children as they emerge. Higher education enjoys this outsized role in large part because many have traditionally viewed the *gaokao* as one of the few relatively egalitarian channels for upward social mobility—the modern incarnation of the imperial Chinese Dream.

But at both extremes of Chinese society, there is now a- steady exit from what has been the core of the social contract for generations. At the top, children of the elite are flocking to American colleges, prompting surging luxury car sales at Mercedes dealerships around schools ranging from Michigan State University to the University of Oregon.[49] And at the bottom, Chinese academics voice concerns of an emerging urban youth underclass, comprising underemployed college graduates and migrant youth excluded from regular educational channels, fueling a "hardening of class differences" (*jieceng gehua*).[50]

Such rising problems in Chinese higher education are but a microcosm of the socioeconomic challenges confronting the nation at large: unreformed state institutions that are legacies of the Maoist era, rising inequality produced by the reform era itself, and the steadily accumulating drag created by decades of binge spending. Contrary to the arguments of those who argue that China today is drawing on its own cultural past to forge a new "China Model" of meritocratic rule,[51] these trends reflect the precise opposite: a closing of the traditional Chinese Dream.

THE COMMUNIST DREAM: EQUALITY UNDER SOCIALISM

The year 1949 presented a new version of the Chinese Dream: equality under socialism. Victorious after the civil war, China's new Communist leaders promised to lift the fortunes of the poor through a fundamental restructuring of society.

Under Mao, results were mixed. The early 1950s saw sweeping land reform. Estates of wealthy landlords were broken up and redistributed to impoverished tenant farmers—all to widespread popular acclaim. But within a decade, this was reversed. Peasants were compelled to turn over farms to rural communes in a process of forced collectivization, while state-imposed *hukou* barriers divided China into two unequal nations—rural and urban, with the former firmly yoked into the service of the latter.

Despite backing away from the planned economy, Deng's initial reforms in the 1980s ironically came closer to realizing the early socialist vision than at any point before or since. The dismantling of rural communes, coupled with the granting of long-term leasehold rights, allowed farmers themselves to reap the benefits of the land they tilled—even absent full privatization. Financial liberalization extended credit to rural businesses. Township and village enterprises boomed.[52] The rising tide of development not only lifted all boats, it lifted those of rural residents *faster* than their urban counterparts. Urban-rural income ratios consequently swung in the direction of greater equality, reaching historical lows in the mid-1980s.[53]

But the past three decades have seen a major shift. Economic stratification in China has risen dramatically, reflected in the steadily increasing Gini coefficient, a statistical measure of a nation's distribution of income between rich and poor (0 representing perfect equality, 1 perfect inequality). (See Chart 2.3.)[54]

China, in the early 1980s, had a more egalitarian distribution of income than European social welfare states such as Sweden or Germany. Since the late 1980s, that has reversed. Official statistics now place China (2015 Gini: 0.46) in the ranks of the top 25 percent most unequal nations in the world, alongside such highly divided societies such as Mexico, Peru, and the United States.[55]

However, even these estimates are questionable. In 2000, as rising inequality pushed China's Gini coefficient past 0.40—the level that many experts flag as a precursor to rising social unrest—China's statistics bureau stopped issuing an official index. It resumed only in 2013—at which point it released the data for the prior decade (depicted in Chart 2.3) showing that inequality had peaked and begun to decline slightly.[56] Others have reached different conclusions. In 2014, a team of

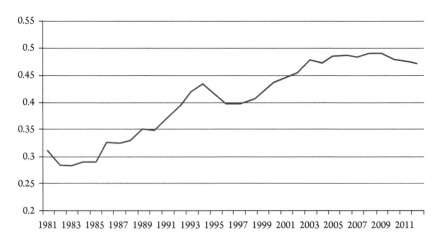

CHART 2.3 China's Gini Coefficient

Source: Terry Sicular/World Bank, 2013

Chinese scholars at the University of Michigan and Peking University derived a figure around 0.53–0.55—situating China's inequality alongside that of Brazil and higher than all but a few economically polarized African and Latin American nations such as South Africa and Haiti.[57] And at least one authoritative Chinese scholar has reached an even higher estimate—placing China's 2010 Gini coefficient at an astronomically high 0.61.[58]

This differs significantly from other East Asian states. Both Taiwan and South Korea, for example, underwent their respective economic boom eras while maintaining relative social equality. Between 1970 and 1988, South Korea's Gini coefficient rose moderately, from 0.33 to 0.40, before beginning to decline in the 1990s. Taiwan managed to hold its corresponding figure nearly constant at around 0.30, before slightly worsening to 0.325 (in 1999).[59] Even among other populous developing nations, China is an exception. Patterns in Indonesia and India resemble those of South Korea and Taiwan.[60] Even Brazil, where absolute levels of inequality have traditionally been far above China, registered a steady decline over the 1990s and 2000s, from 0.625 (1989) to 0.527 (2012).[61]

Of course, China's rising economic disparities do not reflect an absolute decline in the fortunes of the poor. Between 2002 and 2007, incomes of China's least well off increased by 46 percent, causing the absolute poverty rate to fall by half. Rather, increasing inequality is being driven by the fact that—in contrast to the 1980s—China's wealthiest have simply gotten much, much richer than everyone else. During that same five-year period, incomes of China's top 10 percent rose over twice as fast (94 percent) as their counterparts at the bottom of society.[62]

What explains this shift from the relatively egalitarian China of the 1980s to a much more economically skewed one today?

One key factor: a major reversal of the pro-rural state policies that had characterized the early reform period. As economist Yasheng Huang has extensively detailed, the 1990s witnessed a crackdown on institutions of rural finance, the downfall of village and township enterprises, and the adoption of pro-urban biases in state economic plans.[63] The impact of early land reforms also began to fade. The 1980s saw large increases in both agricultural productivity and rural incomes, as farmers received progressively longer lease rights to farmland. But by the 1990s, the bulk of those gains had already been realized, and growth in rural incomes began to slow.[64]

Now, this didn't stop China's economic expansion. GDP continued to rise at blistering double-digit rates each year, while the skylines of major urban areas exploded with new skyscrapers. But the nature of growth shifted. Increasingly, the main beneficiaries were China's established urban residents, particularly those tied to the state sector, rather than the broad rural masses. As Huang notes, "Whereas Chinese capitalism in the 1980s was a rags-to-riches capitalism, the capitalism in the 1990s led to sharp income inequalities, a reduction of social opportunities available to the rural population, slower income growth, and an investment-heavy growth pattern."[65] This is precisely the opposite of the development track followed by Taiwan.[66] Rural farmers leaving the countryside—who in Taiwan formed the foundation for a booming entrepreneurial middle class—in mainland China instead joined a wave of blue-collar migrant laborers working on sprawling construction sites in urban areas.[67]

Subsequent state policies exacerbated these trends. Take housing. In the 1990s, China launched a mass privatization of its state-owned residential housing stock. Existing owners were offered the opportunity to purchase their units at deep discounts. Home ownership among established urban residents surged. Only 11 percent in 1978, it rose to almost 80 percent in 2002.[68] Since rural migrants were generally not state employees, and did not live in state-provided housing, they were commonly outside the scope of such programs. Housing privatization consequently amounted to a one-time windfall for existing urban residents, particularly those tied to the state. As Walder and He note, "Households with a state sector affiliation had barely half the odds of owning a home than others in 1988, but they were around 50 percent more likely than others by 2002."[69]

Concentration of assets in the hands of a narrow urban elite had significant consequences. Housing prices in China boomed in the first decade of the twenty-first century—tripling nationally, and quadrupling in metropolises such as Beijing and Shanghai—driven by a combination of loose lending policies, central stimulus programs that poured massive resources into construction, local government reliance on sales of land rights to developers for revenue, and the lack of alternative investment vehicles.[70] By 2016, Shenzhen had surged past London and Hong Kong to become the second-most expensive housing market in the world, after Silicon Valley.[71] Those who owned property at the outset saw the value of their apartments skyrocket. Others traded up— buying and selling units in a frenetic race to acquire more-desirable properties in new developments. Left out were those who did not share in the initial distribution of assets: rural migrants and the young.

By 2015, the richest 10 percent in China controlled roughly two-thirds of the nation's wealth (heavily concentrated in real estate), while the bottom quarter of all households accounted for but 1 percent. Both the original communist dream and the promise of the 1980s have thus come full circle. In China, a nominally socialist country, levels of wealth inequality now approach those of the capitalist United States—where over 70 percent of national wealth is concentrated in the hands of just 10 percent of the population.[72]

SOCIAL RISKS AND STATE RESPONSES

These trends are not unique to China. In the United States, inequalities in wealth and income have worsened to levels not seen since the Great Depression.[73] A generation of boomers that came of age in an era of low tuition, full employment, and generous pensions is giving way to one of millennials who know only a world of rising student debt and unpaid internships. Popular concern has fed a proliferation of books with titles such as *Inequality*, *The Great Divide*, and *Our Kids: The American Dream in Crisis*.[74] Similar unease is evident in Europe. High unemployment, fraying social-welfare policies, and the multiyear euro crisis have steadily undermined the continental dream of ever-closer political and economic union. On both sides of the Atlantic, national malaise has fueled the rise of radical voices on the right and left alike (Donald Trump, Bernie Sanders, Jeremy Corbyn) and parties (Front National, Syriza).

The frozen nature of Beijing's rule means that such pressures have not—as yet—produced similar shifts in China's political system. But they are bubbling up in society. On the more innocuous end of the spectrum, this consists of phenomena such as the emergence of the term *diaosi* (around 2011) as a self-mocking term adopted by Chinese youth to refer to their generation: unable to purchase houses, obtain well-paying jobs, settle down in relationships, and doomed to struggle for opportunities taken for granted by their parents.[75] English-language media commonly renders *diaosi* as "loser." But to more accurately convey to an American audience the sense of the term as used in China, one needs to invoke more familiar U.S. cultural memes, such as "Starbucks barista with an English degree" or "student debt–ridden millennials living in their parents' basement," even if the precise details of those (such as student debt) do not apply to Chinese youth.

For some, the sentiment that the rules of the game are rigged against them fuels bitter resentment against the powerful, wealthy, and corrupt. This periodically erupts into spectacular outbursts of popular opinion—in social media or on Internet blog posts. Take the 2008 case of Yang Jia, an unemployed twenty-eight-year old who stormed a Shanghai police station, killing six officers, after allegedly suffering abuse at their hands during an earlier interrogation. Or the 2009 example of Deng Yujiao, a young hotel waitress who defended herself against the sexual advances of a local cadre, stabbing him to death in the process. Both incidents quickly metastasized into online sensations. Millions of comments and posts on websites flowed forth. Public sentiment swung strongly in favor of the defendants—lionizing them as symbols of the weak standing up to the powerful.[76]

Such phenomena are not limited to online venues. Recent years have seen a series of violent conflicts between street vendors and urban enforcement personnel (*chengguan*).[77] After a 2013 incident in Hunan province left a watermelon vendor dead, a bloody clash ensued between police and hundreds of angry onlookers who gathered to support the vendor's family. Prominent blogger Li Chengpeng subsequently penned an essay that went viral on social media:

> The authorities dispatched hundreds of police, trying to seize the corpse of the vendor. This is in fact a metaphor for today's China, where the state is seizing property everywhere through a variety of means: businessmen are losing their enterprises and thrown into prison; an anonymous vendor is losing his watermelons. Sometimes it's the urban management officers that seize the property. Sometimes it's the court, or the bank, or the unpredictable policies.

To those business tycoons who have remained silent, please say something.

In this country, nobody is secure. If you choose to stay quiet today, they will be seizing your business empires tomorrow like they seized the watermelons . . .

. . . The watermelon vendor, Deng Zhengjia, lived in a mountain near Linwu County. He wanted to grow sweet watermelons, have a magnificent harvest, and sell his watermelons quickly, so that he could get home in time for dinner. This was his Chinese dream. He took great care of his watermelons.

Why didn't you take care of him? Before we sit down to talk about the Chinese dream, you should protect a watermelon vendor's dream.

Be nice to your people, and to your watermelons. Plant melons, you get melons. Sow beans, and you get beans.[78]

Nor is Li's "reap what you sow" message mere speculation. Ten months later, a crowd of roughly a thousand people in Zhejiang province savagely beat (possibly to death) five *chengguan* officials suspected of killing a local civilian.[79] A litany of other examples could be invoked as well—such as the 2008 case of Xia Junfeng, a Shenyang street vendor who stabbed two *chengguan* officials to death and emerged as a subject of online admiration, or the 2013 incident of a Xiamen villager spraying nineteen *chengguan* with sulfuric acid in the wake of a dispute over the demolition of his house.[80] Such tensions lie inchoate in Chinese society. These are not a clearly focused "social volcano" of pent-up resentment against the Communist Party.[81] Nor are they a wellspring of incipient Jeffersonian liberalism.[82] Rather, they are the product of a myriad of accumulated individual grievances. Tensions surface in a range of ways, with a spectrum of targets. Some take the form of well-organized, carefully calculated protest strategies. Since 2011, there has been a steady rise in the numbers of collective labor protests, with thousands of aggrieved workers blocking roads and stopping work in an effort to apply pressure on employers and local governments alike to address their claims of unpaid back wages and unsafe working conditions.[83]

Others are uncontrolled explosions of mob violence, or what Chinese sociologist Yu Jianrong has termed "anger-venting riots." As he notes, these

> lac[k] a specific grievance. They are precipitated by accidental con-
> flicts between private citizens, but they quickly escalate into large
> and often extremely violent mobs, with most rioters having little
> connection to the causal incident. Bystanders join in the violence to
> vent their own resentment at unfair practices of local governments.
> As news of the incident spreads through modern communication
> channels, mobs can quickly swell to over 10,000 people . . .
>
> . . . Anger-venting riots are often devoid of specific issues, or quickly
> become divorced from the original issue. These riots devolve into
> behavior such as smashing, looting and burning. . . . Unlike a polit-
> ical or economic protest, the vast majority of participants have no
> direct stake in the outcome of the incident. Those involved are usu-
> ally observers, even passerby, simply reacting to perceived injustices.
> They take advantage of the situation to display frustration about
> their own personal grievances, expressing dissatisfaction with social
> injustice. [84]

Frustration can also devolve into random violence. Between 2010 and 2012, China was shaken by an unconnected wave of mass attacks on schools throughout the country. In contrast to American school massacres—often marked by students killing each other with easily obtainable firearms—Chinese attacks commonly featured a middle-aged man storming a kindergarten or elementary school with a meat cleaver or knife and stabbing large numbers of students, often chosen at random.* Some attackers were mentally ill. Others had failed romantic relationships. But a common thread running through many incidents was the decision of the assailant to violently vent anger resulting from

---

* Naturally, death tolls were lower as a result. On December 14, 2012, over two dozen children and teachers were slain by a gunman wielding a semiautomatic weapon at the Sandy Hook primary school in Connecticut. That very same day, a knife-wielding assailant attacked twenty-three students and an adult at the Chenpeng primary school in Henan province. Not one died.

his own economic failings or legal disputes on the most defenseless members of society. When forty-seven-year old Xu Yuyuan, unemployed for a decade, went on trial in 2010 for attacking over thirty students and teachers, he testified that his assault was motivated by rage against society stemming from a string of business and personal failures.[85] In 2017, following a suicide bombing at a Jiangsu kindergarten that killed eight and injured sixty-five, authorities identified the culprit as a twenty-two-year old university dropout holding a range of temporary jobs and suffering from antisocial tendencies.[86] Nor are schools the only target. Recent years have witnessed a spate of bus bombings and arson attacks by Chinese citizens embroiled in legal disputes, apparently choosing to target the public at large as in retribution for their individual grievances.[87]

China's leaders are all too aware of the dangers of these trends. Their own revolutionary past and socialist ideology are omnipresent reminders of the latent risks posed by a combustible mix of disaffected youth, blue-collar workers, and rural poor excluded from the life enjoyed by a narrow urban elite. However, Beijing's instinct is often to focus on controlling the external manifestations of underlying problems. When the Party's flagship newspaper tells Chinese youth to stop using the term *diaosi* and pushes them to transmit "positive energy" instead,[88] one can almost hear aging leaders lecturing a generation of Chinese millennials to "stop being so negative, get off the couch, and do something with your life." Suppressing bad news is another option. Official censors seek to scrub the Internet clean of references to social conflicts that erupt into violence.[89] Since 2013, they have also aggressively moved to silence prominent online critics (such as Li Chengpeng, the blogger quoted above) via intimidation and direct suspension of their social media accounts.[90] Naturally, this merely inhibits the open discussion of the underlying causes of such conflicts, rather than helping effectively address them.

But other state reforms do seek to tackle socioeconomic problems at their roots. The early 2000s saw a sustained push by the Hu Jintao administration to promote pro-rural policies and redress the widening income divide. Agricultural taxes were abolished, direct subsidies extended to rural households, and a nationwide rural cooperative health care program put into place.[91] Such policies helped stabilize the gap between rich and poor (see Chart 2.3), albeit at a relatively high level of inequality.[92] Education was also targeted for reform. In 2005, Chinese authorities announced the elimination of fees for the poorest rural students.[93] Subsequent years saw tuition and school fees lifted throughout the nine years of compulsory education in primary and middle school. And in 2015, central authorities even began to take aim at inequalities in college education, raising quotas for rural students at top Chinese universities, while (slightly) limiting those for their urban counterparts.[94]

Such efforts to reallocate resources encounter deep resistance from those who have benefited from China's reform era. Wealthy urban parents who have splashed out millions of *yuan* to obtain a *xuequfang*—apartments purchased in desirable school districts solely for the purpose of allowing their children to enroll there—viscerally reject requiring their children to share classrooms with, or give up college spots to, rural or migrant children.[95] In the spring of 2016, protests broke out as the details of central plans to reallocate college admissions quotas were announced. Thousands of parents took to the streets in Hubei and Jiangsu, angrily rejecting changes that would negatively affect their children's chances to attend college, and questioning why the bulk of the quota reductions (78,000 out of 160,000 slots) should fall on their two provinces, while Beijing city officials were exempted from making any reductions whatsoever.[96]

Municipal planners find themselves torn between responding to such local pressures and sweeping central orders to provide more services to migrants and rural residents—often without providing additional funding.[97] Some reforms are abandoned as a result. The 2016 college admissions reforms discussed above were shelved in the wake of the social blowback.[98] Others are diluted in practice. As central authorities ramped up pressure to better educate migrant children, Shanghai officials adopted policies in 2008 steering them out of unlicensed private schools and incorporating them into local public schools.[99] But a proliferation of barriers followed. Some schools were set aside exclusively for migrant children. Other adopted explicit spatial segregation policies. Local children take classes in one building, migrant children in another. Different teachers are hired for each group, while class times are staggered to prevent intermixing on the playground.[100] Underlying tensions regularly resurface in new form. In 2016, Beijing announced plans to cap the city's population at 23 million by 2020, and reduce the number of residents in the urban core by 15 percent (compared with 2014).[101] Subsequent months saw an aggressive municipal crackdown on the cheap housing and back-alley stores where migrants live and work, with the aim of driving many out of the city entirely.[102] Pension battles now loom as the next front in these struggles, as central authorities seek to force wealthy eastern provinces flush with years of payments from migrant workers to shoulder more of the burden of paying for their retirements.[103]

Precisely these problems have hampered broader efforts at nationwide *hukou* reform. Over the past two decades, central leaders have made sweeping announcements regarding the need for change—with the 2013 central Party plenum simply one of the most recent examples. Foreign media periodically pick these up, breathlessly announcing that Chinese *hukou* distinctions are to be "abolish[ed]."[104] But implementation details (including the most recent round) have regularly paralleled similar reforms dating back to the late 1990s: relative openness in the smallest cities (with least *hukou*-related benefits), continuing tight controls in the largest cities (with the most), with preferential access limited to the wealthiest and best educated.[105]

A NEW DREAM FOR THE TWENTY-FIRST CENTURY

Facing deeply entrenched social inequalities, China's leaders are attempting to craft a new vision to inspire citizens. Since his rise to power in 2012, Xi Jinping has assiduously promoted his own version of the Chinese Dream (*zhongguo meng*). This signature propaganda effort (analyzed in greater depth in Chapter 4) is a sweeping attempt to shift the ideological basis of Beijing's rule away from the Marxist framework that the Communist Party has embraced since the 1949 revolution to a more explicitly ethnonationalist vision rooted in "traditional Chinese culture," invoking both classical norms and Confucian values.

But Xi's version of the Chinese Dream has another element too. As Chinese leaders have stated in both the current Five-Year Plan (2016–2020) and at venues such as the 2015 Second World Internet Conference, they seek to remake China as an "innovation society." The late twentieth century saw China emerge as a low-cost manufacturing center for the world. Cheap labor fueled China's economic boom. But as wages rise, Beijing wants to see the nation move up the production chain—diversifying away from low-skill, low-value jobs producing cheap products for export (such as to Walmart). The goal: see China produce its own versions of Apple, Samsung, or Google—internationally recognized technology powerhouses, providing high-skill, high-value jobs for the graduates pouring out of China's colleges.[†]

To see this vision taking shape, head to the misty garden city of Hangzhou in eastern China. Pass up the attractions of the West Lake, famed by generations of Chinese painters and poets, and drive into the booming suburbs. There lies the sprawling campus of Alibaba. One of the largest e-commerce companies in the world, it crackles with the energy of Silicon Valley. Young tech and business professionals mingle amid the leafy green concourses, cafeteria, or on the basketball court. A juice bar churns out fruit blends on demand. Those seeking presents for proud relatives back home can stock up in the gift store, which carries a full line of plush dolls bearing the Alibaba logo.

Founded in 1999, Alibaba's growth has been exponential. Each day, it ships four times as many packages as U.S. e-commerce giant Amazon. Since 2009, Alibaba has single-handedly turned November 11 (Singles Day, an invented anti-Valentines Day celebration for the unattached) into the world's largest shopping extravaganza. Total sales on Alibaba's platform on that day alone in 2016 nearly tripled that spent by Americans across all online retail sites during Cyber Monday and Black Friday—*combined*.[106] Unsurprisingly, when Alibaba went public on the New York Stock Exchange in 2014, it marked the biggest IPO in history, raising US$25 billion. Nor is Alibaba content to remain solely focused on e-commerce. Rather, it is moving aggressively into online finance, pioneering new products that are steadily displacing commercial banks. And Alibaba is in the process of expanding its operations

---

[†] Side benefits include strengthening China's influence abroad, and lessening its dependence on American software and hardware suppliers (and the resulting vulnerability to U.S. intelligence agencies).

internationally, opening offices from the United States to Russia, and from Europe to Southeast Asia.

Alibaba's founder, Jack Ma, embodies many of the values that Beijing would like to encourage. His is a classic rags-to-riches tale. An English teacher from an ordinary family (and lacking a tech background), he assembled a team of hard-working dreamers to successfully build a domestic e-commerce giant in the face of stiff competition from foreign competitors such as eBay. He enjoys rock star status in the eyes of many youth. When he announces plans to supplant Walmart as the world's largest retailer, many see an incarnation of their own ambitions to make it big on a global scale.[107] His embrace of green initiatives—purchasing 28,100 acres of conservation land in upstate New York, devoting a set percentage of Alibaba's revenue to environmental purposes—has earned him immense popularity. A generation of aspiring young Chinese look at Ma and see their own version of Steve Jobs or Bill Gates—a new model of the self-made, socially responsible twenty-first-century Chinese tycoon, one distinctly different from exploitative local coal barons or Party princelings parachuted in to run state-owned monopolies.

Indeed, Beijing very much needs them to replicate Ma's success. China's boom years are over. Both the export industries and fixed investment (construction, real estate, and infrastructure) that powered three decades of 10 percent annual growth are tapped out. Xi Jinping himself is promoting the idea that China is shifting to a "new normal" characterized by permanently lower growth. Official statistics indicate that China's GDP growth rate (6.7 percent in 2016) is the slowest in twenty-five years.[108] But others believe China's actual growth rate has slowed much more dramatically—perhaps to 3 percent, or even less.[109] Corporate bankruptcies are spreading. Commodity prices have plunged, leading to massive overcapacity and contraction. Between 2013 and 2015, China's steel industry shed 550,000 jobs, while the coal industry lost 890,000—roughly the same number created during China's stimulus-driven expansion in response to the 2007 global financial crisis.[110]

Faced with these challenges, China's leaders are searching for alternative sources of growth and employment. Beijing hopes that a boom in start-ups and technology firms can employ the surging number of young graduates flowing out of colleges. Leaders also hope that such firms can help China successfully transition to a new economic model—one fueled by domestic consumer demand, rather than speculative real estate bubbles or government construction of half-empty airports. Here, Alibaba is again attempting to pioneer the way. It has announced plans to open rural e-commerce service centers in some 100,000 Chinese villages over the next three to five years. The aim is twofold. On the one hand, developing one-stop centers for rural citizens to make and receive delivery of online consumer purchases. On the other, provide platforms for them to sell rural products directly to urban markets.[111] For Alibaba, this offers the prospect of shifting the half of China's population still living in rural areas directly to online commerce (and thereby entirely bypassing the big box stores and Walmart-style supercenters that characterized the late-twentieth-century American retail evolution). For China, this offers the possibility of better connecting rural consumers to urban markets, fueling employment and wage growth in the countryside. Benefits of economic growth might spread more evenly through the country. And the wave of rural migrants to China's overpopulated coastal cities might slow—or even reverse—as many see the next frontier of economic opportunity beckoning in inland provinces.

At least, this is Beijing's hope. In the summer of 2015, Chinese authorities announced a slew of measures aimed at encouraging college graduates, migrant workers, and army veterans to leave the cities and become rural entrepreneurs.[112] These are but part of a broader state push. China's State Council has promised policy support for small- and medium-sized high-tech start-up companies.[113] National authorities are reworking curricula to promote entrepreneurship and innovation in China's schools.[114] The Ministry of Education is trying to make it easier for students to stop out of college to launch start-up businesses.[115] (An intriguing twist on the traditional Chinese dream of getting students *into* schools!) Last, Beijing is making major efforts to revive vocational training, which had fallen into neglect during China's two-decade-long obsession with four-year university education.[116]

Optimistic China "bulls" view such efforts in a positive light. The former chairman of Morgan Stanley Asia, Stephen Roach, identifies China's expanding services sector (comprising 51.6 percent of GDP in

2015, versus 44 percent in 2010) as evidence of an economy that is successfully shifting away its traditional base in industry and manufacturing and beginning to be driven by internal consumer demand.[117] Such trends boosted the bottom line for some investors. Notwithstanding China's economic troubles, Apple's in-country revenue nearly doubled in the last quarter of 2015, fueling expectations that China would emerge as its largest market by 2017.[118] Starbucks has announced massive expansion plans in China—aiming to open 500 stores per year through 2019.[119]

Others are doubtful. More hiring of Starbucks baristas may not offset the wrenching dislocations that will take place as entire swaths of Chinese industry slip into recession. As one analyst phrased it, "Coal miners do not become internet programmers overnight, or even delivery men."[120] Other barriers exist as well. In summer 2016, Beijing signaled approval for ride-sharing firms such as Uber (subsequently acquired by its domestic rival Didi). A positive omen for laid-off steel workers seeking employment in the urban gig economy? Not exactly. Subsequent months saw major cities such as Beijing, Shanghai, and Shenzhen roll out restrictive draft rules requiring ride-hailing drivers to possess a local *hukou*.[121] Foreign firms have been hit by shifting winds too. Contrary to earlier predictions, stiff local competition and heightened scrutiny by regulators of foreign technology firms led Apple's revenue in China to plunge dramatically, registering regular quarterly declines starting in 2016.[122] Faced with a challenging business climate, other foreign firms, such as McDonald's and Office Depot, decided to sell off their China operations to local ownership in 2017.[123]

Many once optimistic on the ability of China's leaders to manage the nation's economic transition have become very bearish. Back when Xi Jinping announced at China's 2013 Party plenum that Beijing intended to launch thoroughgoing reform of state-owned enterprises, and permit the market to play a "decisive role" in allocating resources, many saw this as a clear central commitment to undertake the necessary structural reforms. Few do now. As Arthur Kroeber, managing director of GaveKal Dragonomics, phrased it:

> Reforms . . . don't seem to have got much traction . . . because that is
> not where Xi's priorities are. . . . His priorities are ensuring that the

party is in the driver's seat with regard to everything, and maximizing his own power in the party.[124]

This perception—that politics are in command—is spreading. Observers once saw China as ruled by a technocratic elite capable of taking tough decisions to steer the country wisely into the future. Now, Party leaders are consumed by internal score settling and driven by an absolute determination to avoid taking any measures that might trigger social dissatisfaction.

Increasingly, economic policy making in China seems disorganized, dominated by a short-term mindset. Take China's 2014–2015 stock market bubble. Starting in 2014, Beijing intentionally began to "talk up" China's stock exchanges, apparently seeing surging markets as an effective means to raise capital for a new generation of domestic entrepreneurs. State media directly encouraged ordinary citizens to buy stocks. Valuations surged. The Shanghai stock market rose 150 percent in a single year. Citizens stampeded to invest, with two-thirds of new investors opening accounts in spring 2015 lacking a high school education.[125] Then—the collapse. In the summer of 2015, stocks collapsed, with the Shanghai exchange falling from the vertiginous heights of 5,166 (June 12) to 3,709 (July 9).

With panic spreading, Beijing unleashed heavy-handed measures aimed at doing whatever necessary to prop up markets. Trading halts froze investors out of three-quarters of traded stocks. Central bank funds were deployed to purchase shares. Public security officials thrust their way into the stock exchanges, issuing vague warnings about the need to investigate "malicious short-sellers."[126] A journalist from a prominent financial magazine was paraded on state television, confessing to bearing responsibility for "fabricating rumors" and contributing to the stock market plunge. Almost overnight, Chinese financiers found themselves the target of measures that they once thought reserved for a narrow fringe of human rights activists and dissidents. Fallout from the stock market collapse remained limited within China itself—less than 7 percent of urban residents are invested in the market, and stock ownership comprises a minuscule proportion of corporate and individual wealth. But the entire episode contributed to a loss of faith in Beijing's management of the economy. In January 2016, the *Economist* magazine captured the sentiment with a front-page cover of Xi Jinping piloting a dragon in flames, spinning into a rapid, uncontrolled descent.[127]

Yet deeper problems loom on the horizon. China managed to surmount the 2008 global financial crisis by a spate of stimulus spending that pumped billions of dollars into the economy, including loose credit policies channeling billions to local governments and SOEs.[128] Now the bill is coming due. National debt-to-GDP ratios have soared, raising the specter of a tidal wave of corporate bankruptcies, and the inability of local governments to pay worker wages. In May 2017, Moody's cut China's credit rating for the first time since 1989. Capital flight has picked up. China's stockpile of foreign reserves declined by US$1 trillion between 2014 and 2017, as funds flowed out of China, seeking safety in overpriced real estate markets from New York to Australia.[129] In turn, this has led to mounting pressure for China to depreciate its currency, prompting the steady imposition of capital controls, and raised the risk of a wave of competitive devaluations from other developing countries. Depending on the analyst one asks, such scenarios could result in anything from an extended period of deflation and slow growth in China along the lines of 1990s-era Japan, to the next worldwide depression.

CONCLUSION

China's rise was intimately tied to its ability to offer citizens hope for a better future. Doors opened for a broad swath of people throughout society.

This is no longer true. The late twentieth century saw go-go capitalism fuse with an unreformed one-Party political system to produce surging economic and social inequalities. Routes for advancement and wealth were steadily choked off; the initial promise of the reform era undermined. The inevitable end of China's three-decades-long boom is amplifying these underlying tensions.

Increasingly, Beijing finds itself constrained in the effort to craft a new Chinese Dream to replace the older, bankrupt ones. Accustomed to deploying mass resources to level mountains or build high-speed railroads to the horizon, Party leaders are now confronting new realities. Austerity politics. Hard budget constraints. Rising debt levels. And behind it all—a deep lack of clarity as to how China's black-box elite political system plans to respond.

Among both Chinese citizens and officials alike, the heady optimism that characterized the early 2000s has given way to a pervasive sense of uncertainty and foreboding as to what the future may hold.

3

Politics: Internal Decay and Social Unrest

THIRTY YEARS AGO, AS communism crumbled, Francis Fukuyama captured the mood of an era with his essay *The End of History* (1989). Liberal democracy was the end-state to which all nations would eventually converge.

But these days, he is more skeptical. Perhaps a touch disillusioned. The plight of weak and failed states from Papua New Guinea to Iraq have led him to shift away from a narrow focus on democracy. He has turned his attention to how strong states arise, publishing *The Origins of Political Order* in 2011. And with Western democracies facing political gridlock, government paralysis, and the financial influence of special interests, he began to look at how developed political systems rot, in *Political Order and Political Decay* (2014).[1]

Given such concerns, when Fukuyama gazed at reform-era China in the 1990s and 2000s, he was understandably impressed. He saw something different. An effective, centralized bureaucracy—i.e. "not Nigeria or Pakistan."[2] Technocratic rule along non-ideological lines—unlike North Korea or Cuba (or Maoist China). State institutions that responded to social pressures, but that remained seemingly immune to capture by powerful interest groups—unlike India or the United States.[3]

Such factors—effective bureaucracy, technocratic rule, and responsive authoritarianism—led Fukuyama to dramatically re-evaluate the merits of China's political system.* But as he considers more recent

---

* "In the hands of good leaders, such a system can actually perform better than a democratic system that is subject to rule of law and formal democratic procedures like multiparty elections." Fukuyama, *Political Order and Political Decay*, 383. "Of the

events, a note of disquiet creeps in. In his conclusion, he finds himself forced to ask: "whether the Chinese regime is itself now suffering from decay"?[4]

The answer: yes.

China's astounding rise over the reform era was strongly tied to one key factor: partial political institutionalization. Naturally, this did not involve *liberal* institutions. China's one-Party system did not (and does not) permit the emergence of independent courts or legislatures. But the reform era saw certain political rules of the game emerge nonetheless. Party cadres found their lives governed by more predictable bureaucratic norms, in stark contrast to the Maoist era. And citizens took advantage of a host of embryonic reforms—village elections, administrative law reforms, increasingly commercialized media outlets—to funnel popular input into the system.

But over the past three decades, efforts to deepen such reforms have bumped up against Beijing's absolute prohibition on challenging one-Party rule. Authorities have regularly intervened to cut back the organic growth of their own reforms, precisely as they appeared to be sinking roots into the soil of China's politics.

This has fueled a destructive chain reaction. If you clear-cut trees and bushes, hillsides will erode. Lands once thought stable will gradually give way. The same is true for political terrain. Beijing's regular moves to curb institutional growth have steadily weakened China's political system. Technocratic rule has given way to crony capitalism. Responsive authoritarianism is devolving into the politics of street protest and state repression. And China's state effectiveness is itself faltering as black-box political struggles generate spreading paralysis and confusion within the bureaucracy.

THE CORE GOVERNANCE PROBLEM

When Fukuyama observed that China's reform-era leaders had reinstituted core features of the imperial system, he was dead-on. Out went politicized self-criticism sessions and Maoist mass movements. In came

nondemocratic alternatives, China poses the most serious challenge to the idea that liberal democracy constitutes a universal evolutionary model." Ibid., 544.

top-down professionalized bureaucracy, civil service exams, and merit-based promotions. But in doing so, Beijing also happened to replicate the centuries-old institutional problem at the heart of China's governance.

Imagine that you are the authoritarian leader of the world's most populous country. Ensconced in your favorite armchair, you contemplate your realm. What is your biggest day-to-day problem? The answer: your own underlings. How can you be sure that they do what you want? How can you guarantee that they don't flagrantly disobey your directives, rob you blind, or worse, plot against you?

In China, this is trickier than it looks. At each level of the bureaucratic hierarchy, power is centralized in the hands of a small group of Party (or imperial) officials. If they want to choke off information to Beijing and cover up their own misdeeds, they have the tools to do so. The very mechanisms used to maintain control over the populace at large—a resilient censorship apparatus, extra-legal security organs—can easily be deployed by local officials to blind their superiors and advance their own interests.[5]

This is a classic principal-agent problem. It is not unique to China. Given the right cocktail of problematic incentives and unchecked power, it can occur anywhere. Take America, for example. The early 2000s saw adoption of high-stakes testing practices in K–12 public schools throughout the nation. Teachers' salaries and school budgets were tied to the performance of their students on standardized tests—the very same exams that educators themselves were charged with collecting and grading. The result? A wave of cheating scandals stretching from Pennsylvania to Texas. The largest outbreak—in Atlanta—saw some 178 teachers and administrators at 44 schools accused of a massive conspiracy to erase wrong answers and insert correct ones.[6]

Such problems are magnified immensely in a country of 1.4 billion people and more than 60 million state employees, lacking a free press and effective external checks on power. In 2005, provincial authorities in China's northeast simply blacked out all information regarding a massive benzene spill on the Songhua River—for over a week—provoking an international incident with Russia, limiting the ability of national environmental authorities to respond, and generating panic among hundreds of thousands of local residents denied accurate information as to why their water supply had been shut off.

In China, these are not simply isolated incidents in specific sectors or companies. They are part of a latent crack stretching through the entire system of governance. No less a figure than China's current premier, Li Keqiang, admitted (in 2007) that official Chinese GDP statistics are unreliable, "manmade" figures, manipulated by local authorities seeking to please their superiors and dress up annual work evaluations.[7] Put simply, China is one big principal-agent problem.[8]

THE SEARCH FOR SOLUTIONS

This problem is not new. Generations of emperors faced the same challenge as their modern Party counterparts. How to assess the work performance of the district magistrates dispatched to manage the far-flung imperial domains? Was the local magistrate telling the truth that declining tax receipts from his county were the result of external factors? Or was he simply covering up his own corruption or incompetence? [9]

China's dynastic rulers adopted a range of strategies in response. Increased top-down supervision was one option. The best-known example: the imperial censorate. Emperors established a group of high-level authorities (censors) and endowed them with wide-ranging authority to investigate governance problems throughout the realm. Such efforts were an imperial end-run around the bureaucracy, allowing censors to bypass ordinary reporting channels and provide recommendations directly to the throne.[10]

Such efforts at top-down supervision faced key constraints. Censors were few in number. No guarantee existed that their reports were entirely free from bias or self-serving political ingratiation. Most important, the censorate's nature as a tool for the emperor's *personal* supervision of the bureaucracy imposed inherent limits. Censors could serve as a myriad of "eyes and ears" to funnel a mass of information directly to the emperor. But they were not allowed to usurp his ultimate power of decision.[11] Reliance on a single individual (or "brain") to take action meant that the utility of such mechanisms depended on the emperor himself. Faced with an overworked emperor, or one who preferred spending time with the imperial concubines instead of managing the affairs of state, unread censorial reports piled up, and the system lost effectiveness.

The victory of Communist forces in the civil war, and the establishment of the People's Republic of China in 1949, led to the creation of a new bureaucratic structure to govern the nation. Again, the age-old problem presented itself: how were Party leaders in Beijing supposed to supervise the cadres they deployed across the vast Chinese countryside, and whom they entrusted with managing all levers of state power? The 1953–1954 Gao Gang incident threw this problem into sharp relief. A key revolutionary figure during the civil war, Gao rose to assume joint command of all Party, state, and military forces in northeast China, from where he mounted a challenge to ascend to the very top of the Party hierarchy. Purged for attempting to set up an "independent kingdom," his case stands as an early example of inherent difficulties faced by China's Party leaders in managing their own ranks.[12]

For Mao, the answer to this problem lay in his revolutionary experience during the 1930s and 1940s—bottom-up supervision of the bureaucracy through frequent (and chaotic) rectification campaigns, marked by mass rallies, public denunciations, self-criticisms, and regular purges. Campaigns served to expose work errors of local officials and ferret out disloyalty or incompetence.[13] They also fanned massive uncertainty and fear, whipped up ideological fervor among society at large, and rendered cadres acutely sensitive to Mao's every utterance.

Such policies ensured Mao's total domination of political life during the radical decades stretching from the 1950s to the 1970s. But they incurred massive costs. Politically, it is hard to run a state when your subordinates are regularly purged. Under Mao, Deng Xiaoping himself famously fell from grace three times—including a stint laboring as an ordinary worker in a tractor factory.[14] Economically, the single-minded focus of officials on class struggle contributed to decades of stagnant growth.

These concerns led Deng Xiaoping to chart a new course after his rise to power in 1978. Mass political campaigns faded. Authorities turned down the dial on class struggle. But the question of how to manage local officials remained. Beijing pursued two strategies in response. Both sought to build institutions to resolve China's core governance problem.

First, starting in 1979, central Party officials began to revive top-down cadre management systems—evaluation systems used to assess and grade local cadres. Quantifiable performance targets, such as foreign investment or GDP growth statistics, rose in importance.[15] The role of ideology fell. Success in meeting targets was tied to promotion or salary bonuses. Such efforts rippled through the bureaucracy. The 1980s and 1990s saw legal institutions (such as courts) and administrative organs (such as birth control agencies) adopt parallel evaluation mechanisms. Judges and state employees were rewarded for success (and disciplined for failure) in meeting targets—deciding a specific number of cases per year, or holding annual numbers of births under a set limit. Such efforts were not entirely new.[16] They represented a revival of early 1950s-era Party mechanisms that had fallen into disarray during the decades of radical Maoism, and that themselves were rooted in yet earlier systems used by Chinese emperors to manage the imperial bureaucracy.

Second, Chinese authorities launched major efforts to build new institutions to control the exercise of power by local officials. Some sought to impose external legal checks. Others aimed at harnessing bottom-up citizen input to help monitor local authorities. Drawing on his own bitter experience during the Cultural Revolution, Deng Xiaoping set the tone in 1978:

> [W]e must strengthen our legal system . . . so as to make sure that institutions and laws do not change whenever the leadership changes, or whenever the leaders change their views. . . . Very often, what leaders say is taken as the law, and whoever disagrees is called a law-breaker. That kind of law changes whenever a leader's views change. So we must concentrate on enacting criminal and civil codes, procedural laws, and other necessary laws.[17]

Unsurprisingly, the 1980s were the heyday of legal reform. Hundreds of new statutes were enacted. Beijing breathed life into the previously moribund national legislature, the National People's Congress.[18] In 1987, it extended legal recognition to local experiments with village elections that had sprung up spontaneously in the early 1980s as Maoist agriculture communes were disbanded.[19]

By the late 1980s, Chinese reformers had even begun to tentatively tackle the thorniest of all issues—Party control. They recognized that excessive centralization of power in the hands of a few leaders posed an obstacle for the growth of institutions. In response, they attempted to disentangle Party and government power. In 1988, university presidents (rather than Party committees) were given control over day-to-day management of their schools.[20] The national Party political-legal committee charged with supervising the courts, prosecutors, and police was abolished (at least in name).[21] It looked—just perhaps—that China might be on a gradual road to building meaningful institutions to address the latent governance problems that had bedeviled generations of prior rulers.

ONE STEP FORWARD, ONE STEP BACK

Many of these hopes died in 1989. After the brutal crackdown on the Tiananmen protests, China sank into a political deep freeze. Some reforms were annulled outright. Party authorities were again vested with leadership of China's colleges; the national Party political-legal committee reconstituted and expanded.

And yet, not all was reversed. Take the Administrative Procedure [or Litigation] Law. Issued in 1989, it allowed citizens to challenge state actions in court. One could easily imagine that in the conservative backlash of the early 1990s, this would have been yet another example of a late-1980s era reform destined for the dustbin of history. But the opposite occurred. In 1991, at an internal Party conference aimed at strengthening China's security apparatus in order to avoid the fate of the Soviet Union and Eastern European Communist regimes, one finds Qiao Shi—the then-Party chief in charge of China's domestic security organs—arguing:

> Historically, it was the case that officials brought suit against citizens. [Now,] the newly implemented Administrative Procedure Law authorizes citizens to bring suit against officials—this must be regarded as an advance for democracy and the rule of law. Implementation of some laws will increase "trouble" (*mafan*). But this trouble is extremely necessary, and is beneficial to better protect citizen rights.[22]

Nor was this idle talk. During the 1990s, China's courts moved to implement the law. Administrative tribunals opened nationwide. Suits against the government rose from zero to roughly 100,000 by 2001.[23] Other reforms followed in tandem. Chinese authorities professionalized the judiciary, moving away from the practice of staffing courts with former military officers. They removed definitions of lawyers as "state legal workers" and privatized the bar. By the early 2000s, state-owned law firms had given way to an explosion of private firms, domestic and foreign alike. In 1997, central authorities adopted "rule according to law" (*yifa zhiguo*) as a core Party slogan. Parallel constitutional amendments followed two years later.[24]

Similar trends occurred elsewhere. Immediately after 1989, internal Party resistance coalesced against experiments with local village elections. Hardline opponents viewed these as examples of a dangerous "bourgeois liberalization" associated with deposed reformist leaders. They clamored for repeal of the 1987 law legitimating such practices. At this critical juncture, key Party elders spoke up in defense of the law. One in particular: the nearly ninety-year old Peng Zhen, one of the so-called Eight Immortals (retired revolutionary-era Party officials whose advanced age and record of service allowed them to wield substantial influence behind the scenes during the 1980s and 1990s). Such support proved crucial in overcoming Party resistance. With central backing assured, officials within the Ministry of Civil Affairs (MOCA) sprung into action. The 1990s saw MOCA authorities assemble a coalition of forces—ranging from Chinese villagers aggrieved by local governance abuses to foreign funders such as the Carter Center and the International Republican Institute—to promote village elections nationwide, often in the face of entrenched opposition from local officials.[25]

How to explain this? Did top Party figures such as Qiao and Peng somehow have a sudden change of heart? Were they seeking Western-style democracy or legal checks on one-Party rule? No. Both were Party loyalists. During the 1930s and 1940s, they had struggled side-by-side with the masses in bitter battles against Japanese invaders and Nationalist oppressors. They remained convinced of the Party's absolute role in leading China to a better future. But both had also suffered under Mao—Peng's purge in 1966 being one of the opening acts in the Cultural Revolution. And they were deeply aware of the need to build institutions to address the principal-agent problem at the heart of Chinese governance.[26]

Peng himself is a good example. While serving as Beijing's mayor and deputy director of the central Party-political legal committee in the 1950s, he had supported the establishment of grassroots elections as a tool to channel public opinion and ensure Party officials successfully stood on the same side as the masses. When village elections begin to spread during the 1980s, he was one of the most fervent supporters, seeing them as crucial to rehabilitating Party governance. Li Lianjiang and Kevin O'Brien vividly recount his role in the passage of the original 1987 law:

> Peng's lobbying [of national legislators] was characterized by nos-talgic memories of how close Party-villager relations had been before 1949 and a warning that rural rebellion was possible if self-government was put off. . . . Peng argued that village democracy was a matter of "life and death" for the Party. . . . Peng went on to lament how relations between cadres and villagers had deteriorated over the years, noting that . . . not a few [rural cadres] had become corrupt and high-handed "local emperors" (*tu huangdi*). If such trends were not reversed, he cautioned, villagers would "sooner or later attack our rural cadres with their shoulder poles" [i.e. work implements]. To prevent further erosion of in cadre-mass relations, Peng claimed that top-down supervision was not enough: "Who supervises rural cadres? Can we supervise them? No, not even if we had 48 hours a day."[27]

The only option, in his view, was to open bottom-up channels—building institutions to permit citizens themselves to supervise the exercise of power by local officials.

Such concerns inspired other reforms too. During the 1990s, Beijing embraced the idea that China's increasingly commercialized media could play a limited watchdog function. Under the slogan *yulun jiandu* (public opinion supervision), Party authorities actively encouraged tel-evision and newspaper outlets to report on local governance abuses and scandals. Hard-hitting investigative news programs such as CCTV's *Focus Interview* became smash hits, drawing 300 million viewers a day. Visits from figures such as Premier Zhu Rongji (in 1998) raised their profile even higher.[28] In the early 2000s, top Party authorities similarly flirted with limited governance reforms aimed at increasing "intra-Party democracy" (*dangnei minzhu*).[29] These sought to increase bottom-up input in the selection and promotion of local Party officials, via soliciting recommendations or nominations from a broader swath of the public at large.

Central officials did not see such efforts as incompatible with authoritarian rule. Rather, they saw them as crucial to maintaining China's one-Party system. Courts could help handle the mounting local conflicts produced by rapid economic development and urbanization. Media supervision and electoral mechanisms would allow Beijing to harness popular opinion to help better monitor grassroots officials.

Unsurprisingly, as each of these channels opened, people flocked to use them.

Take China's legal reforms, for example. In the 1990s, farmers began aggressively using the new rule-of-law rhetoric by Party authorities to challenge illegal local exactions and land seizures. Numbers of court cases multiplied. Some sought to wedge the door open yet wider. By the early 2000s, a cadre of public-interest lawyers (such as Teng Biao and Xu Zhiyong) and activists (such as Chen Guangcheng) had emerged. They fused public-interest lawsuits and savvy media strategies to focus public attention on official abuses and push for deeper institutional reform. Indeed, these met with some resounding initial successes, including prompting the State Council to abolish a nationwide detention system of questionable legality in 2003.[30]

Officials, too, began to aggressively use the space granted to them. Some agitated for spreading elections yet higher up within the bureaucracy. In the late 1990s, for example, several impoverished areas of northern Sichuan experienced outbreaks of citizen protests and riots caused by aggressive local tax-collection efforts. Local Party authorities began adopting more-inclusive voting practices and semi-competitive elections as a way to restore a degree of trust with the local population. This included altering practices of choosing township officials—a qualitative leap from prior efforts aimed at selecting (comparatively powerless) village heads. The 1998 Buyun election witnessed perhaps the pinnacle of these efforts. Roughly six thousand registered voters (Party and non-Party members alike) took part in more-or-less direct elections for township head. The experiment garnered national attention after the *Southern Weekend*—a liberal-leaning newspaper just beginning to make a name for itself with its penchant for aggressive, investigative journalism—broke the story in an extensive report.[31]

What did top Party leaders in Beijing think of all this? Were they thrilled to view their reforms begin to take on an organic life of their own? Well, no. If you are a paranoid authoritarian ruler committed to maintaining one-Party rule at all costs, you see things very differently.

When China's leaders looked at their society, they perceived their own limited governance reforms being hijacked to engage in precisely the kind of activities that they most feared. As Chinese lawyers and activists came together to form public interest groups such as the Open Constitutional Initiative (after 2003), piloting new forms of legal activism and exploring the idea of creating branch offices throughout the country—Beijing saw the seeds of an incipient political opposition. When Beijing's leaders cast their gaze at their own ranks, they saw similarly disturbing trends. Chinese judges seemed to be taking the legal framework that Party authorities had created increasingly seriously. Some used it to push yet further, exploring the idea that the constitution could be a source of rights in the Qi Yuling case (2001), or that courts might be able to independently exercise the power of judicial review to invalidate local regulations in the Seed Law case (2003). China's leaders saw such things, and they began to worry that they were losing control of the show. And they had to act.

And that's precisely what has happened—repeatedly—since the 1990s.

This follows a depressingly familiar cycle. At the outset, each reform is marked by a burst of enthusiasm. Public-interest lawyers are hailed in state media for their contributions to the development of rule-of-law. Scholars proclaim "deliberative democracy" the solution to China's governance challenges.[32] News headlines blare that rising online activism in new social media forums are opening new channels to resolve local abuses.[33] Then comes the counter-reaction. Voices warn that nefarious forces are mobilizing to threaten Party rule. Reforms run up against the internal political limits imposed by adherence to Leninist lines of control. Supporters are marginalized. And just as reforms appear to be gathering a life of their own, Beijing systematically withdraws central support or directly steps in to neuter them.

For precisely such reasons, central authorities clamped down on experiments with direct local elections after the late 1990s. Support for "intra-party democracy" faded by 2005.[34] Party authorities began to turn against their own legal reforms around the same time.[35] Steadily, they closed down the legal rhetoric (constitutionalism), channels (open court trials), and social forces (lawyers) that activists had used to mobilize for greater change. New political campaigns within the Chinese courts and government (such as the 2007 Three Supremes) reminded judges of the supremacy of Party policy. Pressure on China's public-interest lawyers increased. Harassment came first. Then denial of bar licenses. Open Constitution Initiative was shuttered on tax charges in 2009. By 2011, arrests and enforced disappearances had become regular events. Media controls steadily increased. In the early 2000s, publications such as the *Southern Weekend* were weakened by regular purges. By 2011, Party authorities had decided on the need to reclaim control over social media sites such as Weibo, which have emerged as freewheeling public forums for exposing corruption and governance abuses.[36] A wave of arrests and tightened regulations followed, successfully reimposing central authority and inducing self-censorship among users. By 2013, Party propaganda hacks reemerged as deans of China's journalism programs.[37] The once-dynamic field of investigative reporting in China was steadily smothered—caught between tighter political controls and increasingly unfavorable economic trends for print media. Talented young reporters began to leave the profession in favor of other careers, such as web startups focused on investment research or online education.[38]

Naturally, heightened repression does not end pressure for change. The core principal-agent problem remains. Party authorities are always looking for new mechanisms for supervising their subordinates. Consequently, there is always someone in some corner of China's bureaucracy promoting various useful reforms. At the time of writing (early 2017), current examples include: continuing efforts to implement the 2007 Open Government Information regulations, and moves by the Supreme People's Court to create cross-jurisdictional tribunals. The former aims at introducing a degree of bottom-up transparency to monitor officials, while the latter seeks to partially decouple judicial power from local governments and enlist courts to check their power.

But critically, these are never permitted to mature. Because of Beijing's unwillingness to permit fundamental political change, Party power is regularly deployed at critical junctures to torpedo its own reforms. Since the 1990s, China's internal reforms have consequently remained locked in a one-step forward, one-step backward cycle. Political institutionalization never deepens. And China's governance institutions remain blocked from evolving in a healthy, organic manner.

FROM TECHNOCRATIC RULE TO CRONY CAPITALISM

This has been deeply corrosive. China's classical governance model relies on a coherent, centralized bureaucracy. It must respond to central mandates set in Beijing. While it may be called on to respond to social pressures or local interests, it must avoid being co-opted by them. And it has to be able to effectively monitor and control its own lower ranks. But as Beijing's own limited governance reforms have repeatedly stalled out, all of these have degraded over the course of the reform era.

Back in the 1980s, even after the chaos of the Cultural Revolution, China's aging revolutionary Party leaders constituted a relatively cohesive entity.[39] Policymaking might be marked by internal disagreements. But agreement could be reached on key issues. And once elite consensus has been obtained, Beijing could mobilize the Party machinery to impose its will. Unpopular policies could be imposed on a resistant society, as with the implementation of the one-child policy during the 1980s and 1990s. Fragmented state actors could be corralled to follow central desires. Deng Xiaoping did this with his famous "southern tour" (*nanxun*) in the early 1990s, relaunching market reforms in the face of conservative opposition. Premier Zhu Rongji did the same in the wake of the 1998 Asian financial crisis. Between 1998 and 2003, he wielded bureaucratic levers to carry out systematic economic reform. Control over China's banks, insurance, securities companies, and regulatory agencies was recentralized in an elite Party leading group. Massive reorganization followed, marked by regular monthly meetings across state bureaucracies, comprehensive personnel reshuffling, and extensive recruitment of personnel with overseas experience.[40] For some observers, this represents China's top-down governance at its best—an example of how authoritarian Party institutions can flexibly respond to head off pressing social and economic problems.

But the late reform era saw the sinews of China's technocratic machine atrophy. Elite cohesion eroded. The tight-knit revolutionary generation of leaders (such as Deng) passed from the stage in the 1990s. Power disseminated among a wider range of cadres. Internal frictions increased. By the late 1990s, with Beijing's redefinition of Party ideology to allow private entrepreneurs to be accepted as members of the Communist Party, any semblance of meaningful unity around shared principles of socialism vanished. Factions coalesced around shared financial interests. Zhu's reforms had left large sectors of the economy in the hands of massive oligopolies (such as PetroChina or China Telecom)—now organized as state enterprises (SOEs) rather than creaking Soviet-style ministries. Endowed with vast resources (many listed on the Hong Kong or New York stock exchanges) and deep political ties (often with children of top Party officials as CEOs or board members), these steadily emerged in the early 2000s as quasi-feudal satrapies highly resistant to outside pressure.[41]

Lacking effective bottom-up checks on power, China's closed political system fused with rapid accumulation of wealth. A spreading plague of corruption resulted. Starting in the 1990s, China experienced a qualitative intensification in corruption, with "high-level, big-stakes corruption increas[ing] more rapidly than 'ordinary' corruption and other forms of official malfeasance."[42] Partial privatization transferred large swaths of valuable public assets such as urban land to private hands (see Chapter 2). Both the scale of corruption and the ranks of Party cadres involved rose dramatically. As the American scholar Andrew Wedemen has noted:

> [Economic crime] cases involving senior officials climbed from a scant 4 per 10,000 cases filed in 1982, to 277 in 1988, and 313 in 1993. Thereafter, the number doubled to 658 per 10,000 in 1998, and hit more than 1,000 in 2007. In other words, one in ten of those charged held leadership positions at or above the county level.[43]

No longer was corruption an individual matter. Networks of cadres began to conspire with real estate developers and other financial interests to lay claim to massive shares of wealth produced by escalating valuations. In resource-rich Shanxi province, for example, rapidly rising energy prices in the early 2000s led to the emergence of corrupt networks that tied local coal tycoons to the very highest officials in the province—including over half of the members of the Party standing committee.[44] Even the brother of Ling Jihua, the chief of staff to China's then-top leader, was implicated. Relatives of the Party elite accumulated fabulous wealth of unclear provenance. In 2012, the *New York Times* and Bloomberg launched a series of exposés on their corporate holdings—revealing that the family members of premier Wen Jiabao had alone accumulated assets worth some 2.7 billion U.S. dollars.[45]

Unlike countries such as Russia or Venezuela, deepening corruption during the 1990s and early 2000s did not choke off China's economic growth.[46] But it gradually altered the nature of the Chinese Communist Party itself. Once unheard of, bribery of higher officials for political advancement (or even the outright sale of offices) became regularized.[47] As opaque ties between political and economic elites deepened, the autonomous identity of the Party eroded. "Crony capitalism" began to eat away at the beating technocratic heart of Chinese governance. Looking at these trends, scholars such as Minxin Pei have concluded that at some point over the past two decades, China's ruling elite devolved from a tightly organized Leninist one-Party system into an outright "kleptocracy."[48]

Nor is this merely the view of a few foreign observers. In a sharply worded January 2016 speech to China's central Party disciplinary committee, Xi Jinping himself warned darkly that:

> There are careerists and conspirators existing in our Party and undermining the Party's governance. . . . [S]ome officials have been forming cabals and cliques to covertly defy the CPC Central Committee's decisions and policies . . . [that] risk[s] compromising the political security of the Party and the country.[49]

As the Party's core lost technocratic cohesion, problems spread. Forging consensus became steadily more challenging. Imposing central mandates on recalcitrant actors became increasingly difficult. Key economic reforms faltered. Central efforts to extend Zhu's reforms and impose market discipline on the capital markets and the banks fizzled out by 2005.[50]

Eight years later, it was the same story with regard to state-owned enterprise reform. The 2013 announcement by China's Politburo that the market was to be the "decisive factor" led to high hopes among financial analysts. Finally, they thought, Beijing would curb the bloated state-owned enterprises that were consuming cheap bank credit, generating escalating levels of debt, and pumping out vast quantities of iron and steel no longer needed as China's construction sector tanked. State leaders announced dramatic plans to curb overcapacity—cutting 500 million tons of coal production (9 percent of the annual total), and 100–150 million tons of steel output (13 percent of capacity) by 2020.[51] But unlike the reforms of the 1980s and 1990s, concrete implementation lagged.[52] Signs of policy disarray and inaction proliferated. Rather than undertake comprehensive SOE reform, massive state firms were simply merged into larger (and less productive) behemoths.[53] Steel mills briefly shuttered reopened.[54] In order to juice growth, Beijing regularly stepped on the gas pedal, flooding the system with yet additional stimulus spending. Debt levels surged to new highs. Meanwhile, confusing and contradictory signals emerged from Beijing—a highly placed "anonymous official" (speculated to be one of Xi Jinping's top economic advisers) appeared in the Party's mouthpiece *People's Daily*, warning of the dangers of pursuing precisely such policies.[55] Increasingly, China resembles less a finely tuned racing yacht manned by an elite cadre of technocratic specialists, and more a lumbering ocean liner driven forward into rough waters by its own inertia, as the muffled sounds of struggle among the captain and crew echo forth from the locked bridge.

Corrosion also crept into crucial levers that Beijing relied on to steer lower levels of the bureaucracy. As mentioned earlier, the early reform years of the 1980s and 1990s saw the adoption of top-down evaluation systems to guide local cadres to achieve key targets, particularly in the high-priority fields of birth control, economic growth, and social stability. But as time wore on, each of these became "locked-in"—highly resistant to change—a form of regulatory capture somewhat analogous to, say, American or European farm subsidies, but with far more serious consequences.

Mandatory population planning targets created strong incentives for local cadres to control births in their jurisdictions. To hit their assigned numbers, some resorted to compulsory sterilizations, or even forced abortions. More common were compulsory fines of violators. By the early twenty-first century, this had evolved into a profitable income stream for revenue-strapped local governments, some $3.1 billion in 2013, according to one estimate.[56] China's policies also created vested interests—such as the 500,000-person-strong family planning agency—whose very existence depended on the enforcement and continuation of state policies.[57]

By 2000, China's demographers recognized that population policies were contributing to a host of unfavorable trends—among them, plunging fertility rates and soaring imbalances in male-female sex ratios at birth (as a result of sex-selective abortions). Were the voices of experts heard? No. Their vigorous internal lobbying in favor of relaxing policies was stymied by internal bureaucratic resistance. After all, what would happen to employees of the national family planning committee? Only after it was folded into the Ministry of Health in 2013 (and China's population police began retraining as early childhood development specialists), was its power weakened sufficiently to permit one-child restrictions to be relaxed into a two-child policy (in 2016).[58] But as one leading Chinese expert noted, "It's an event that we have been waiting for for a generation, but it is one we have had to wait much too long for . . . it won't have any impact on the issue of the aging society."[59] The damage had already been done. China is now graying more rapidly than any other major economy in history.[60] Between 2010 and 2030, the proportion of elderly in China's society will double—from 8 percent to over 15 percent. By 2050, it will have tripled, to roughly 25 percent—with dramatic implications for everything from the size of China's labor force to the stability of its national pension system.[61] As one academic study concluded:

> History will remember China's one-child policy as the most extreme example of state intervention in human reproduction in the modern era. History will also likely view this policy as a very costly blunder, born of the legacy of a political system that planned population numbers in the same way that it planned the production of goods. It

showcases the impact of a policymaking process that, in the absence
of pubic deliberations, transparency, debate, and accountability, can
do permanent harm to the members of a society.[62]

Economic growth was a similar story. GDP targets drove local cadres
to pursue development with little regard to pollution. Building dirty
chemical manufacturing facilities boosted short-term growth statistics.
But long-term harm to the environment or the health of neighboring residents was not factored in. By the late 1980s, some in Beijing
had recognized the problems with this development track, creating
the National Environmental Protection Agency in 1988. But efforts
to enforce China's nascent environmental rules sputtered during the
1990s. NEPA's weak status (a mere bureau-level entity) meant that it
was outranked by more powerful state-owned oil and gas enterprises,
as well as construction and development bureaucracies, all of which
enjoyed ministry-level ranks.[63] Further, the overriding importance of
GDP growth targets gave local cadres little reason to cooperate with
environmental protection efforts that could potentially harm their promotion prospects.[64]

In the early 2000s, national environmental officials joined forces
with the statistics bureau to try to change this dynamic. They drew on
United Nations expertise to develop a "Green GDP" metric that dis-
counted economic growth by levels of environmental degradation, and
promoted it as a more accurate tool to assess the performance of local
cadres. But immense blowback resulted after preliminary adjusted figures revealed some provinces actually had experienced *negative* adjusted
growth rates. Officials who had relied on heavy industry to aggressively
develop their jurisdictions saw their careers within the Party hierarchy
at risk. Quietly, the entire project was shelved.[65]

Recent reforms have been more successful. Since 2006, central
Party authorities have made environmental issues a higher priority.
A cabinet-level Ministry of Environmental Protection (MEP) was
established in 2008. China's Politburo has extended strong support
for a new set of environmental cadre performance targets—including
reductions in sulfur dioxide, energy intensity, and PM2.5 levels.[66] Some
positive effects have resulted. Emboldened by their increased prestige,
MEP regulators have begun aggressively denying approvals to polluting

or resource-intensive projects. Progress remains mixed. Data falsification by self-reporting polluters is pervasive, while large state-owned enterprises continue to use their considerable resources to foil enforcement. Will such top-down enforcement strategies help China address the environmental damage resulting from decades of go-go development policies—80 percent of groundwater in China's major river basins labeled as "unsafe for human contact," severe air pollution resulting in the world's highest mortality levels from asthma? [67] Can they succeed, given Beijing's limited willingness to couple them with bottom-up monitoring, such as by environmental NGOs or specialized courts?[68] The jury remains out.

These examples do have a positive side. Beijing can alter course. With both population planning and the environment, China's leadership has taken halting steps to reverse core policies when confronted with their negative consequences. But instead of carefully laid plans set by technocratic managers, the picture that emerges is a very different one. China's reform era has produced deeply entrenched vested interests desperately battling to resist change—precisely the kind of political decay that Fukuyama flagged as confronting societies ranging from India to the United States.

Beijing's efforts to curb the evolution of bottom-up checks on power fuel such decay. As Party leaders tighten restrictions on activists and civil society, they stifle alternative voices that might help identify problems or counterbalance vested interests. Such policies are not limited to fields traditionally regarded as "sensitive." They are spreading. Faced with slowing economic growth, Beijing began instructing economists and corporate business analysts in 2016 to avoid overly pessimistic estimates of the nation's woes, and instead infuse their financial reporting with "positive energy" (*zhengnengliang*).[69] This carries more than a whiff of pre–reform era practices of altering weather reports or harvest figures to appease political masters. This is dangerous. China's leaders risk encasing themselves in a house of mirrors, with sycophantic underlings reflecting back a Panglossian version of reality, while outside, China's society finds itself starved of the oxygen needed to accurately evaluate pressing social and economic challenges.[70]

Of course, information controls are far from what they were under Mao. Reports of local malfeasance can still filter up to the rarefied air of central Party compounds via a partially commercialized media or vibrant (albeit heavily censored) Internet. And Beijing's rulers have massive resources at their disposal—people, money, and organizational skill—to throw at problems. But increasingly, they are reactive. Local governance abuses often have to worsen and explode—either figuratively (such as the 2008 milk powder scandal that sickened hundreds of thousands of infants across the nation) or literally (the 2015 chemical blasts that leveled the warehouse district of Tianjin's port, killing nearly two hundred)—before Beijing pivots to address the social problem of the day.

China's early reform era was characterized by technocratic rule—long-term planning at the center, flexible experimentation at the local level. But that has slipped. With political rot and crony capitalism setting in, the early twenty-first century saw China slide toward political deadlock in Beijing, and governance by scandal and crisis in the localities.

FROM AUTHORITARIAN RESPONSIVENESS TO SOCIAL RADICALIZATION

It began simply enough. In fall 1996, residents of Faxi village, in the arid northern province of Shaanxi, began suspecting that their Party secretary was skimming local finances for his own purposes. Anonymous posters accusing him of crimes began to circulate. He responded by using the village public address system to criticize his opponents.[71]

Dozens of villagers started streaming up the bureaucratic hierarchy to township authorities, petitioning them to impeach the Party secretary. Faced with this pressure, they caved in. Township authorities relieved him of his post, further announcing that villagers would be allowed to elect fifteen representatives to represent their interests in an inspection of local finances.

Conflict steadily escalated over the next five years. Township manipulation of village elections was met with protests and mild violence; reinstatement of the fallen Party secretary confronted by a mass petition of some 120 villagers to the provincial capital and blockage of nearby road construction projects. Legal and political grievances snowballed together. In 2000, three of the key petition leaders were arrested and convicted on a variety of charges, including inciting social disorder. Sentences ranged from six months to four years in prison. Villagers responded with repeated demonstrations. They aggressively circulated appeals throughout the province to higher-level Party authorities, seeking to trigger their intervention in the dispute.

In this case, the villagers were successful. Provincial Party authorities dispatched a high-level work team to inspect affairs in Faxi. After a massive investigation, they issued their 588-page report in summer 2001. They concluded that Faxi suffered from multiple governance failures. Examples included: a general lack of openness in village affairs, a tendency for a few leaders to decide key issues without seeking the participation of (or even informing) residents, and a failure of township and county officials to thoroughly investigate citizen grievances. These created fertile ground for individual grievances to mushroom into mass petitions.

Local officials were directed to quickly resolve village grievances to restore stability; the judges handling the legal appeals of the convictions of the protest leaders instructed to reverse their criminal sentences. In November 2001, the county Party secretary expressly visited Faxi village to apologize to the assembled residents for the official handling of their grievances. But instead of resolving the matter, his apology was viewed by villagers as insincere. The result? Yet another cycle of mass petitions to higher level Party authorities seeking further redress. . . .

Faxi is far from unusual.[72] So-called mass incidents in China surged from 10,000 in 1994, to 74,000 in 2004, to more than 120,000 in 2008.[73] Security officials have since ceased releasing reliable data. Speculation periodically emerges as to more recent statistics. In 2010, Tsinghua professor Sun Liping estimated the number at 180,000.[74] Such figures include a wide range of activities: bar brawls that spill out onto the streets, peaceful sit-down protests by a few dozen plaintiffs dissatisfied with court verdicts, organized rallies by several hundred citizens opposed to the construction of a waste incinerator in their hometown, violent riots by thousands (or tens of thousands) enraged by interethnic tensions or accumulated abuses of local employers.

Such activities have increasingly moved online. The Lei Yang case is one such example. Lei, a young graduate of one of China's elite colleges, died in Beijing police custody in May 2016 after being arrested in an anti-prostitution raid. Bruises on his body and suspicious failures of video recorders sparked allegations of police brutality; the heavy-handed official reaction raised suspicions of a cover-up. Thousands of classmates and alumni of his alma mater, Renmin University, aggressively took to organizing online petitions calling for justice. One (subsequently deleted) read:

> We are outraged by the Changping police's assortment of hypocritical and evasive rhetoric! . . . [I]t looks more like a malicious act of randomly targeting ordinary people or middle-class urbanites than an accident. . . .
>
> Whether or not Lei Yang visited a prostitute (what one can do with just 200 renminbi at a massage parlor?), he was not involved in any criminal offense. Even if he had moral shortcomings, like the rest of us, he didn't deserve to die. . . .
>
> As senior fellow students of Lei Yang, we have been working hard for many years amid the waves of reform and opening-up. Most of our fellow alumni can be found in various specialty areas like Lei Yang, but they dare not call themselves the elite of society. We painfully feel that today, more than 30 years after the reform and opening-up, our personal safety and civil rights have not been guaranteed.
>
> At a time when citizens are routinely confronted with a wide range of lawlessness such as demolitions and the kidnapping of children, it is difficult for them to be guaranteed their personal safety from the police. The relationship between public security departments and citizens is extremely abnormal.
>
> So, the death of Lei Yang was by no means an accident. It was a tragedy arising from the system. We call on the top authorities to conduct an independent and impartial investigation into Lei Yang's death. We demand that his killers be severely punished and that discipline within the public security departments be corrected. We want our most basic rights to personal safety, civil rights and urban order.[75]

As such petitions went viral on social media, pressure increased on Beijing authorities to respond to stem the public outcry. One month after Lei's death, they did—with prosecutors announcing arrest of two of the police officers on suspicion of misconduct, after an autopsy revealed that he had died as a result of suffocation.[76] But their decision on December 23, 2016, to abandon criminal charges stirred deep anger among Beijing's established urban residents, many of whom viscerally identified with Lei more strongly than any number of similar victims of police abuses in rural China. Online criticism surged. The next day, some 1,500 professors, lawyers, and Renmin alumni signed a petition challenging the decision of Beijing prosecutors. Once again, officials hastened to respond with a mix of sticks and carrots. Censorship of the incident on social media escalated. Five days later, Beijing police announced the police officers involved had been fired.[77]

Outside China, there is a tendency to try to fit such events into familiar narratives. The "budding of democracy" is a popular one. In 2011, thousands of residents in the Guangdong village of Wukan drove out Party officials as part of extended protests against local land seizures. After provincial authorities entered into a brokered agreement recognizing villager demands, foreign media hailed the incident as an example of "fledgling democracy" in China.[78] Five years later, when authorities detained the Wukan Party secretary (previously a key leader in the 2011 uprising) on bribery charges, amid his calls for additional protests, the story was run in reverse. As the *Washington Post* put it, "Wukan symbolized hope for Chinese democracy. A new crackdown may change that."[79] Online activism receives similar treatment. Under the rubric of "technological transformation," social media is depicted as the tool that is empowering the next generation—in China, just as in Missouri or Tunisia—fundamentally altering the relationship between state and society.[80]

Such depictions miss the point. These activities are not new. They are the modern parallels of imperial ones. During the Qing dynasty, unkempt petitioners from remote regions of China straggled into Beijing to bang the grievance drum and summon imperial officials to hear their capital appeals (*jingkong*). Now they gather in front of the State Bureau of Letters and Visits, gripping faded copies of paperwork detailing decades-long battles—sometimes won, but more often lost—against local officials over land seizures or unpaid wages. Official "letters and visits" (*xinfang*) bureaus receive millions of such individual petitions each year.[81]

Just as today, things could escalate. Carefully examine a petition by Sichuan residents against malfeasance by local officials in the 1870s, and you see shades of Faxi or Wukan. All the key elements are there. The unheard capital appeal. Efforts by dissatisfied petition leaders to mobilize local support. Spreading demonstrations. Finally, the decision by central authorities to crack down, resulting in riots and violent clashes.[82] Or study a 1746 collective petition by members of a Buddhist sect seeking to overturn the detention of their leader. Watch their appeals for assistance go viral, with incense-bearing sectarian representatives from across the province crowding into the lobby of government offices to pressure officials handling the case, and the echoes of Lei Yang (or Falun Gong—see Chapter 4) are unmistakable.[83]

Nor did imperial officials look any more favorably on such activities than their modern Party counterparts. China's dynastic records are replete with complaints by local magistrates of "unruly people" (*diaomin*) being stirred up by "litigation tricksters" (*songshi*, or "litigation instigators").[84] Change the date, update the language, and presto—you have the televised broadcast Party authorities aired in the summer of 2015, following their mass detention of roughly two hundred rights lawyers and activists, accusing them of organizing petitioners and rabble-rousing at courthouses.[85]

This is what local politics looks like in China. Many aspects resemble other societies. Elites have means—both formal and informal—to ensure their voices are heard, their grievances handled. The powerful mingle with their classmates from Beijing University (or Yale). The wealthy can buy access to their local congressman (or Party secretary). As elsewhere, it is a different story for the poor. Faced with an abusive encounter with police resulting in broken bones, or a lengthy land dispute that endangers family finances, their choices are limited. Many simply lump it. Lack of information or resources means that only a small fraction of disputes ever reach the official justice system (roughly 6 percent in rural China, 15 percent in developed Western systems).[86]

Beijing is all too aware of the dangers of leaving the urban proletariat and rural farmers without adequate recourse. After all, Party leaders themselves rose to power through a Communist revolution in 1949. For that reason, since the beginning of the reform era, Beijing has attempted to steer citizen grievances into legal channels. The 2008 Labor Contract Law is one recent example. This worker-friendly legislation attempted to address abuses suffered by China's vast population of migrant laborers. Notably, it required employers to sign written contracts with their employees, and increased severance payments to laid-off workers. The law also gave workers a private right of action to sue their employers for violations, rather than requiring them to wait for state officials to take action.[87]

Beijing actively encouraged workers to use the new law to protect their rights. State media touted its benefits. Party authorities rapidly built out the national legal aid system, seeking to channel the disputes of migrant workers into the legal system (see Chart 3.1).[88] Numbers of labor disputes filed with mediation committees and arbitration boards surged following its passage (see Chart 3.2).[89]

However, as labor scholars such as Aaron Halegua, Eli Friedman, and Mary Gallagher, and Ching Kwan Lee have documented, these efforts encountered extensive problems in practice. Examples include:

- Limited access to legal representation[90]
- Mixed results for individual claims by workers[91]
- Strict political controls on trade union activity[92]
- Crackdown on labor NGOs[93]

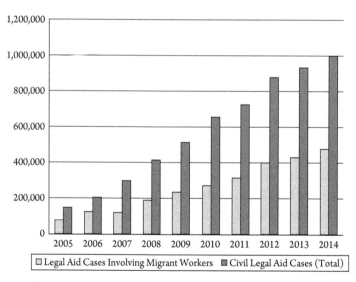

CHART 3.1 Migrant Workers Receiving Legal Aid and Total Civil Legal Aid Cases (2005–2014)

Source: Aaron Halegua (2016). Reproduced by permission

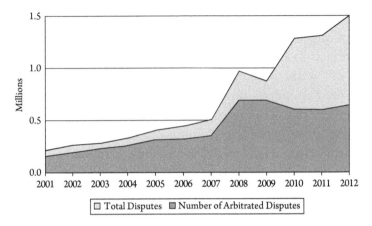

CHART 3.2 Labor Disputes 2001–2012
Source: Mary Gallagher (2017). Reproduced by permission

These are not unique to labor conflicts. Make a few additions (pervasive problems enforcing court judgments), tweak the content a bit (a more plaintiff-friendly atmosphere for environmental claims in recent years), and the same list could be replicated for a wide range of legal disputes in China.

So are China's marginalized completely lacking in recourse? Not exactly. Ironically, Beijing's obsession with stability gives them a powerful (albeit risky) tool. Among the numerical cadre performance targets used to evaluate local officials, maintaining social order is among the most important (alongside the GDP growth and population figures discussed above)—a "priority target with veto power" (*yipiao fojue*), in China's bureaucratic parlance. Large-scale citizen protests, or mass petitions to higher levels of the government, can result in career or financial sanctions for the local officials who fail to keep their jurisdictions in order. These are not simply individual in nature. Just as in the imperial era, collective liability is at the heart of Party evaluation systems. All members of the land bureau (or court tribunal) that issued the decision (or opinion) triggering popular unrest can be held responsible.[94]

Chinese citizens aren't dumb. Sure, state officials and ivory-tower academics may lambast them. When 30-odd taxi drivers from Heilongjiang converge on Beijing and collectively drink pesticide in the middle of one of the capital's busiest shopping districts, appealing for the right to renew their taxi licenses,[95] or when 150 workers at a major

Apple supplier in southern China scale the roofs of their dormitories and threaten to commit suicide to protest working conditions,[96] the denunciations are predictable. "Low quality" (*di suzhi*) rural migrants. A shocking lack of legal consciousness. Such hand-wringing misses the point. Most know exactly what they are doing—bypassing legal channels they perceive as stacked against them in favor of trying to hit the button most likely to generate a flash alert to the desk of the local Party secretary, prompting him to order local officials and judges to show up at the negotiating table and address their grievances.

Precisely this dynamic is behind the widespread resort in China to the extra-legal politics of petition and protest. Labor disputes again provide a good example. As Mary Gallagher has noted, those workers who do struggle through China's formal labor dispute system end up with "higher levels of disillusionment and more negative perception of the legal system's effectiveness and fairness."[97] Many decide that "extra-legal weapons such as demonstrations, sit-ins, and petitioning [are] necessary to raise the stakes and attract public sympathy and government attention."[98] Strikes and other forms of labor protest have surged in recent years as a result (see Chart 3.3). In China, collective disputes aren't ending up in court. They're ending up in the streets.

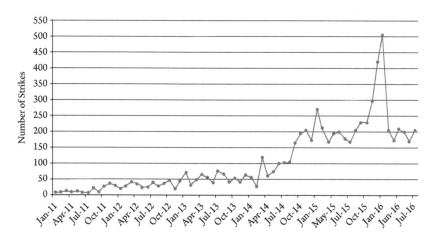

CHART 3.3 Strikes Reported in China: 2011–2016

Source: China Labour Bulletin (various years), http://maps.clb.org.hk/strikes/en. Reproduced by permission

Officials are all too familiar with these risks. American city councilors know the rules of the political game they face: potential primary challengers, poll numbers, and the general election schedule. So too are local officials in China intimately aware of those confronting them: when inspection teams from higher levels are scheduled to show up in their jurisdictions, or which dates are most likely to see mass petitions to Beijing by, say, disgruntled elderly pensioners in their jurisdictions (answer: twice a year, right before the annual fall conclave of the Party elite, or the spring meeting of the national legislature).

Some view this in a positive light. For Fukuyama, such petitions and protests are crucial "feedback mechanisms" that help impose a degree of accountability on local Chinese officials in an otherwise closed one-Party state.[99] But this depiction is incomplete. It overlooks the corrosive effects this process has on state and society alike.

Individual petitioners are generally left embittered and angry. Many start with high hopes. Upon arrival in Beijing, 95 percent agree with the statement that "central authorities welcome peasant petitions." But after only a week in the capital, their attitudes shift dramatically. Only 39 percent believe central officials welcomed rural petitioners. Half assert that central leaders feared petitioners or retaliated against them.[100] Risks are higher for leaders of collective petitions. Organizing mass protests can result in severe criminal sanctions. Or intimidating nighttime visits by impressively muscled youth hired by local authorities to carefully "explain" to you why it might not be such a good idea to continue organizing workers in the local factory. Obviously, this can change people's outlook. A figure such as the blind activist Chen Guangcheng may start out viewing himself as a loyal Chinese citizen seeking to inform his neighbors of their legal rights, and alert central authorities as to local abuses by birth control officials in Shandong. But take a four-year criminal sentence for "organizing a mob to disturb traffic," tack on years of house arrest for him and his family under the watch of dozens of local thugs hired by the local government to keep him isolated from the outside world, and perceptions shift.[101] Once-moderate civil activists steadily morph into political ones.

What about so-called successful protests? Under severe pressure to head off social unrest, local officials sometimes find that simply folding—giving in to large groups of well-organized protestors—makes rational sense, regardless of whether their demands actually have any merit. In such situations, as one study of worker protests in southern Chinese courts has shown, legal norms can get thrown out the window. Evidentiary and procedural standards can be abandoned; unrelated parties (bearing no actual legal liability) ordered to pay workers' wages. This includes courts or government agencies literally paying off protesting workers out of their own budgets to get them off the streets.[102] Such policies are so common that they have given rise to their own parlance. Officials refer to *yong qian lai mai wending* (buying stability with cash). Petitioners speak of *danao da jiejue, xiaonao xiao jiejue, bunao bu jiejue* (make a big stir, get a big result; make a small stir, get a small result; stay quiet, and nothing happens).

For many Western observers, there is an understandable tendency to view such events through rose-colored glasses tinged with nostalgic memories of their own participation in 1960s-era protest movements. Long-suffering workers receiving compensation. Aggrieved villagers forcing the local Party boss to capitulate. But look deeper. This back-and-forth between China's state and society is not producing positive change. In reality, Beijing's short-term efforts to respond to outbursts of popular anger are steadily undermining China's institutions and norms.

Take the effect on law first. Contrary to popular belief, law itself does not bring social stability. Most people don't resolve that minor traffic accident or their workplace dispute with their boss by going to court. They instead settle issues between themselves in "the shadow of the law"—i.e., based partly on their perceptions of what the outcome might be if they took it to formal legal institutions.

But in China, the reverse is taking place. Many aggrieved parties conclude—entirely logically—that launching a coordinated Internet protest or a mass petition of hundreds of disgruntled farmers to the provincial capital is the best way to get what they want, regardless of the underlying legal merit of their grievances. This is fueling a "populist threat" to Chinese courts,[103] as Ben Liebman has noted, "in which the formal legal system operates in the shadow of protest and violence."[104] This is not limited to land disputes, labor conflicts, or environmental pollution cases. It is pervasive. Take medical malpractice. One local judge notes that his county experiences roughly "ten to twenty major medical protests a year . . . in which patients or their families cause significant disruption, block access to a hospital, or place dead bodies inside hospital lobbies [as escalation tactics to increase pressure on local authorities to offer concessions]".[105] The result? As Liebman has found, "The threat of violence [from patients' families] leads hospitals to settle claims for more money than would be available in court and also influences how judges handle cases that do wind up in court."[106]

This wasn't supposed to happen. China's late-twentieth-century reforms—village elections, local people's congresses, court challenges to state actions by public interest lawyers—were supposed to steer such tensions into more institutionalized forms. But as China's political climate tightens, these channels are closing down. The underlying tensions are not disappearing. They are mutating into new forms.

This can be seen in China's beleaguered community of liberal activists. Back in the early 2000s, they were attempting to use what channels existed. Xu Zhiyong stood for (and won) election in 2003 to a district legislative seat in Beijing. The petition he brought to the national legislature challenging the state "custody and repatriation" detention system reflected a belief that China's own constitutional and legal norms could themselves be employed to promote change. But by 2011, state space for such activities had decreased. Xu's work shifted in response. His new focus: forming loose networks of citizens around the country to discuss political and social reform (the New Citizens Movement), and organizing migrant families to combat educational inequality.[107] Groups such as Yirenping working on gender and disability issues began to eschew simple reliance on legal challenges in favor of pop-up street demonstrations (*xingwei yishu*, or "performance art"). A steady "radicalization process" took place, with previously moderate lawyers shifting tactics away from courtroom lawyering and toward social organizing.[108] Prominent rights lawyer Teng Biao notes their activism has become progressively "*zuzhihua, zhengzhihua, jietouhua*" (organized, politicized, and pushed towards street action) in the face of heightened state repression.[109] Nor is this evolution finished. Since 2014, Yirenping has been suppressed, Teng exiled abroad, and Xu sentenced to (and served) three years in prison. Undoubtedly, the next generation of activists will pioneer a new set of strategies. It remains as yet an open question what they will be.

Similar shifts are found elsewhere too. By the late 1990s, scholars had noted the emergence of a polished "elite" among the ranks of China's petitioners. These individuals were capable of not only fluidly expressing their own grievances, but also organizing groups of workers or villagers to engage in collective petitions. Many had previously served in the military.[110] But since the early 2000s, their activities have shifted. Simply beseeching higher officials to intervene in local disputes is out. More confrontational "direct action" strategies are in: blocking roads and construction projects, or mobilizing hundreds of supporters to encircle government buildings and engage in defiant, face-to-face negotiations with officials.[111]

Repression can lead to unpredictable escalation. For example, popular passions in the eastern province of Zhejiang were inflamed by a 2005 crackdown on a restrained sit-down blockade mounted by elderly protestors against polluting chemical factories. The deployment of 1,500 police to clear the demonstrators prompted local villagers to rush to their assistance. A full-scale riot ensued. More than 200 villagers and over 100 police or officials were injured; some sixty-eight government vehicles damaged. Protestors abandoned restraint in the wake of the crackdown. They "began denouncing local leaders, carrying out mock funerals, interrogating factory owners, and ransacking homes of 'traitors'."[112] Spectators started to flow in from neighboring counties to look at the burned-out cars and hear excited participants recount their own dramatic participation. Faced with the prospect of spreading disorder, county authorities backed down, ordering closure of the chemical park.

Beijing is acutely sensitive to these trends. It has steadily upgraded the security apparatus in response. Starting in the early 1990s, Party authorities began increasing the importance of maintaining social stability as a factor in evaluations of local officials. Domestic security portfolios ballooned. Each new crisis—suppression of the Falun Gong after 1999, heightened fears of social unrest after the 2003–2005 "color revolutions" in Eastern Europe, widespread citizen protests in Tibet in 2008, ethnic violence in Xinjiang in 2009—provided yet another reason to throw yet further resources into the ever-expanding security apparatus. From the 1990s to the early 2000s, the political-legal officials charged with managing them regularly rose in bureaucratic rank (see Chart 3.4).

Name	Term in Office	Party Rank
Ren Jianxin	1992–1998	Central Committee (≈200 members)
Luo Gan	1998–2002	Politburo (≈25 members)
Luo Gan	2002–2007	Politburo Standing Committee (9 members)
Zhou Yongkang	2007–2012	Politburo Standing Committee (9 members)

CHART 3.4 National Political-Legal Committee Chairs (1992–2012)

By the early twenty-first century, such policies reached new heights. Under the reign of former security czar Zhou Yongkang, one of China's nine most powerful officials from 2007 to 2012, spending ballooned. In 2011, combined central and local spending on public security surpassed—for the first time—the military budget.[113] China's security apparatus had emerged as a massive, sprawling fiefdom. Just as economic development and population planning targets adopted by China's reform-era leaders had steadily warped its institutions by the beginning of the new millennium, so had Beijing's preoccupation with social unrest become baked into the fabric of the state.

One way to appreciate this is to examine how China's institutions and strategies for maintaining social control have changed. Back in the 1980s, Party political-legal committees were the fulcrum for these efforts. They exercised direct control over the courts, police, and prosecutors. Internally, their composition changed little over the first several decades of the reform era. (see Chart 3.5). These were perfect for the social control strategies of the early reform era: conducting highly mediatized "strike hard" anti-crime campaigns or locking up individual dissidents for extended periods.

But as the reform era wore on, these were no longer sufficient. Heading off an imminent mass petition by laid-off workers to the provincial capital required coordinating the intervention of a much broader range of actors. Social media accounts of key protest leaders needed

- Supreme People's Court
- Supreme People's Procuratorate
- Ministry of Public Security
- Ministry of State Security
- Ministry of Justice

CHART 3.5 Membership of the Party Political-Legal Committee (2007) to be cut off, state banks instructed to extend the overdue loans of the indebted employer so that back wages could be paid. For precisely this reason, starting in the 1990s, so-called committees for the comprehensive management of public security (CMPS) began to proliferate within China's bureaucracy. Co-located with the Party political-legal committees and chaired by the Party political-legal chief for a particular jurisdiction, these committees were charged with coordinating official responses to outbreaks of social unrest. Their key function: creating channels for Party political-legal chiefs to call a spectrum of different state organs to the negotiating table to try to hammer out a response. By the late reform era, these had evolved a sprawling bureaucratic reach. (see Chart 3.6).

- **Supreme People's Court**
- **Supreme People's Procuratorate**
- **Ministry of Public Security**
- **Ministry of State Security**
- **Ministry of Justice**
- Standing Committee of the National People's Congress
- Ministry of Information Industry
- General Administration of Customs
- General Administration of Quality, Supervision, Inspection, and Quarantine
- Chinese Communist Party Youth League
- Propaganda Department of the Chinese Communist Party
- Chinese People's Political Consultative Conference
- State Administration of Radio, Film, and Television

- Security Department of the Political Department of the People's Liberation Army
- Ministry of Civil Affairs
- Ministry of Railways
- Ministry of Culture
- General Administration of Civil Aviation
- General Administration of Press and Publication
- Headquarters of People's Armed Police
- State Council Office for the Prevention and Control of Cults
- All-China Federation of Trade Unions
- Ministry of Health
- Min istry of Education
- State Administration of Work Safety
- Mobilization Department of the General Staff Headquarters of the People's Liberation Army

- Central Disciplinary Commission
- Ministry of the Treasury
- Ministry of Communications
- National Population and Family Planning Commission
- State Administration for Industry and Commerce
- Insurance Regulatory Commission
- Organization Department of the Chinese Communist Party
- General Office of the State Council
- All-China Women's Federation
- Ministry of Labor and Social Security
- People's Bank of China
- National Tourism Agency
- Ministry of Personnel
- Ministry of Construction
- Ministry of Supervision

CHART 3.6 Membership of the Committee for the Comprehensive Management of Public Security (2007)

Reading this list, one might be tempted to view it as impressive feat of institutionalization, corralling a panoply of different bureaus and forcing them to talk to each other. But the reverse is actually the case.[114] It illustrates the steady breakdown of reform-era practices. The name of the game in China's early reform era was specialization—the retreat of indiscriminate exercise of power by ill-defined Party bodies, the emergence of financial professionals in the Ministry of the Treasury and educational experts in China's schools and colleges. Now, the evolutional clock of China's government is running in reverse. Ever-expanding fields of domestic governance are being "securitized," with policies drafted and managed in light of their potential for triggering social unrest.[115] The ill-defined Party bodies are reemerging. Partially established norms that were built up in the reform era—whether corporate debt limits or labor contracting rules—are dissolving in light of the overriding pressure to stave off social unrest. Mid-level officials accustomed to viewing themselves as pursuing technocratic policies flexibly responding to long-term national needs are finding themselves pulled in front of their superiors to justify projects in light of the short-term imperative to do whatever it takes to maintain social stability. Precisely this dynamic is behind the slow death of efforts by China's central bank in 2015–2016 to liberalize the yuan, or the 2017 decision by Shanghai housing authorities to back off from cracking down on commercial properties that had been illegally converted into residential apartments.[116]

Beijing's effort to strengthen its ability to address social unrest have also led it to move away from crudely packing dissidents off to labor camps in favor of more fine-tuned repression. Tools drawn from China's own history have been updated. Collective sanctions against relatives of protest leaders are one example. Family members employed by government agencies or receiving state benefits are often pressured to contact striking workers and plead with them to cease their actions, or watch as their relatives lose their jobs or social security checks.[117] This has results. Starting in 2011, Tibetan monks began resorting to a wave of self-immolations to protest harsh Chinese rule. Authorities responded by applying collective sanctions on the family members of anyone who set themselves on fire. In one Sichuan county, these included: a three-year bar on family members traveling overseas, obtaining government employment, or receiving bank loans or business permits.[118] Numbers of self-immolations dropped off dramatically. As one monk stated in an interview with the *South China Morning Post*, "I can choose to destroy this body for my ideas, but I cannot make a decision like that for others. . . . Many monks do not want to endanger their families."[119]

Observers who examine local protests for signs of China's imminent collapse will search in vain. Beijing retains a firm grip. It has the money to buy off protestors, security forces to suppress them, and organizational skills to stave off the emergence of networks linking different social groups (such as those between striking workers, religious dissidents, and nationalistic students) that might threaten their control. Moreover, the vast majority of protests and demonstrations simply are not aimed at challenging Party rule.[120] They instead represent the daily grind of local grievances in any society—anxious workers demanding their back pay, local communities incensed by the decision of zoning officials to locate a trash incinerator in their neighborhood. In short, these are retail politics with Chinese characteristics.

The real danger is a deeper one—one arising from the fact that the dynamics surrounding petitions and protests are steadily becoming "mere" grassroots Chinese politics-as-usual. The back-and-forth swirl of local politics is the training ground in which opposition figures and political insiders alike are formed worldwide. Almost without exception, whether it is Vladimir Putin or Mahatma Gandhi, they all pass through the K–12 political classrooms of their respective societies. There, they internalize the rules of the power games played on their home turf; they pioneer the strategies that they will employ later in their careers. But what is taking place in local Chinese politics today is a slow radicalization of both state and society alike. Amid Beijing's intense emphasis on stability maintainence (*weiwen*) policies, the leading edge of citizen activism is being driven toward mobilized protest strategies and underground communications, local officials away from institutionalized governance and toward knee-jerk decisions to repress and/or concede.

This is a problem. This is not "responsive authoritarianism." Still less is it a transition toward democracy. As Chinese scholar Yu Jianrong has pointed out, it is "rigid stability," where local authorities "find themselves trapped in a vicious cycle, wherein the harder they try to preserve stability, the greater instability they face."[121] Ironically, it is China's authoritarian system *itself* that is inducing society to drift toward increasingly disruptive forms of social unrest.

LOSS OF BUREAUCRATIC COHESION

With China facing spreading decay inside the Party itself, and new forms of social activism emerging outside, Xi Jinping ascended to power in 2012.[122] He was convinced of the fierce need to act. Since then, Xi has shaken the Party to its core with a tough anti-corruption campaign, while dramatically recentralizing political power in himself and a few trusted aides. He has also launched the most severe domestic crackdown on dissent, civil society, and the media since the immediate aftermath of 1989 (see Chapter 1).

Naturally, this has led to a loss of hope among many who had hoped that the twenty-first century would see China gradually transition to a more liberal, more open society. As veteran legal activist Teng Biao phrased it:

> Xi has done much to bring back the ideological patterns of the Mao Zedong era, including the recycling of old slogans, the shutting of NGOs, the arrest of dissidents and enhanced controls on the spread of information.[123]

Not all are so negative. Since 2012, there has been a strand of opinion that runs along the following lines. Sure, Xi is tough. He is harsh. He is running roughshod over state and society alike. But tough times call for a strong leader. Xi is addressing the dangerous weakness and ineffectiveness that had characterized Hu Jintao's administration. He is centralizing power. And at the end of the day, he is building new institutions to govern China. Naturally, these will be highly illiberal, authoritarian ones. But regardless of how one might normatively feel about these trends, they represent a renewal of the Party's rule.

Such arguments aren't just coming out of China's state media. They resonate with those advanced by serious academics outside the mainland as well, who draw attention to key shifts launched by Beijing since Xi assumed power in 2012.[124] A partial list includes:

Judicial Reforms

- Construction of circuit tribunals of the Supreme People's Court in regional centers like Shenzhen and Shenyang
- Creation of cross-jurisdictional courts cutting across existing administrative boundaries
- Moves to decouple control over local court funding and personnel decisions from local governments, vesting it with provincial courts instead

Party Disciplinary Reforms

- Increased numbers of disciplinary personnel at the central level
- Strengthened power of the central Party disciplinary committee, via the establishment of branch offices in all central Party organs and state-owned enterprises
- Increased control of central disciplinary officials over provincial disciplinary heads

One could point to such developments and assert—correctly—that they reflect a trend toward centralizing power. One could try to go yet further and assemble this together into an argument that China is seeing an evolution of a new, more centralized, more institutionalized one-Party state—a "perfect dictatorship" (Stein Ringen), or a swing back toward "hard authoritarianism" (David Shambaugh).[125] Still others assert they represent the next step in the development of "rule-of-law with Chinese characteristics," purged of deviant Western liberal notions that had crept in during the reform era, and more faithful to China's own authoritarian Legalist traditions.[126]

This may indeed be Xi's intention. He appears to be searching for a way to reinstitute some version of China's classical top-down governance system—a hybrid fusion of imperial Chinese and early 1950s Party practices. Think of this as the "red dynasty" scenario: power highly concentrated in the top leader in Beijing and his courtiers, a tamed and reformed Party apparatus disseminating the center's will to the provinces, and with Party disciplinary inspection commissions (DICs) playing the modern role of the imperial censorate.

Law does play a role in this model. As one mantra currently circulating in Beijing's halls of power puts it: "use law to govern the country, use internal regulations to govern the Party" (*yifa zhiguo yigui zhidang*). Law and Party regulations are to be twin handles by which a new generation of red emperors rules China. This is behind a host of seemingly contradictory policies. Even as Beijing aggressively instructs cadres on the need to "look toward the Party center" (i.e., Xi himself),[127] it simultaneously pushes forward with efforts to install legal counsel in all government organs and state-owned enterprises.[128] Of course, such a disconnect—between legal norms and central bureaucratic dictates—is itself deeply rooted in China's history.[129]

Nor is this vision entirely bad news. It even holds some faint promise for those who hope China's institutions of governance might gradually evolve in a different direction. Take judicial reform. Back in 2010, China's court system was in a locked in a deep freeze. Under the iron grip of the then political-legal head Zhou Yongkang, security hacks had been charged with running the Supreme People's Court (SPC), late-twentieth-century reforms aimed at creating a professional judiciary reversed, and revolutionary-era populist judging practices revived. (This author himself had characterized such developments as amounting to "China's turn against law."[130]) Now, many of these trends have themselves been reversed. Since 2012, control over the SPC has been vested in professionals with deep legal expertise. Reforms currently being pursued within the court system now echo many of those pursued in the 1990s and early 2000s—a professionalized judiciary, emphasis on trials, and efforts to immunize judicial decisions from external interference (but not from Party "guidance"). All of these had previously fallen into disrepute during the second half of Hu Jintao's administration (2007–2012).

So isn't this cause for optimism? Well, yes and no. Talk to the judges in the ponderously named SPC Leading Small Group Office for Judicial Reform, and you quickly realize their caliber. You also sense the extent to which Xi's new central vision has given them a degree of central support, and range of space to maneuver.[131]

But neither law nor courts exist within a vacuum. As much as it may pain American law professors to hear, law is merely an artifact of politically institutionalized governance. During China's reform era, central officials were committed to wide-ranging governance experiments across multiple different fields. This included space for bottom-up reforms funneling citizen participation into the system. It also embraced (if cautiously) openness to outside ideas. This is no longer the case. Space for bottom-up participatory reforms has been curtailed; relevance of foreign models strictly cautioned against. Judicial reforms in China increasingly resemble a lonely outlier. Moreover, they are beginning to bump up against internal limits—skyrocketing workloads, bureaucratic infighting with other organs resentful of the greater attention being lavished on judges, and an exodus of trained personnel.[132] Even those within the system voice worries. As one expert in the Supreme People's Court sighed, "I just hope that when the history of this period is written, people will recognize that we really tried our best."

Perhaps they will succeed. But intentions are one thing; actually turning them into political institutions, quite another. The mere desire to centralize power is not the same as institution-building. And there are three key reasons to doubt that political institutionalization—defined by Huntington as the creation of "stable, valued, recurring patterns of behavior"—is taking place.[133]

First, many of the trends currently playing out in Beijing are less about building up institutions, and more about wresting control of specific bureaucracies to strengthen Xi's personal rule. Rapid concentration of power in the hands of a single individual in the midst of a heated struggle for power should not be confused with greater institutionalization of an authoritarian system.

Recent years have seen a proliferation of nebulous leading small groups (lingdao xiaozu) chaired personally by Xi Jinping. These bypass other Party leaders and allow him to directly exert a broader influence over a wider range of state power. Economic reform is one example—the small group chaired by Xi has effectively marginalized the role of the premier (Li Keqiang), who had borne responsibility for this portfolio in prior administrations.[134] Domestic security is another. By 2010, the expansion of the Party political-legal apparatus as a tool to handle social unrest had produced a vast fiefdom under the thumb of the former security czar, Zhou Yongkang. The purge of Zhou in 2013 gave Xi the opportunity to seize control of this turf. The newly created National Security Commission absorbed the domestic security portfolio (along with agencies aimed at foreign threats) and rendered them directly responsible to Xi.[135] Not to existing Party institutions, such as the Politburo standing committee, but to Xi himself.[136] But since then, there has been no clear definition regarding how this new commission is to actually operate. What was an ill-defined political-legal apparatus has been upgraded to an even less well-defined security apparatus under the control of China's top leader.

Or look more closely at developments in the Party's own internal disciplinary apparatus. Scholars who had examined its evolution up until 2012 found a steady trend toward centralizing control over disciplinary inspection commissions (DICs) in the hands of provincial Party standing committees, and (since 1992) a greater professionalization in their work. DICs appeared to be increasingly focusing on anti-graft work rather than (as in the past) rectification of political errors.[137] Notably, even when they *were* used to eliminate high-profile rivals (such as Jiang Zemin's toppling of Chen Xitong in 1995, or Hu Jintao's removal of Chen Liangyu in 2006), the charges brought were for corruption, rather than for politically challenging China's top leader. One could plausibly assert that such developments represented a shift—albeit partial and incomplete—toward greater institutionalization.

Now consider what has taken place since 2012. Control of the Party disciplinary apparatus has been centralized in the hands of Xi Jinping's close ally Wang Qishan. The massive campaign that has unfolded over the past several years has begun to mutate. It is moving beyond mere anti-corruption work. New targets include Party cadres suspected of disloyalty to the top leadership (i.e. Xi),[138] government employees who exhibit sloth or inaction,[139] and professors who voice improper opinions in class.[140]

This is a reversion to patterns drawn from the 1950s and 1960s—one where the discipline committees are being used as a top-down political tool to shake and purge the entire Party apparatus. Nor is this being accomplished by the organic evolution of China's institutions of supervision and oversight. Instead, it is marked by the expanded use of central inspection teams that descend on designated government and Party organs in sudden raids, detaining targets according to black-box rules.[141] Since 2015, official Party parlance has shifted to warn cadres against violating unclear "political rules" (*zhengzhi guiju*),[142] in addition to the specific (but still extralegal) mandates of the Party's own charter and internal regulations. Many interpret this as a sweeping catch-all provision aimed at allowing Xi to pursue all behavior and opinions he finds objectionable.[143] A pervasive sense of uncertainty and fear has descended across the Chinese bureaucracy. Suicides have multiplied, with fifty-four cadres perishing from "unnatural causes" between January 2013 and April 2014.[144] All of this represents devolution away from institutionalized governance, not progress toward it.

Second, centralization of power in Xi's hands reflects a broader trend. Partially institutionalized elite political norms that *had* emerged under China's reform era are breaking down. Xi's takedown of Zhou, which flagrantly violated tacit norms exempting current or former Politburo Standing Committee members from prosecution, is but one example. The 19th Party Congress in fall 2017 saw others topple as well. In a decisive break with reform-era norms, Xi was elevated to a level within the Party ideological canon approaching that of Mao. And contrary to practices dating back to the 1990s, no obvious successor to Xi was designated. Both raise the possibility that Xi might seek to continue to rule on in some form after the end of his second term as Party general secretary in 2022. As veteran China watcher Willy Lam has noted, this would "constitute a body blow to the institutional reforms that Deng [Xiaoping] introduced in order to prevent the return of Maoist norms."[145]

Third, the mechanisms that Beijing is using to influence society at large are sliding toward deinstitutionalized channels. Consider other recent trends—all of which break with patterns established since 1978.

- Cultivation of a budding cult of personality around the central leader, complete with fawning videos bearing titles such as "If You Want to Marry, Marry Someone Like Big Daddy Xi [Xi Dada]."[146]

- Pivoting away from the Communist Party's revolutionary roots in favor of the revival of an ethno-nationalist ideology rooted in history, tradition, and Confucianism (see Chapter 4).
- Return to Maoist-era tactics—televised self-confessions by journalists and lawyers, unannounced disappearances of state officials and civil society activists alike—inducing what Minxin Pei has aptly termed a "rule of fear."[147]

Rule by fear, tradition, and personal charisma. These are not efforts to promote institutions of governance. As the sociologist Max Weber pointed out, these are the *antithesis* of institutionalized, bureaucratic rule.[148]

And that's exactly right. China's reform-era trajectory is being reversed. As discussed in Chapter 1, Beijing's failure to deepen political reform when it had the chance to do so—during the last two decades of the twentieth century and in the first decade of the twenty-first—is now leading the entire system to cannibalize itself and its own prior efforts at political institutionalization. Step by step, Xi finds himself needing to break more and more of the system in order to combat internal opposition, protect his position, and advance his own interests. Under these pressures, China's tradition of coherent bureaucratic rule (which Fukuyama had identified as the third element of stability in the reform era) is beginning to wobble.

Observing the political tightening in China, some argue that Xi is a new Mao. In the spring of 2016, both the *Economist* and *Time* magazines published editions with eye-catching cover art showing Xi morphing into Mao. As Hannah Beech wrote in *Time*, "[Xi] has retreated into the world of Mao: personality cults, plaudits to the state sector and diatribes against foreigners supposedly intent on destroying China."[149] In response, Beijing added both magazines to the steadily expanding list of banned websites, blocking users inside China from accessing them.[150]

Such a comparison misses the mark. For all of Xi's invocation of Maoist language, and despite his centralization of power and adoring throngs gathered around him in camera shots, there is still a crucial difference. He has not resorted to mass campaigns as a political tactic.

Until that reoccurs, one cannot claim that Xi is a revived version of Mao. And that simply has not happened.

Pessimists would interject—"and that has not happened . . . yet." For Beijing to even attempt to resort to mass political mobilization, one would have to first see certain shifts in China's political terrain: the top leader purging his opponents among the ruling elite, re-establishing tight control over media channels, and laying the groundwork for a cult of personality among the population at large. Inconceivable a decade ago, all of these have come to pass in the past five years. Given that, one has to at least ask the question: faced with a looming crisis—a leadership split, a clash in the South China Sea, or a debt-fueled economic crash—might Xi decide to try to break the final taboo of the reform era, call the masses to the streets, and sacrifice the institution of the Party itself in a last-ditch effort to preserve his own power?

CONCLUSION

Unlike a decade ago, the breakdown of China's reform-era norms is no longer confined to discrete areas such as judicial reform or the treatment of civic activists. It is now mutating like a virus across many different fields. This is why China is moving from "the turn against law" to "the end of the reform era."

Care to see these trends play themselves out in miniature? Just travel to China's bustling southern metropolis of Hong Kong.

When the former British colony reverted to the People's Republic of China in 1997, it more than any other region under Beijing's jurisdiction embodied the norms that observers such as Fukuyama associate with effective Chinese governance. It had a highly effective bureaucracy, capable technocratic managers, and an authoritarian executive branch with responsive channels of governance (limited electoral mechanisms, firm rule of law, an independent anti-corruption commission) with wide popular support. By the terms of the retrocession agreement, Beijing assured Hong Kong a high degree of autonomy under the rubric of "one country, two systems." Chinese authorities largely respected this principle in the decade that followed.[151]

But as China's politics chilled, frigid winds swept into Hong Kong. Starting in 2012, local school curricula began to be modified to emphasize "patriotic" themes and the role of the Communist Party. Media outlets at odds with Beijing came under pressure. Mainland Chinese banks withdrew advertising dollars. A string of violent attacks by unidentified assailants targeted their editors and owners.[152] Such political trends fused with social ones. Tighter economic integration with mainland China brought more tourists, an influx of money that drove up property values, and increased usage of Mandarin rather than the local Cantonese dialect. Resentment spread.

Society radicalized. After Hong Kong's legislature rejected Beijing's proposed reforms to the process for selecting the territory's chief executive, latent tensions devolved into acrimonious recriminations. Pro-democracy forces launched a civil disobedience campaign aimed at pressuring Party leaders into adopting more liberal reforms. During the fall of 2014, activists occupied the streets of Hong Kong's central business district for roughly three months. But the aging moderate pro-democracy leaders schooled in the rules of parliamentary debate found themselves surprised by the emergence of a much more aggressive youth movement. A generation of college and high school students that previously saw the purchase of the newest model iPhone as their highest goal in life emerged as vocal leaders—facing down tear gas, participating in hunger strikes, and organizing the distribution of food to protest camps. Nor did tensions ease after the street occupations faded in the winter of 2014. Subsequent months saw flash protests erupt in shopping malls frequented by mainland Chinese tourists, with groups of masked local demonstrators shouting slurs and being dragged away by police.[153] Steadily, the scent of rural Chinese politics has begun drifting into the once-urbane commercial districts of Hong Kong.

Since the 2014 protests, Beijing seems to have decided that Hong Kong's relative liberties are a political problem. Pro-government figures are being installed in key positions in universities, their critics blocked.[154] Such developments have led to a "dramatic decline in academic freedom" in Hong Kong.[155] Critical commentators in papers such as the *South China Morning Post* and the *Hong Kong Economic*

Journal are finding their columns canceled. And when the former was taken over by mainland China's Internet giant Alibaba in 2015, self-censorship spread yet further.

As these pressures build, cracks are emerging in Hong Kong's long-stable institutions of governance. The once-respected anti-corruption commission has been tarnished by accusations of politicized interference amid a probe into the financial dealings of Hong Kong's chief executive.[156] Corporate analysts fear that heightened mainland pressure is eroding the integrity of local financial markets and the transparency of corporate information—particularly that of Hong Kong–listed mainland Chinese companies.[157] Other concerns are even more direct. In 2015–2016, Beijing's security forces seized five Hong Kong booksellers responsible for the publication of salacious exposes of the lives of top Chinese officials. The fact that security forces seized two from outside mainland China (in Thailand and Hong Kong), and that they all subsequently made highly unconvincing televised confessions, generated significant alarm among citizens.[158]

Such developments have led many to fear that Hong Kong's unique autonomous status is fast eroding, as the internal reform-era political consensus in Beijing underlying it is breaking down. This has further radicalized some opposition leaders. Early 2016 saw youth activists form a National Party expressly advocating Hong Kong independence. Founder Chan Ho-tin argued that "staging marches or shouting slogans is obviously useless now. Regarding using violence, we would support it if it is effective to make us heard."[159] The decision of Hong Kong authorities in summer 2016 to ban their candidates from standing for legislative election inflamed activists.[160] After several "localists" from other parties successfully won legislative seats, two vented their ire at their inauguration—raising Hong Kong independence banners and using a derogatory World War II–era Japanese expression to refer to China.

Unsurprisingly, Beijing's response has been to double down. Consider the moves seen in the first half of 2017 alone. A highly unusual interpretation of Hong Kong's Basic Law by China's national legislature. Efforts to purge ten legislators from the pro-independence and pro-democracy camps from Hong Kong's seventy-person legislature (potentially eliminating the opposition's few procedural checks on pending legislation). Revival of calls for mainland-style national security legislation. A nationalist campaign by pro-Beijing forces attacking the reliability and loyalty of non-Chinese judges serving in Hong Kong courts. New moves clamping down on Hong Kong schools and universities to curb spreading localist sentiment among youth.

This is precisely how once-firm norms erode, and how seemingly stable institutions regress. Start playing some of these trends forward (a slightly more violent replay of the 2014 protests, or a more aggressive push by Beijing to assert control over Hong Kong courts), envisage the likely set of reactions and counter-reactions, and one ends up with some scary consequences. Moreover, all of the above has taken place within just a few years, in China's wealthiest area—one where the rules of the political game were thought to have been relatively established, with society relatively docile and politically inert. If this could occur in Hong Kong, what might take place across the border in mainland China, with its much deeper history of political turmoil?

4

Religion and Ideology: What Do We Believe?

CHINA TODAY IS THE Wild West of religion.

Take a society scoured clean by a decades-long repression of tradition. Introduce an ideological vacuum caused by the collapse of communism as a belief system. Relax state controls. Add hundreds of millions of people searching for meaning, values, and community in a world turned upside down by frenetic social change. The result: an explosion of beliefs of all kinds.

Many are searching China's own past for a golden age to which to return. Underemployed left-wing college graduates railing against capitalist exploitation, blogging late into the night about reviving true Maoist values (Nationalism! Socialism!) of the 1950s. Elderly academics attempting to reintroduce Confucian teachings in schools in order to cleanse a country stained by Western doctrines such Marxism and liberalism. Yellow-clad monks seeking to spread a humanistic version of Zen Buddhism dating back to the Tang dynasty (AD 618–907), but since corrupted by superstition. A willowy self-taught fortune teller who claims she obtained unique powers after sequestering herself away for months on an extended fast, and holds unnervingly intense eye contact while informing you that the answers to everything—*everything*—can be found in the *Yi Jing*, the classic divination text dating to the second century BC. And that doesn't even include the surging interest in more recent faiths to land on China's shores—such as Protestantism and Catholicism. China literally has it all.

Official statistics obscure how big the boom is. Since the mid-1990s, authorities have held to bland assertions that China has roughly 100 million believers of all religions, pointing to membership rosters of state-run patriotic religious associations. But the real increase has come in unregistered groups. Outside estimates place the true total of all believers much higher—300 million folk religionists, 250 million Buddhists, 68 million Christians, and 25 million Muslims.[1]

Many see hope in the spread of religion. Chinese officials stress narrowly utilitarian benefits, pointing out the role for believers in helping care for the elderly and sick. Others take heart in the emergence of an unshackled spiritual individualism. Authors such as Evan Osnos (*Age of Ambition*) or Ian Johnson (*The Souls of China*) portray in exquisite detail how the past three decades have set millions set free to chart their own journeys of faith.[2] Still others endow China's religious revival with deeper meaning. Evangelical Protestants associated with the "Back to Jerusalem" movement interpret Christianity's spread in China as part of a divinely inspired plan—one assigning Chinese believers a special role in a final push to convert Muslims, Buddhists, and Hindus throughout Asia and North Africa in order to fulfill the conditions for Christ's return.[3]

But just as with China's booming economic wealth and surging citizen political demands, we need to look deeper. What is mounting Chinese religious faith being funneled into?

THE GRAY ZONE—UNREGISTERED FAITHS

An ordinary newspaper article. That's how it started.

For Mr. Zhang, the elderly professor in front of me, it changed his family for the better. Perched on the sofa of his family's cozy Beijing apartment, his wiry fingers traced the air as he remembered.

He had been searching. Spiritually, he had felt vaguely empty. In the late 1980s, he first encountered religion. Popular Buddhist and Taoist tracts had begun to circulate again after decades of enforced atheism. These spoke to him. The Marxist slogans he preached in his political philosophy class suddenly seemed shallow and void. As his son and daughter-in-law silently exchanged glances, he enthusiastically recounted his participation in the *qigong* fervor that had swept the country at the time.[4] Millions flocked to public parks, auditoriums, and stadiums to practice these traditional Chinese mediation and health exercises. A shifting array of self-taught masters emerged as overnight celebrities. Each promised that correct posture and diligent practice of their methods could improve health, clear the mind, and calm the spirit. "Or even acquire special powers," said Mr. Zhang with a broad smile and dramatic sweep of his hands. Pausing, he looked around the room, adding, "Of course, we later realized that was just our subconscious minds talking to us."

In 1994, Mr. Zhang read the article that altered everything. Just a few dry paragraphs, it described a new faith—one that emphasized the unity of humanity. He excitedly perused the limited details. This was it. This was what he had been looking for. But he had no actual contact with believers. Even the religion's name remained a mystery. Nonetheless, he shared his experience with his family. Two years later, his son encountered foreign teachers at his college. They spoke of their beliefs in passing. They stressed the unity of all world religions. His son immediately recognized this as the faith his father had spoke of. On the next school vacation, he brought his father to meet the foreign teachers. Both quickly became members of China's small, but growing, Baha'i community.

Why? "Ah," sighed the daughter-in-law, "Many people today are *fuzao*—restless, and lacking in real consistency or morals." Smiling at her husband, she continued, "In contrast, when I met him at the Baha'i event in college, I just knew he was different. He had depth. He had values."

Many are searching for purpose amid China's dizzying social changes. Paths differ. A few days earlier, I had been on a bus winding its way through misty hillsides in the southwestern city of Chongqing. Through rain-slicked windows, a large billboard caught my eye. "Help quiet the restless feelings of your youth." I tried to mentally guess what the sign might be referring to. Yoga studio? Motivational speaker? One of the newly popular self-help books reinterpreting Confucian teachings for the twenty-first century? As we rounded a bend, the sign came into closer view: an advertisement for luxury apartments in one of the posh gated communities that had spread like wildfire on the outskirts of the city. For the newly monied classes seeking to live out their dreams, the pursuit of such affluence is so common as to be unremarkable. When, in 2010, a female contestant on a hit television dating show crushed the hopes of her unemployed suitor with the memorable rejection, "I would rather cry in a BMW [than smile on a bicycle]," it immediately became a catchphrase for a generation.[5] Only the truly ostentatious now merits mention: a young woman posting online photos of herself dressed in a paper dress given to her by her *gandie* (sugar daddy) and stitched together with bills allegedly worth $32,000;[6] or the incongruous $16.5 million gold, gem, and jade-encrusted statute of Mao Zedong unveiled in Shenzhen for the 120th anniversary of the birth of the Communist revolutionary who had once decried such displays of wealth.[7]

Such worship of blind materialism worries the Zhangs. They have seen families of coworkers erode and collapse under the relentless search for the next marker of success—spacious apartments, imported cars, vacations abroad. Their beliefs help the Zhangs keep their priorities straight. To spend more time with his family, Mr. Zhang's son has just left his lucrative position at a big law firm for a less demanding job. Religion helps there too. "It gives me a compass to deal with the moral challenges that come with doing business today," he adds, "pressures for self-serving behavior, or even corruption."

They are also troubled by what they see in the schools. Intense test-driven competition drives parents to push children beyond all reasonable bounds in order to squeeze out a few more points on their exams. Mr. Zhang's son and wife worry about their own child—that he might internalize the message that grades are the entire measure of his life's worth. The close-knit Baha'i community helps balance such pressures. Believers host weekly study sessions in their homes. Children discuss questions not adequately taught in school—responsibilities toward friends and family, how to be a good person. This appeals to nonbelievers too. Several of the Zhangs' neighbors send their children to attend, precisely because they like the values being transmitted.

But still, why Baha'ism? Why this tiny offshoot of the Judeo-Christian-Muslim tradition, originating in nineteenth-century Persia, with but a few million members worldwide and perhaps several thousand in China? Why not Buddhism, rooted in nearly two thousand years of Chinese history? Or one of the rapidly expanding Protestant congregations? "Oh, we do not reject any of those," says the son. "All of those have their place in helping people find their path." "But Baha'ism just moved us," notes the daughter-in-law. She pulls down a religious text, thumbs to a passage from 1917, and reads it aloud:

> The Bahá'í teacher of the Chinese people must first be imbued with their spirit, know their sacred literature, study their national customs and speak to them from their own standpoint, and their own termi-nologies. . . . China is the country of the future.[8]

This resonates with them. They are struck by the acceptance of China's own culture and traditions. Daoist, Buddhist, and Confucian sages (as well as Christian and Muslim prophets) are not simply rejected out of hand. Rather, they are embraced as earlier incarnations of one universal faith.

As they reminisced over family photos, I sat back and reflected. What I was witnessing was the early days as a faith spread into new lands. For many religions, this era has already faded into history. Sure, there was once a time when early Christians could share first-hand memories of Peter's debate with Paul over dinner in Antioch. But that is long past. Even the birth of more recent faiths such as Mormonism is gradually receding into yellowed diary pages recording the harsh trek to Utah and the years of conflict with the U.S. federal government. But the people in front of me could point to pictures of the earliest Baha'is in Beijing and ask, "Oh, was Sandy at your wedding too? What is he up to now? I should give him a call."

RELIGION: THE BIG PICTURE

New faiths have not had an easy time in China.

Fearing the seeds of possible resistance, imperial authorities viewed religion with a wary eye. Dynasty after dynasty adopted a dual strategy. Pick a state-sponsored ideology. Restrict competing doctrines.

Confucianism—the philosophy most associated with China today—was one of the earliest targets of state repression. To the Qin rulers who first unified the country in 221 BC, the itinerant teachings of Confucius and his disciples looked weak. These emphasized family,

moral self-cultivation, and adherence to historical tradition. This con-
flicted with the harsh Legalist values espoused by the Qin court: state,
rule by coercion, and absolute obedience to the emperor's will. For a
newly ascendant despotic regime under the control of an increasingly
paranoid leader, there could be only one response. The resulting policies
have gone down in one of the most vivid expressions in the Chinese
language—*fen shu keng ru*. Burn the Confucian books; bury their scholars alive.[9]

The fortunes of different beliefs in China have since followed a regular ebb and flow. After the collapse of the Qin dynasty, Confucianism
emerged as the new state orthodoxy. Legalist texts went into remission.
When Buddhism entered China from India in the first millennium AD,
it was initially embraced. Emperors converted. They sponsored construction of temples through the land. But as monasteries grew wealthy
and powerful, the imperial state became fearful. In AD 842–845, Tang
emperors launched a brutal purge—obliterating shrines, seizing lands,
and defrocking monks and nuns.[10] In the following centuries, the imperial state and its resurgent Confucian advisers smothered religion with
bureaucracy. Licensing systems were established for monks; ordination
barred without government approval. Such moves broke the back of
Buddhism as an autonomous force in Chinese society.[11]

After Western missionaries reached China in the sixteenth century, it was Christianity's turn. Early Jesuits such as Mateo Ricci
became trusted imperial advisers. Prominent intellectuals converted to
Catholicism. But attitudes shifted as Christianity spread. During the
nineteenth century, Confucian literati grew suspicious of the expanding influence of churches. Local officials and citizens alike resented the
regular appeals of converts to Western embassies for diplomatic intervention in civil disputes.[12] Emperors watched with horror as heterodox
Christian movements and anti-Christian nativism alike fused explo-
sively with latent citizen discontent, producing bloody uprisings such
as the Taiping (1850–1864) and Boxer (1898–1900) Rebellions.

The founding of the People's Republic of China in 1949 brought a
new secular religion: communism. Communist leaders asserted strict
control over all competing beliefs. Foreign missionaries were expelled.
New "patriotic" religious organizations administrated by Party authorities were created for the five officially recognized religions—Buddhism,

Catholicism, Daoism, Islam, and Protestantism. These organizations assumed responsibility for managing religious sites, training clergy, and harmonizing religious doctrine with Marxist theory.[13]

As China descended into the national political madness of the Cultural Revolution (1966–1976), even these harsh controls were abandoned in favor of a new goal: total eradication. Religious believers were compelled to publicly renounce their beliefs; Buddhist and Catholic clergy forced to marry. Rampaging mobs of Red Guards were unleashed on religious sites, desecrating churches, temples, and mosques. Thousands of years of priceless cultural heritage went up in flames. As religion was repressed, the personality cult of Mao surged. His words became scripture—immortalized in little red books read fervently by hundreds of millions in regular study sessions. Sobbing students shouted out their devotion in mass rallies. Young couples married in front of his photo. Radical activists engaged in worship-like rituals in front of his statues.

Such radicalism receded with the onset of the reform era. Ideological crusades faded; economic development emerged as the new state priority. When central authorities announced a new direction for religious policy in 1982, it amounted to a U-turn back to the 1950s and imperial eras.[14] To be sure, Party authorities remain deeply suspicious of religion.[15] Atheism is promoted among the ranks of cadres. But control, rather than elimination, is the watchword for society at large.

Religion in China today is a complex spectrum, carefully detailed by sociologist Fenggang Yang.[16] Revived state-sponsored ("red") patriotic churches and temples are sites for approved religious practices. Officially banned ("black") groups are severely repressed. Between the two lies a shifting zone of "gray" beliefs and practices. This includes everything from entire sects—Mormonism, Judaism, and Baha'ism—to booming Protestant and Buddhist house congregations gathering privately outside official structures, to an eclectic mélange of traditional and new spiritual movements. Not officially recognized, not always harassed, they remain perpetually cautious for the knock on the door, the phone call in the night, signaling they have crossed an invisible line.

Boundaries can be fluid. Believers might visit both registered and unregistered groups in search of faith and community. Official Protestant churches might help distribute translated religious works to underground house churches. Sometimes this is in outright defiance of official rules. Sometimes it is with the tacit approval of local Party authorities who prefer that citizens receive religious instruction from figures deemed safe.

State attitudes also differ dramatically from place to place. In Wenzhou, authorities strictly suppress Catholics who stubbornly insist on swearing allegiance to the Vatican rather than Beijing. Down the coast in Ningde, the same believers enjoy an exceptionally high degree of tolerance—including openly celebrating Catholic masses, organizing religious activities, and even registering religious sites—precisely because local officials have decided to reach a pragmatic accommodation with a large, well-organized local underground movement rather than risk social unrest with a crackdown.[17]

What does this mean in practice for ordinary believers of unapproved "gray" groups?

For Baha'is such as the Zhangs, they do not openly tell strangers about their beliefs. But colleagues and friends all know. Youth study groups of Baha'i values and ethics are fused with English teaching. After all, who could object to children improving their foreign language skills? Consistent with Baha'i teachings, they try to comply with state rules about religious practice. House meetings are kept small—no more than twenty attendees at a time. Foreign Baha'is are not invited to major festivals. And believers carefully stay away from attempting to create anything like a formal Baha'i organization such as those in other countries. Instead, a loose network helps organize study sessions, distribute religious works, and translate materials.

But clashes do occur. To wary police eyes, a "loose network of believers" can look a lot like an anti-state cabal. In the late 1990s, authorities at Mr. Zhang's school called him into a meeting with stern-faced public security and religious affairs officials. They accused him of spreading a cult and demanded he hand over Baha'i religious books. After vigorously defending the merits of his beliefs, he reluctantly complied. "But without giving them the core texts!" he clarifies with a vigorous thrust of his index finger.

Faced with such suspicion, Baha'is in China are currently engaged in a delicate dance. Since the 1990s, the Macau-based, Baha'i-inspired Badi Foundation has conducted anti-poverty and education initiatives in rural China. Such social service work has won a measure of recognition, including regular cooperation with Chinese authorities charged with development and women's affairs.[18] Similarly, Baha'is cooperate with state academics seeking to understand their religion. In 2001, the Chinese Academy of Social Sciences opened a research center on the Baha'i faith.[19] Scholarly works on Baha'ism have since followed.

The Zhangs and other Baha'is see the bright side of religion in China today. They have carefully used the zone of tacit state tolerance since the late 1970s to share experiences and build their community—including opening a summer camp for dozens of Baha'i youth. And they hold out hope that Beijing might at some point extend their faith some kind of official recognition as well.

THE BLACK ZONE—REPRESSED BELIEFS

Not so for another spiritual group. For them, recent decades have seen a dramatic reversal in fortune, making them one of the most harshly repressed of all organizations.

In the early 1980s, as China emerged from the ashes of the Cultural Revolution, many turned toward traditional practices suppressed during the heights of Maoist radicalism. Like Mr. Zhang, millions took a renewed interest in *qigong*—health and meditation exercises deeply rooted in Chinese history. Thousands of competing books and groups emerged. For some, the benefits resembled any other form of exercise. Others veered into the paranormal. Newspapers carried fevered reports on miraculous cures and feats of extrasensory perception. Despite criticism of such claims by members of China's scientific establishment, *qigong* enjoyed strong state support. Aging Party cadres flocked to masters for treatment. Sports and health officials sponsored conferences on the merits of different practices. Top universities conducted experiments on claims by *qigong* grandmasters that they could use biophysical energy to manipulate objects over great distances.[20]

As the *qigong* boom spread, some began to import more and more religious trappings into their teachings. When Li Hongzhi, a former trumpeter for a provincial forestry police band, emerged as a national sensation in 1992 with his new form of *qigong* practice—Falun Gong—his initial public lectures and healing sessions featured him clad in sober business attire. These gradually gave way to explicitly Buddhist and Daoist symbolism and clothing. A hagiography of Li's life followed. His journey toward enlightenment was described in a framework closely resembling that of traditional Chinese spiritual figures throughout history—an auspicious birth, a youth marked by miracles, rigorous self-cultivation under the tutelage of various masters.[21]

Falun Gong grew rapidly. During the 1990s, the movement evolved many of the core elements of a religion. A single text—the Zhuan Falun—provided a semi-organized set of core beliefs. Content extended far beyond simple exercise to encompass teachings on the origins of the universe, life after death, and instructions for ordinary living. A national organization—the Falun Dafa Research Association—oversaw a network of regional branches, which in turn supervised a hierarchy of local practice groups. These disseminated reports purporting to show a wide range of health benefits resulting from their practices. Popular interest spread, particularly among those unable to afford the spiraling costs of health care as China moved toward a more market-based system. Millions of practicioners, often elderly, filled public squares to carry out prescribed rhythmic breathing exercises.

By 1995, official attitudes toward *qigong* started to shift. Party authorities launched campaigns attacking "feudal superstition" and "pseudoscience." State papers carried editorials by noted scientists attacking the claims of various sects. Propaganda officials banned publication of Falun Gong works. Sensing the changing winds, many casual adherents began to disassociate themselves from *qigong* practice. But not true believers. Falun Gong adherents organized protests against negative media commentary. Reactions varied. In some cases, residual support within government (particularly the sports ministry) fused with an official desire to avoid social unrest to produce retractions, apologies, or even firings of journalists. Others encountered an iron hand. In April 1999, following a demonstration in Tianjin, riot police were deployed, and dozens of adherents detained.[22]

The result: the largest demonstration in Beijing since 1989. On the evening of April 24, Falun Gong adherents filtered into the capital in small groups. By the following morning, over ten thousand practicioners, mostly middle-aged and elderly, had gathered in neat lines stretching for kilometers around Zhongnanhai—the complex in the heart of the city housing top Chinese leaders. The demonstrators did not unfurl banners or shout slogans. Instead, they sat silently until authorities called their representatives in for discussions. After presenting their requests—release of the Tianjin detainees, recognition of their movement, and a guarantee of freedom from prosecution—they dispersed just as quietly as they had come, having picked clean all litter on their side of the street, while that of the police forces observing them remained strewn with plastic lunch containers and discarded chopsticks.[23]

Now, if there is one thing that authoritarian rulers dislike, it is waking up to their morning tea (or coffee) and finding that their leadership compound has been surrounded. Particularly by a highly organized group previously ignored by their security forces.

Chinese leaders went ballistic. In July 1999, after a brief strategic pause, they launched a brutal campaign to wipe out Falun Gong. A tidal wave of state propaganda demonized the sect as a "cult." Top leaders were rounded up in mass arrests; ordinary members subjected to intense pressure to repent and denounce Li Hongzhi (himself having immigrated to New York in 1996) for deluding and twisting their minds. Subsequent years witnessed persecution far exceeding that experienced by students arrested in the 1989 democracy protests: lengthy prison sentences, torture, psychological abuse, and thousands of deaths in state custody.[24]

State suppression has had three key effects.

First, Falun Gong has been driven deep underground in China. Some kind of network continues to exist, if the extent is unclear. Adherents have periodically hacked into state cable channels to disseminate pro–Falun Gong information. And in a James Bond–style scenario characterized by hidden messages passed in a fruit market, fake IDs, a network of unidentified activists, and a two-week journey from Beijing to Thailand, adherents successfully staged the 2009 escape of the wife and children of an activist lawyer noted for his defense of persecuted Christian and Falun Gong adherents—from under the noses of the security cordon monitoring his house.[25]

Second, the movement outside China has been radicalized. Adherents initially focused their ire on individual leaders responsible for their suppression, filing dozens of (largely symbolic) lawsuits in courts worldwide against former top leader Jiang Zemin and his security chiefs. But since 2004, the struggle has been reinterpreted in sweeping cosmic terms. Falun Gong materials such as the *Nine Commentaries* now depict the Communist Party as representing an "anti-universe force" that has "pushed civilization to the brink of destruction," and will eventually be destroyed.[26]

Third, state suppression has prompted Falun Gong to metastasize. Twenty years ago, this was a group of elderly retirees gathering in parks. Now, it is by far the most organized of all anti-Beijing political movements within the Chinese diaspora.

The next time you are in a Chinese restaurant anywhere in the United States, take a look in the stack of papers gathered near the door. Odds are that you will find the *Epoch Times* (*Dajiyuan*) there. Behind the ordinary headlines on national politics and Hollywood stars, you will find stories carefully following a specifically selected set of talking points: Party corruption, Chinese state-sponsored organ harvesting from prisoners, perhaps a selection from the *Nine Commentaries*. This is but the tip of an extensive media network built by scratch by Falun Gong adherents over the past two decades. Websites such as *Minghui* transmit doctrine and allow believers to share experiences. The New Tang Dynasty cable TV station beams out a steady stream of counter-propaganda responding blow for blow to that produced by Beijing. Nightly news programs air the dirty laundry of internal Party struggles, sitcoms parody inept cadres mouthing political slogans, while evangelical speeches discuss the nature of enlightenment.[27]

Naturally, Beijing fulminates that this is all the CIA's work. The truth is far more prosaic. Individual adherents mortgaging their homes to support a new radio station. Silicon Valley engineers using their evenings to devise new software to circumvent state Internet controls. Elderly volunteers dedicating their weekends to gathering outside the tourist attractions of New York, Paris, or Hong Kong to urge mainland Chinese visitors to quit the Party—or using telemarketing software to randomly mass-dial phone numbers in China for the same purpose.

Most notably, Falun Gong is challenging Beijing's effort to ground the legitimacy of the Communist Party in Chinese culture. In New York and California, adherents have established state-licensed high schools and colleges, with a heavy emphasis on traditional dance and arts. Many graduates go on to participate in Shen Yun, the Falun Gong–affiliated performing arts troupe. Founded as a loose group of expatriates in 2006, it has since grown to several hundred artists and three touring companies. Styling themselves as the authentic representation of "5000 years of civilization" destroyed by Beijing, they perform in national and community theaters alike around the world, raising money for the cause.[28] About 90 percent of the artistic content is immediately familiar to anyone who has seen parallel official performances in China. Traditional music. Acrobatic feats. Displays of martial arts skill. Synchronized mass performances in swirling silk outfits. Even the obligatory minority nationality dances are included. But exiting the auditorium, one invariably overhears voices of confusion from non-Chinese who thought they were simply attending a New Year's culture performance. "Great dances, but I didn't really understand that bit in the fourth act where Buddha descends from heaven in a beam of light to obliterate the cruel authorities persecuting those other guys. What was that?"

Overlooked is the real nature of what they have just witnessed: a slick twenty-first-century version of the revolutionary dance troupes pioneered by Party authorities themselves during the civil war era of the 1930s and 1940s. The propaganda teams of stalwart (and comely) soldiers reworked traditional operas and folk songs to infuse them with socialist themes. Performed by the flickering firelight of countless village squares, Chinese nationalism was awakened, the peasant masses mobilized, and the gospel of liberation spread.[29]

The true irony is that Beijing's crackdown is producing exactly what the state fears most—a well-organized, highly motivated force of true believers who are adopting many of the Party's own methods in order to survive.

For most Americans, this dynamic is simply too unfamiliar to even recognize. Our own blinders mean that we see the people who most resemble ourselves as representing the "real" China. Liberal East Coast intellectuals instinctively identify with secular Ivy-educated Chinese lawyers who speak a common language of human rights. Religious conservatives gravitate toward Christian activists who share their faith. A neo-Buddhist/Daoist sect that borrows Leninist united front tactics and situates itself as the rightful inheritor to the nationalist mantle of Chinese civilization? Doesn't even register.

The full moon shone down on the temple. Under its glow, we feasted on *yangmei*—succulent red Chinese strawberries.

Around me were the elite of Chinese society: executives of booming private companies, retired Party cadres, the head of an overseas Chinese association in Latin America. In ascending this quiet, cool hillside in the coastal province of Zhejiang, they had left behind the steamy summer heat and smog of the overcrowded cities.

For them, the past decades had been very good indeed. Now they wanted something more. Seeking spiritual enlightenment and intellectual growth, several had enrolled in a short course on classical Chinese culture led by the yellow-robed monk to my left. A man of many hats, he simultaneously served as a professor at Peking University, a deputy director of the state-run national Buddhist Association, and the newly appointed abbot for the temple where we were sitting. For a few days each month, busy corporate lives were placed on hold as his students jetted across the country to reassemble at the feet of their master. There they could briefly relive the simple camaraderie of their school days. Tonight, they erupted in delighted laughter as a middle-aged CEO of a medical device firm read aloud a poem that he himself had composed— one humorously rearranging the teachings of their master into verse.

For some, the quest was more consuming. Take our host for the evening. A wealthy entrepreneur in a stylish gray suit, Mr. Pan had found religion after his business ventures and self-confidence briefly fell on dark times some fifteen years ago. Reflection led him to a Taiwanese master instrumental in reviving Chinese Buddhism after the chaos of the twentieth century. Now Mr. Pan had turned his formidable energies to a new task: commemorating his master with a grand project that would continue his legacy. Since 2007, he has poured millions of dollars of his own money (as well as funds borrowed from outside investors and local authorities) into building the massive temple complex around us.

How to convey the project's scale? Simply describing it as the "largest single imperial-style temple in China," with vermilion hues modeled on the Forbidden City, fails to do it justice. The ability to receive (and feed) millions of visitors each year? But a petty detail. No, to fully appreciate the scope of Mr. Pan's plans, you have to focus on the lotus-shaped skyscraper under construction on a mountain in the background. Architecturally, it is a representation of one of the Buddhist heavens. Lighted, it is visible for dozens of miles in the distance. As Mr. Pan explains, inspiration came to him while visiting televangelist Robert Schuller's Crystal Cathedral in southern California. "In America, you have such striking buildings dedicated to spreading Christianity. I realized we needed something like that here to spread our own cultural values, such as Buddhism." This is his vision. A mega-temple for a renewed twenty-first-century China. The complex seeks to unite a multitude of different Buddhist sects divided by history—radiating their values out to a China desperately in need of faith. A hoped-for influx of paying tourists is to support this effort. Their numbers will bring national attention; their ticket purchases help defray costs.

Not all inspiration is religious in nature. The dancing water fountains in the manmade lake? "Oh, I saw those at the Bellagio in Las Vegas. You simply *have* to have things like that in China today, otherwise people won't take you seriously."

Like many in China today, Mr. Pan has chosen to work with state ("red") religious institutions. Outside China, simple generalizations ("state toady") are often thrown around to describe Christians, Buddhists, or Muslims who follow this path. Reality is more complicated. True, some patriotic clergy are simply career-minded bureaucrats. When I sat down with the head of one of the largest Beijing temples, conversation casually flowed just as it might with any mid-level official. Possibility for advancement within the state apparatus. Recent Party slogans. Relative prices of cars and jewelry. Religion was just a job that paid the bills.

Others are different. Take Bailin temple in Hebei province. An important Zen (Chan) Buddhist center during the Tang dynasty, it had been reduced by the late 1980s to a single decrepit pagoda infrequently visited by religious pilgrims. But in the last twenty-five years, it has undergone a massive revival and expansion. The temple now boasts spacious grounds, hundreds of monks, and (since 1998), the Hebei Buddhist Academy—a training center for novices. The leader in this effort: Master Jing Hui, an energetic elderly monk who remerged in the late 1970s after decades of Maoist persecution. He has since been followed by a new generation of college-educated monks who turned to religion after the suppression of the Tiananmen Square protests. Good connections have aided their work. Jing Hui, for example, served as founding president of the official Hebei provincial Buddhist Association. The temple's expansion has also received support from a complex web of official interests. The local government views religious pilgrims (and their pocketbooks) as valuable economic tools to develop a dusty corner of the north China plain, while religious affairs officials see utility in encouraging the expansion of Buddhism—perhaps particularly in a province with a heavy Catholic minority.[30]

But the Bailin monks are far from passive executors of Beijing's will. They are carefully promoting their own spiritual vision. Drawing inspiration from Taiwanese Buddhist sects that emphasize charity projects and social activism, they have reinterpreted doctrine that they believe has become excessively remote from human concerns. They have purged many of the commercial influences, such as ticket sales and fortune telling, that dominate the practices of many Chinese temples. And they are reaching out to youth. For the past twenty years, with strong state support, the temple has sponsored summer programs that attract hundreds of college students and promote Buddhist values in a structured environment.[31]

Nor are these efforts limited to officially sanctioned venues. Enter a certain nondescript Beijing building labeled as a teahouse, and you find yourself in an unregistered private Buddhist religious center. An elegant wooden interior surrounds you. Spacious rooms provide a serene environment for group meditation and study. The facility periodically arranges for local monks to meet with believers. The day I visited, Bailin monks were conducting a mass initiation rite for a hundred new lay members ranging between twenty-five and fifty years old. Those familiar with mainline Sunday services in the United States would find the two-hour event vaguely familiar. And with good reason. The monks freely acknowledge importing elements from Christian services to render once highly stylized and ceremonial Buddhist practices more popularly accessible. Thus, a lay choir provides inspirational music. A sermon delivered in colloquial Chinese gives both spiritual guidance (grasping for transitory pleasures such as money or power will not bring long-term satisfaction) and practical life counsel (maintain open communication with your spouse, avoid business trips with members of the opposite sex, don't drink . . . but if forced to, absolutely stay away from the hard stuff). Ritual vows allow new initiates to commit themselves to a new moral code. Last, informal mingling with the monks permits parishioners to broach personal challenges they face. Some raise problems with their relatives. Another proudly notes that she recently closed her café and is converting the premises to other uses, after one of the monks had visited and commented that the gambling taking place there was bad for social morals.

The Bailin monks walk a careful line. Little in their teachings could be considered controversial, except by radical leftists opposed to all religion. Publicly, the monks repeat official slogans on the need for patriotism. Believers are assured that state birth-control policies comply with Buddhist law. But they are not simple mouthpieces for Party doctrine. True, they give the standard disclaimers on avoiding superstitious belief in miracles. But when the bright-eyed monks usher you into a back room of the temple to examine the *śarīra*—sacred pearl-like remnants left among the cremated remains of the temple's former masters, similar to Catholic or Orthodox relics—you sense something different. These are true believers, not Party hacks. Within the tight confines set by Party authorities, they are advancing their spiritual vision.

RELIGIOUS EVOLUTION

Similar stories could be told about other faiths. The same spectrum exists across all of them as well. Entirely state-run groups such as the Daoist Association of China wrap the major beliefs into a tight embrace.[32] Closely state-affiliated organizations such as the Amity Foundation (chaired by a former head of the official Protestant church) sponsor international exchanges and run a range of social service activities, including operating one of the largest Bible publishing operations in the world.[33] Small, unrecognized associations are left alone. And a handful of underground Christian and Muslim movements have been aggressively targeted for elimination.

On the surface, this system has served Beijing well. It has allowed Chinese rulers to control the development of religion since the beginning of the reform era. No space exists for spiritual belief to coalesce into an organized political opposition. Phenomena such as Catholic priests openly preaching liberation theology from the pulpits of South American churches, or the Muslim Brotherhood organizing their own nationwide social welfare network among the Egyptian poor under the Mubarak regime—all of these are utterly foreign to China.

But there is a problem. Just as in the political sphere (see Chapter 3), China's frozen religious institutions are generating perverse effects. They are pushing believers away from existing religious institutions. They are stymieing the evolution of new ones. And they are funneling mounting citizen spiritual demands into new and problematic directions.

Start with China's "red" religious organizations. Many believers are repelled by efforts to "harmonize" sacred teachings with Party doctrine. Requiring Catholics to deny the Pope, or Muslims to eat during the Ramadan fast—these are not exactly effective ways to win the hearts and minds of the devout. Even those who initially find comfort in official institutions can be subsequently driven off. Noted Christian activist Bob Fu lost faith in the state-run Protestant church when Party authorities not only forced a popular pastor to retire, but physically silenced him in front of his congregation, arresting all who dared intervene.[34]

Official sects also face problems familiar to any state monopoly or large bureaucracy—which is exactly what many of them they are. Think of them as the 1970s IBM of the Chinese religious world. Resource-rich, sure. But slow in adapting to the booming demand for religion. This works if you are the only supplier in a restricted market. However, as soon as you face sharper, nimble challengers, problems emerge. And this is precisely the challenge posed by more enterprising spiritual movements such as Falun Gong or Christian evangelicals. These are the startups of Chinese religion. They proselytize aggressively (and illegally), deeply believe in their values, and continually experiment with new channels to reach believers.

China's state-run faiths struggle with this competition. So do those who work with them. Erecting expensive churches, mosques, and temples is easy. Building community and content is harder.

The second day of my visit with Mr. Pan, roughly two hundred volunteers and invited guests gathered to hear the new abbot deliver one of his first public lectures. After the audience joined in singing a hymn composed the day before by one of the volunteers, the abbot delivered a PowerPoint presentation sketching out his vision for the temple's future. To term it wide-ranging would be an understatement. The American gangster film *The Godfather*, Japanese telecom firm NoDoCoMo, McDonald's, and a Chinese businessman in Brazil trying to save the rainforest——all were packaged together in a convoluted argument that Buddhist values had an important role to play in doing business in the world today.

Interesting? Compared with many state-run religious speeches, certainly. But did it really touch the audience, composed largely of elderly women seated in the back of the auditorium? No. It felt like it was directed at the handful of wealthy donors comfortably seated up front—a MBA class on corporate social responsibility delivered by a highly educated religious academic. Sensing the disconnect, Mr. Pan stepped in at the end to steer the audience back to the one element that had united all in common purpose. "Let's all close out by singing that song again. Say, three times?" The physical edifice had been constructed. But he was still grappling with how to fill it.

Dissatisfaction with state sects has fueled the boom in unregistered ("gray") religious groups. Citizens are flocking to these for their spiritual needs. There, they face the blank stare (or hostile gaze) of Chinese officials. In response, some try to keep off the state's radar. Stay small. Focus on personal self-cultivation. Avoid high politics. Over the millennia, countless Daoist, Buddhist, and folk religious sects have adopted just such an approach—rising and falling in quiet obscurity.

Problems come when they start to expand. Then the calculus alters. Potential for confrontation increases. Tacit arrangements begin to break down. Such policies toward unregistered religious groups—particularly rapidly growing, evangelistic ones—end up steering their evolution in key ways.

First, it politicizes them. Believers cannot simply hive off their faith from politics. Everything from municipal zoning battles to major crack-downs against religious leaders form a pervasive background against which they must define themselves.

Second, it prompts them to adapt organizationally. Barred from developing religious institutions of significant scale, many have no choice but to go underground. There, they face a key question. How to survive and propagate their faith in the face of constant state surveil-lance? They borrow a page out the Communist Party's own history. In her study of the China Gospel Fellowship, a major underground house church movement numbering over a million members, Karrie Koesel notes how it replicates all the classic Leninist organizational features.[35] Underground communications. Membership cells tightly binding individuals into the group. Semi-autonomous branches with limited knowledge of other members, curtailing damage in case of detection. Such practices, more or less common in all underground Christian congregations today, parallel those adapted over the centuries by heter-odox Buddhist and Daoist sects facing similar pressures from imperial authorities and their Confucian advisers.

Third, this state-society interaction feeds a millennialist streak in Chinese political history. Oddly enough, it just so happens that forcing large numbers of religious believers into secretive networks turns out to be a pretty good breeding ground for radical cults—particularly when you suppress the emergence of independent religious organizations that might help moderate theological teachings. This is how "gray" religious groups evolve into "black" ones.

Historically, this has fueled the spread of a range of apocalyptic sects in China. Centuries of imperial repression of heterodox Daoist and Buddhist beliefs pushed them underground, into the vastness of the Chinese countryside. There, they fragmented, multiplied, and mutated. Some evolved into simple clan rituals. Others passed quietly from the stage upon the death (or arrest) of a charismatic founder. But still others developed messianic ideologies and complex organizational capabili-ties.[36] In times of crisis, these genetically recombined with latent popu-lar discontent in an explosive manner, generating widespread uprisings that could paralyze a county . . . or topple an empire. Precisely this dynamic has produced many of the colorfully named rebellions that litter Chinese history, such as those of the Red Turbans (1351–1368) or the White Lotus Society (1796–1804).

Of course, these trends are not unique to China. Some should be familiar to Americans as well. Take the nineteenth-century U.S. experience with the Mormon faith. The birth of a new evangelical movement with unorthodox views. Pervasive hostility from society and the state. Murder of the founding prophet at the hands of a lynch mob. A desperate trek to remote western deserts in the face of overwhelming odds, hardening group identity and belief in divine protection. Decades of conflict with federal troops and courts seeking to assert central rule. Radicalization. The emergence of a hardcore anti-government ideology among some believers, coupled with isolated incidents of violence such as the 1857 Mountain Meadows massacre of some 120 settlers—including men, women, and children—passing through Mormon-occupied territory.[37]

So why does this stop there? Why does it not evolve into early-twentieth-century squads of Mormon suicide bombers blowing up tracks of Union Pacific trains crossing Utah? Why does the skyline of Salt Lake City not feature temples glorifying martyrs who successfully assassinated U.S. federal judges?

The answer: liberalization and institutionalization.[38] Federal and Mormon authorities reached a political accommodation, resulting in the admission of Utah as a state in 1896. Mormonism shifted from a quasi-revolutionary sect to an openly organized church. Rather than existing outside of, and in opposition to, the state and mainstream society, it began to operate within them. Anti-government attitudes faded. Divine revelations became less common. The Mormon church began to evolve all of the institutions of an organized faith—a more coherent doctrine, a bureaucratic hierarchy, a welfare system. Theology moderated. Polygamy was renounced in 1890 (and again in 1904); racial discrimination in church leadership positions banned in 1978. Once regarded as a fringe cult, it is now a mainstream conservative faith, the religion of the 2012 Republican presidential candidate, and the subject of a Tony Award–winning Broadway musical. Today, only a handful of obscure fundamentalist Mormon splinter groups in isolated communities of southern Utah and northern Arizona remain—reminders of a historical path not taken.

Think this unique to the United States? Try another example. In the late nineteenth century, just as Mormons, Christian Scientists, and Seventh-day Adventists were emerging on the American spiritual landscape, China experienced its own burst of new religious movements. Yiguandao was one. A Buddhist/Daoist sect practicing spirit writing and led by living incarnations of Buddhist deities, it was labeled as a heterodox cult and repressed both by the Qing dynasty and its Nationalist successors.

Along with many other redemptive societies emphasizing imminent salvation, Yiguandao expanded dramatically during the wartime chaos of the 1930s and 1940s. The "apocalyptic message of many of these societies (notably in the case of Yiguandao) readily made sense to populations brutally exploited by repressive regimes and falling prey to war, roving bandits, and natural disasters."[39] By the early 1950s, official statistics placed the total number of believers at some 13 million, three times as many as Catholics and Protestants. In many areas of northern China, Yiguandao ranked among the strongest and most organized popular institutions, and a serious social, political, and military contender to Communist rule. Unsurprisingly, it was ruthlessly eradicated starting in 1949—one of the earliest targets of Mao's purges.[40]

Yiguandao believers who fled with Nationalist forces to Taiwan in the wake of the Chinese civil war fared only marginally better. Under Chiang Kai-shek's iron rule, Yiguandao remained tightly suppressed through the 1970s, subject to frequent police raids. Believers were accused of financial extortion, intimidating unbelievers, and rape of female believers. Such charges parallel those brought by Beijing today against groups ranging from underground Christian congregations to Falun Gong—as well as those faced by early Mormons in the United States.

But all this changed with Taiwan's political liberalization in the late 1980s. Martial law was lifted; spiritual life deregulated. With this, Yiguandao ceased being "an isolated, separated, and secret religion."[41] Organization changed as a result. Fragmented underground master-disciple cliques gave way to a stable bureaucratic hierarchy. A professional clergy gradually replaced the charismatic folk lay leaders of earlier years. Doctrine changed. New leaders began to filter and reinterpret earlier texts. Taboos against physicians, medicine, and public swimming faded. Religious figures announced the end of the messi-anic period—no new living deities would be born, the practice of spirit writing halted. Today, Yiguandao is highly integrated into Taiwanese society, with members totaling some 3–4 percent of the population. Their activities now resemble those of religious minorities in many other countries. They offer free courses on the Chinese classics, operate an extensive school system (and summer camps) for their children, and run many of Taiwan's tasty vegetarian restaurants.

CHINA TODAY

This is not what is happening in China today. Rather, like a windup clock spinning crazily in reverse, state policies are producing exactly the opposite effect.

Beijing's revival of imperial religious policies has produced modern, Internet-savvy versions of the sectarian groups that plagued celestial emperors of the past. Of twenty-odd officially banned "cults," one of the most notorious is Eastern Lightning (also known as the Church of the Almighty God).[42] Since emerging around 1990, it has spread widely across northern China. It asserts Christ has been reborn as a Chinese woman from central China. Her advent announces the arri-val of the apocalypse. Human corruption will be swept away; the reign of Satan (symbolized by a red dragon, and embodied by the Chinese Communist Party) ended. Adherents aggressively target underground Protestant house churches for evangelization, apparently concluding that they are less likely to seek the aid of the police. Conversion efforts can be extreme. Threats, abductions, and sexual blackmail are com-mon. Nor is violence unknown. In May 2014, patrons of a McDonald's in Shandong province watched, horrified, as six Eastern Lightning members beat to death a woman who had rejected their proselytization efforts and refused to provide her mobile phone number.[43]

Just as with their historical antecedents and modern competitors, Eastern Lightning has evolved a decentralized, cell-like structure. This allows it to survive in the face of state repression. Intense secrecy makes the movement's claims of millions of adherents impossible to verify with any accuracy. But China's underground Protestants clearly view it as one of the most serious threats they face. When an assortment of house church leaders came together to issue an unusual joint statement of faith in 1998, two of their key requests were that state authorities no longer mistake them as cults . . . and that Beijing aggressively crack down on the real heretics—Eastern Lightning.[44]

Do such trends threaten the power of the state at present? No. Sects such as Eastern Lightning remain socially marginalized by their own extreme beliefs. Instead, the risk is a longer-term one. State repression and the decaying legitimacy of official religious institutions are pushing the most evangelical of religious groups underground, where they mix with a whole range of those at society's edges—migrants, petitioners, the rural poor. They become politicized. And they develop new organizational tactics to survive.

But wait, isn't that good? If you are Protestant, perhaps you think of the Southern Christian Leadership Conference, and the part it played in organizing African American activists during the 1960s American civil rights movement. Or if Catholic, that of the Church and John Paul II during the Polish struggle against Communist rule in the 1980s. And if Buddhist, the evolution of the lay pacifist movement Soka Gakkai in postwar Japan, coupled with the emergence of its affiliated political wing, the New Komeito party.

But China leaves little space for such groups. Beijing simply does not permit it. Unrecognized evangelicals are less Martin Luther King and more Martin Luther. Except that they are never, ever allowed the institutional autonomy to evolve into stable religions. Sure, one can imagine an alternative world where Chinese underground house churches would be allowed to register, to operate freely. Should this happen, they too would evolve organizationally. They would marginalize extreme theologies such as Eastern Lightning. But this is not the way of the Chinese state. Instead, Beijing drives them all—the pious reverend, the self-proclaimed messiah, the venal huckster, and the aspiring revolutionary—together, into a bubbling, explosive stew of political, religious, and social grievances.

This is not a remote concern. Historically, this is precisely how challenges to a weakening Chinese state emerge in times of crisis. In the mid-1800s, this is how you get a failed imperial civil service exam-taker proclaiming himself the younger brother of Jesus, raising an army of miners and peasants, and launching the Taiping Rebellion against the Qing dynasty—the bloodiest civil war in history, in which some 20 million perished.[45] This is not unique to Christian offshoots. Parallel stories could be told about Buddhist or Daoist-inspired uprisings, such as White Lotus (1796–1804) or Boxer (1898–1900) Rebellions. Rather, it is the process of state repression—of being driven underground, of being forced to adapting to a new environment—that molds Chinese spiritual beliefs into revolutionary discontent.

Recent developments are exacerbating these risks. As China's reform era ends, the zone of tacit state tolerance that characterized it is rapidly narrowing for many beliefs.

Such trends are most extreme in western China, where ethnic relations have worsened dramatically since the 1980s. Tough state controls over the expression of religious identity have combined with latent economic disparities and massive in-migration by Han Chinese to fuel a dangerous cycle of radicalization among both Tibetan Buddhists and Muslim Uighurs. After severe ethnic rioting shook the Central Asian region of Xinjiang in 2009, Beijing flooded city streets with an overwhelming security presence. Rank religious oppression followed. Under the Orwellian-titled "Project Beauty," veiled women are stopped at checkpoints and taken in for lectures on proper, secular dress.[46] Local authorities bar bearded men from public transportation.[47] The results have been sadly predictable. Unimaginable a decade ago, radical jihadist ideology and underground militant cells have begun to take shape. Since 2013, terror attacks on Han civilians and assassinations of state imams viewed as collaborators have become regular events. In response, Beijing has redoubled its efforts: mobilizing big data in order to better track and control the population, and promulgating monetary rewards for interethnic marriages to encourage ethnic assimilation.

Similar pressures exist in ethnic Tibetan areas. After large-scale protests against Beijing's rule erupted in 2008, massive state security forces descended on the Himalayan plateau. Monasteries were once again subjected to stifling controls. But the residual influence of an elderly Dalai Lama committed to pacifism continues to hold in check a generation of angry Tibetan youth. For this reason, self-immolations (over 100 since 2009), rather than attacks on others, remain the most extreme form of protest so far.

Of course, since minorities comprise but a fraction of China's total population, the dangers are limited. In a worst-case scenario, as the *Economist* has noted, Xinjiang might become to China what Chechnya is to Russia—a violent, running sore, but hardly a threat to national stability.[48]

But there is a broader problem. Beijing's leaders recognize that the Marxist slogans still ritually invoked by Party leaders have become little more than punchlines for water cooler banter. They are looking for a new ideological packaging to support one-Party rule. Since 2012, state television and media have begun to beat to the tune of Xi Jinping's new ethno-nationalist propaganda narrative: the "China Dream." Under this rubric, Party leaders are pivoting back to China's own history and culture to fill the ideological void left by decades of now-empty Communist rhetoric, rampant capitalist excess, and bureaucratic corruption.

One viscerally feels this in walking the streets of Beijing today. Brightly colored propaganda posters line the walls, wrapping classical artwork, Chinese nationalism, and one-Party rule into an attractive whole. On newsstands, Party papers that once denounced China's feudal past now regularly invoke "traditional values." Television dating programs that soared to national fame by highlighting the stark materialism of China's youth have been toned down, or replaced with family-friendly game shows emphasizing contestants' abilities to write Chinese characters or identify classical idioms.

As part of this, Party authorities are reviving beliefs deemed to be more authentically Chinese. Confucianism is one. Top Party leaders, including Xi Jinping himself, have made pilgrimage to the birthplace of the sage whose teachings were inextricably linked to centuries of imperial rule. The Confucian classics are being extolled once again, the Party depicted as the "standard-bearer" in upholding their values, and their content increasingly wrapped into official propaganda campaigns.[49] Official attitudes toward Buddhism have also quietly softened. Buddhist groups are increasingly viewed both an important channel to improve cross-straits relations with Taiwan and – nothwithstanding the faith's origins in South Asia - a potential bulwark against ideologies and religions perceived to be foreign.

Such efforts have their flip side as well. Pressure has increased on religions viewed as "foreign." Take the example of Wenzhou, "China's Jerusalem." Decades of relatively tolerant local religious policies had led to the rapid spread of Protestant groups in this this well-heeled port city. Estimates place the total number of believers at around 15 percent. Wealthy businessmen funded the construction of massive, oversized churches—many belonging to officially approved, "red" congregations—while municipal authorities turned a blind eye at violations of zoning ordinances. But in late 2013, amid growing state concerns over the spread of Christianity, provincial Party authorities on an inspection tour of a local development zone were disturbed to see large crosses dominating the skyline. Within months, Chinese authorities were embroiled in a selective demolition campaign. Repeated struggles broke out as hundreds of churchgoers attempted to form human shields to block bulldozers from encroaching on their places of worship.[50] The campaign subsequently spread province-wide. By 2016, between one and two thousand crosses had been torn down from churches throughout Zhejiang, and harsh prison sanctions handed out to pastors and lay members who dared resist.[51]

Mounting indications now suggest that the Zhejiang campaign may be the forerunner of a much broader crackdown—one national in scope, tougher in nature, and extending to a range of "red" and "gray" religious organizations as well. At the 2016 work conference on religious affairs, central Party authorities signaled their intention to more aggressively promote theological interpretations of Christianity (and Islam) deemed "compatible" with Chinese culture.[52] Subsequent regulations have tightened controls on the overseas ties and funding of domestic groups. Pressure has ramped up on the obvious targets (with Xinjiang officials banning Uighur parents from giving their children "overly religious" names and encouraging citizens to inform on those who "lure" their children into religion)[53] as well as minuscule sects that had previously enjoyed a degree of tolerance (for example, municipal authorities in Kaifeng curtailing the limited religious activities of the tiny population of Chinese Jews, including barring them from gathering to celebrate Passover).[54]

Such state efforts to promote ideological conformity are not limited to religion. They are spreading more broadly. Indie film festivals held since the early 2000s with little state interference are encountering unexpected headwinds. One of the most well-known—the Beijing Independent Film Festival—was shuttered in 2014, and forced to move in 2015 to . . . New York. Controls are now tightening noticeably within China's colleges. Dire warnings have begun to flow forth—regarding the need to tighten control over foreign contacts, to remold social science textbooks to be more politically correct, and to ensure that young academics have the proper ideological orientation.

Arts and literature have been targeted too. State media has devoted heavy coverage to a major 2014 speech by Xi on the need to "clean up" art and culture. Stressing patriotism, it warns against an excessive focus on "foreign" cultural products. Major state projects now seek to redirect attention to China's own heritage (ironically, the very same heritage once targeted for destruction by Maoist student radicals in the 1960s). These range from *Confucius*—a new dance interpretation of classical philosophy currently being performed by the national opera troupe— to *The Great Wall* a joint Sino-U.S. sci-fi action film supported by Beijing's largest state-run film company, released in early 2017. (Spoiler alert: Matt Damon fighting mythic beasts on the Great Wall during the fifteenth-century Ming dynasty in a B-grade action flick panned by audiences and critics alike is apparently an approved expression of "traditional" Chinese culture and history.)

CONCLUSION

Naturally, Chinese leaders hope that these efforts will contribute to national stability. Remodel the remnants of a dead Marxist ideology imported from the West. Fashion a new state-sponsored ideology for a twenty-first-century China out of material drawn from its own history. Simultaneously surmount the spiritual vacuum facing Chinese society, and create a firm, lasting basis for authoritarian rule.

But Beijing's pivot back to the past may produce precisely the opposite effect. The renewed drive for ideological conformity is eroding the relative openness for belief and thought that characterized China's reform era. It risks steering the country back to yet earlier historical periods, where self-imposed intellectual isolation sapped national dynamism. And it threatens to further fuel the underlying unstable dynamic at the heart of religious evolution in China today. In returning to history, Beijing may be at risk of repeating it.

Xi Jinping

Xi Jinping (above) is China's strongest leader in decades. (AP Photo/ Luis Hidalgo) He has recentralized power in his own hands and deftly eliminated his opponents. Since his rise, tacit political norms that had held sway during China's post-1978 reform era – collective leadership, avoidance of a cult of personality, immunity for China's top Party elite from criminal prosecution – have begun to buckle or give way.

Coupled with Xi's pivot back towards concepts and language drawn from the imperial and revolutionary eras, such shifts have led many observers overseas to compare him to yet earlier Chinese leaders. Below are two examples: revolutionary Communist leader Mao Zedong (1893–1976), and the Qianlong emperor (1711-1799), ruler of the Qing dynasty at its height. (right - illustration by David Parkins for the Economist) (left - illustration by Jon Berkeley for the Economist)

The reform era has dramatically changed China. Nowhere is this more evident than in the boomtowns of eastern China. In 1980, Shenzhen (above) was a sleepy market town of some 30,000 people in Guangdong province, across the border from Hong Kong. By 2015 (below), it was a vibrant international commercial hub, with over 18 million residents in the greater metropolitan area. (above - Brian O'Hagan) (below - Imaginechina via AP Images)

Social and Economic Shifts

But the rich-poor divide has surged over the past three decades. Official statistics place China alongside Peru, Mexico, and the United States in levels of inequality. Unofficial ones place it much higher. China's explosive urban growth means this division is no longer a case of poor rural farmers and wealthy urbanites. Rather, sharp social cleavages are evident within Chinese cities themselves, between disadvantaged migrant workers and established urban residents. Above, an aerial view of a Shanghai shantytown with old houses next to clusters of modern high-rise residential apartment buildings, January 11, 2017. Chinese central authorities started a three-year project to rebuild urban shantytowns in 2015, aiming to construct a total of 18 million new homes in all. (Imaginechina via AP Images)

Politics and Protest

China's frozen one-Party system offers ordinary citizens few meaningful institutional channels to have their voices heard on the political decisions that affect their lives, and limited ones to obtain redress of their legal grievances. Many resort to a wide array of protest and petition strategies as a result.

Two schoolgirls dressed in Superman costumes hold up protest signs demanding unpaid wages for their fathers in Zhengzhou, Henan province on July 9, 2013. According to them, their fathers had been hired to renovate a local expressway toll station but were not fully paid. Efforts to contact local authorities to demand back wages proved fruitless. Needing money to pay their tuition for next semester, the two sought to call public attention to their plight. (Imaginechina via AP Images)

Thousands of parents gather outside the department of education in Nanjing, Jiangsu province on May 14, 2016 to protest proposed changes to university admission quotas that would disadvantage their children in the fierce competition to enter top colleges. The reforms would have increased numbers of slots for students from poorer provinces, at the expense of others (such as Jiangsu), while leaving Beijing unaffected. (Imaginechina via AP Images)

Amid a mass riot on June 28, 2008 involving tens of thousands of people, the county government offices and police headquarters of Weng'an, Guizhou province were torched. The incident's trigger: the drowning of a local teenage girl, which sparked rumors regarding the involvement of local officials in her death. Family grievances fused with latent popular discontent regarding land seizures by local authorities for hydroelectric and mining projects. Protests rapidly escalated in size and violence over six days, before being suppressed. (Kyodo via AP Images)

Politics: Back to the Future

Recent years have seen Beijing experiment with reviving practices drawn from China's Maoist era. One example: forced public confessions as a political tool. Below, an example drawn from 1960s-era Cultural Revolution. On the following page, the modern version — televised confessions by a range of public and private figures.

Provincial Party Secretary Wang Yilun, being criticized by Red Guards from the University of Industry and forced to bear a placard with the accusation "counterrevolutionary revisionist element," Harbin, China, August 23, 1966. [© Li Zhensheng/Contact Press Images from "Red Color News Soldier" (Phaidon, 2003)]

(clockwise from top left)

Charles Xue – Chinese-American entrepreneur and social media celebrity (2013)

Peter Dahlin – Swedish rights activist (2016)

Peter Humphrey – British corporate investigator (2013)

Zhang Kai – Chinese Christian human rights lawyer (2016)

Gui Minhai – Chinese-born Swedish publisher, co-owner of a Hong Kong bookstore known for political gossip involving elite Chinese leaders. (2015)

Wang Xiaolu – Chinese journalist for Caijing magazine, confessing to fabricating and spreading false information about China's stock market amid the 2015 rout.

(Screenshots from Chinese state broadcasts on CCTV, CNTV, and Wenzhou TV.)

Religion and Ideology: Return to the Past

China's rise has led many citizens to take a revived interest in their own history and culture. Beijing has also begun its own pivot towards the past. Marxist dogma is giving way to millennia-old imperial traditions as the ideological rationale for one-Party authoritarian control.

Eye-popping contradictions are resulting. Confucianism and Buddhism, once targeted for eradication by Mao, have found renewed favor among China's Communist rulers. Above, newly enrolled primary school students, dressed in replicas of traditional costumes, take part in a reimagined version of an ancient educational ritual at the Confucian Temple in Nanjing, Jiangsu Province. (Imaginechina via AP Images).

Above, the massive Longhua temple complex near Shaoxing, Zhejiang province. Privately-funded, but with significant government support, it purports to be the largest single imperial-style temple in China, with ambitions of spreading Buddhism worldwide. (Photos by author)

In contrast, pressure has mounted on beliefs viewed as "foreign." Above, lay leader Tu Shouzhe stands on his Protestant church's roof in Zhejiang Province in this July 2015 photo. His church, like many others, was targeted by a massive government campaign to cut down the crosses from thousands of Christian churches that dot the province. (AP Photo/Mark Schiefelbein)

Religion and Ideology: Building Tensions

Beijing is also looking overseas, portraying itself as the rightful successor to thousands of years of Chinese tradition. Above, two competing performances at Lincoln Center in New York City within mere days of each other. On left, the American debut of *Confucius*, a dance drama performed by the state-run China National Opera & Dance Drama Theater (and directed by a 77th direct descendant of Confucius). On right, the annual performance of Shen Yun, a Falun Gong-affiliated performing arts group that combats Beijing's narrative, and promoting itself as "reviving 5,000 years of traditional, divinely-inspired Chinese culture." (Photo by author)

5

China in Comparative Perspective

AMERICANS LOVE POLITICS. FLIP on the television on Sunday morning, and you can find analysts of all stripes endlessly speculating on the latest developments in Washington.

But when it comes to how political systems actually evolve in other countries, we are remarkably blind. Blame history. The United States was born a democracy, with a functioning set of political and legal institutions largely inherited from the United Kingdom. Many Americans assume this is simply the natural state of affairs. We underestimate how difficult it is to actually create a working state—any state—in the first place. And then we overestimate how easy democratization is.

As a result, Americans have a unique faith in big political change: that autocratic regimes ("bad guys") can quickly and successfully transition to democratic ones ("good guys"). Some believe economics is key. Just allow capitalism to work its wonders, let a modern middle class rise, and democracy will flourish. Development experts in the 1950s and 1960s took this as scripture. They plowed money into pro-American military regimes from Chile to South Vietnam, rationalizing that this would turn them into stable democracies. Others emphasize the role of leaders and ideology. They search the ranks of Iraqi opposition forces for a Washington or Jefferson, convinced that if only the right person could emerge, holding the right liberal views, he could lead the country to a better future.

Such views reached their zenith after 1989. The collapse of the Soviet Union and Eastern European communist regimes, the rise of Vaclav

Havel, Lech Walesa, and Nelson Mandela, and the global spread of republican forms of government seemed to provide the ultimate proof. Democracy was indeed inevitable. Authoritarian states such as China were only retrograde holdouts. Eventually, the sprouts of capitalism, the winds of freedom, and perhaps the sounds of good old-fashioned American rock-and-roll would lead to change there as well.

The problem is: it didn't quite work out that way. Wracked by revolutionary violence and political turmoil, Cold War–era American allies in Latin America and Africa remained far from bastions of democratic progress. Visions of a post-1989 democratic world crashed on the cold, hard rocks of the failed states created by authoritarian collapse—in the former Yugoslavia during the 1990s, in Iraq after the 2003 American invasion, and in Syria and Libya after the 2011 Arab Spring. In contrast, during the 1960s and 1970s, Taiwan and South Korea registered some of the highest economic growth rates in the world, even as both remained tightly controlled authoritarian regimes.

In response, new voices emerged. Beginning in the 1960s, Samuel Huntington advanced the concept of "authoritarian modernization."[1] Authoritarian regimes and military strongmen were not simply historical missteps on the road to democracy. They were necessary stages. As dramatic economic and social changes swept through developing nations, authoritarian rule was required to maintain order, build state institutions, and shepherd unruly societies. Democracy could wait.[2] Such views were not limited to the ivory towers of academia. In the 1980s, Huntington served as an adviser to both military rulers in Brazil and the South African apartheid government, cautioning both to proceed carefully with their respective transitions to more liberal political systems, so as to avoid losing control of the process.

For many, China is the prime example of a nation in the middle of authoritarian modernization. Under one-Party rule, the Chinese economy has expanded tenfold since 1978. Hundreds of millions of rural farmers have moved to the cities. Education rates have soared. And Party authorities have sponsored a plethora of legal and institutional reforms. These developments have led foreign scholars such as Randall Peerenboom to assert that China is successfully following an "East Asian Model" pioneered by Taiwan and South Korea—rapid economic reform under authoritarian rule, with democratization delayed until a relatively high level of wealth is attained.[3]

But such comparisons are incorrect. China is not following in the footsteps of others. Rather, over the past three decades, Party authorities have stymied the emergence of precisely the types of institutions that facilitated gradual reform in other authoritarian regimes. China is not only failing to democratize; its leaders are progressively undermining the very things that might make any form of stable transition possible.

TAIWAN AND SOUTH KOREA: THE EAST ASIAN MODEL?

Naturally, it makes sense to look at Taiwan and South Korea for clues as to China's future. Their shared cultural heritage, deep historical ties, and similar political histories make them logical choices for comparison.

As with China, both experienced decades of blazing economic growth and massive social change under authoritarian rulers—in Taiwan, the Nationalist party; in South Korea, a series of military dictators. Both also built effective administrative states during this period. In the late 1980s, both went through democratic transitions. Military rule ended, press controls were lifted, and nationwide multiparty elections held. Subsequently, the 1990s and 2000s witnessed a steady deepening of democracy. National legislatures became meaningful political actors. Courts asserted their independence. Opposition forces peacefully won the presidency via free elections in both South Korea (1997) and Taiwan (2000). And then they peacefully lost control—also via free elections— to political parties that were the direct successors to former authoritarian rulers. Indeed, in South Korea, this even involved electing as president (in 2012) the daughter of the military dictator who had ruled during the 1960s and 1970s, only to impeach her (yet again peacefully) five years later in the wake of a massive corruption scandal.

So might this be China's future too? Might China be in the early stages of the same process that Taiwan and South Korea have gone through—one that might eventually lead toward a relatively stable political transition? And are Chinese leaders drawing the correct lessons from Taiwan and South Korea in delaying political liberalization until the country is wealthier?

Unfortunately, no. China's experience has diverged in two critical aspects.

First, China has already blown past the relevant levels of economic development that Taiwan and South Korea experienced during their own transitions.

Remember that proponents of authoritarian modernization focus on the need for the state to exert an iron hand in addressing the rising social conflicts generated by rapid economic development and rapid social change—waves of rural peasants flowing into rapidly expanding cities, the spread of polluting industries and accompanying environmental destruction, and so on. Chinese authorities embrace this. Official state propaganda surrounding the Party's "harmonious society" campaign launched in 2006 noted:

> [I]nternational experience indicates, when a country progresses from per-capita GDP of $1000 USD to $3000 USD, all forms of social and economic tensions become heightened. This leads to increased internal conflict. If handled well, social and economic progress can move to the next level. If handled poorly, economic progress will halt or even regress.[4]

According to supporters of authoritarian modernization, rulers should not attempt political liberalization during this period. Instead, they should "sequence" their reforms. Only after economic reforms are well advanced, only after implementing a range of institutional and legal reforms, can states be opened to the rough-and-tumble of representative politics.[5] Otherwise, liberalization risks adding fuel to fire—generating uncontrollable explosions of social and political violence. Some attempt to quantity levels of economic development at which liberalization might be "safe," based on examples of successful transitions. According to Fareed Zakaria, CNN journalist (and former student of Samuel Huntington), "a country that attempts a transition to democracy when it has a per capita GDP of between $3000 to $6000 will be successful."[6]

On the surface, Taiwan and South Korea support such conclusions. Chart 5.1 shows the per capita GDP of both economies since the 1970s (given in constant 2010 US dollars to facilitate comparisons).[7] As per

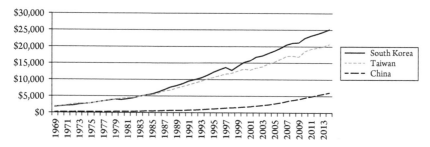

CHART 5.1 GDP Per Capita 1969–2014 (constant 2010 USD)
Source: Economic Research Service, USDA (2015)

capita GDP rose from the $2,000 USD level (1970) to the $5,000 USD level (mid-1980s), both experienced increasing social turmoil. Student and labor protests increased. Dissidents escalated their calls for political reform. Authoritarian rulers responded with harsh repression of mass citizen demonstrations, such as the Kaohsiung Incident (1979) in Taiwan or (more violently) the Guangju Massacre (1980) in South Korea, in which hundreds lost their lives. Then, as both passed through the $6,000 USD level in the late 1980s, a sea change occurred. In 1987, Taiwan lifted martial law and legalized the opposition party, while South Korea held its first free presidential elections. Consistent with scholarly predictions, the political transitions of both have subsequently unfolded in a peaceful, stable manner—free from military coup d'états or mass killings of former regime members.

Now contrast this with China. From 2001 to 2014, China's per-capita GDP surged from under $2,000 US to $6,000 US—precisely the point at which Taiwan and South Korea experienced political transitions. For those who would try to directly extrapolate from Taiwan and South Korea to draw predictions for China, democracy should be breaking out right about . . . now. This isn't happening. Social tensions are rising. Protests are multiplying. But leaders continue to hold Chinese society in a tight grip.

Of course, Taiwan and South Korea are small. China is big. Perhaps it is unreasonable to expect their paths to be exactly the same. For this reason, many back off from sweeping arguments that democratic political transitions are foreordained to occur at specific levels of economic development. But the belief that wealth matters—that richer countries are more likely to experience stable democratic transitions—still carries enormous weight. This is true for authoritarian modernizers such as Peerenboom.[8] But it is also true for their critics in the democracy promotion camp. For example, one finds a 2013 Council on Foreign Relations treatise arguing that:

> [G]rowth in GDP per capita does not in and of itself make an autocracy more likely to democratize. . . . Increased national income does, however, make democracy more likely to endure once it arises. . . . [A] serious economic contraction would be a major threat to China's one-party regime. But the prospects that enduring democracy will result from such an economic crisis improve as China reaches higher levels of economic development.[9]

Such arguments, however, share a common flaw. To draw broad comparisons between nations, scholars code countries (for example, as "democracies" or "dictatorships"). They then tick off years with dramatic shifts, such as free elections of chief executives or national legislatures, and note the relevant national per-capita GDP levels.[10] In the case of Taiwan or South Korea, this leads to a focus on the dramatic events of the late 1980s and early 1990s, such as the first contested national elections. But democratization is not a discrete event. South Korean and Taiwanese opposition activists and authoritarian rulers did not simply wake up in the late 1980s and decide to become a democracy. Rather, democratization is an extended *process*—a lengthy push and pull between state and society. And in both South Korea and Taiwan, this began decades prior to the political shifts of the 1980s and the 1990s.

This leads to the second key difference with China. For China today not only differs from 1980s-era Taiwan and South Korea—when all three were roughly equally wealthy. It also differs from the path followed by Taiwan and South Korea since the early 1970s—when their moves toward democratization actually began, and when both were much poorer than China is today.

Take Taiwan first. From the standpoint of the twenty-first century, we often forget the extent to which 1970s-era Taiwan was boiling under pressure.

After decades of frozen authoritarian rule, disaffected Taiwanese chafed against the political and social controls exerted by Chiang Kai-shek and the Nationalist (KMT) Party. Some resorted to terrorism—the 1970 assassination attempt on Chiang's son (and political successor) at the Plaza Hotel in New York, and a 1976 mail bomb that blew off the hands of the governor of Taiwan. Social discontent periodically exploded into violence. One example: the 1977 Chungli incident, where revelations of KMT ballot stuffing resulted in a mass riot of over ten thousand people and the torching of the local police station. Such developments, along with growing environmental pollution and quality-of-life concerns, led many of Taiwan's best and brightest to emigrate to the United States. Taiwan faced the real possibility of a very dark future.[11]

But that did not occur. Why? Because Taiwan began to politically liberalize. And not in the 1980s, as is commonly believed, but in the 1970s. The reasons are complex.* But the personal commitment of Nationalist leader Chiang Ching-kuo to gradually open the political system was one crucial factor. By the mid-1970s, despite periodic state suppression, an increasingly organized group of *dangwai* (outside the party) opposition activists were publishing political journals (the social media of the day) and competing in local elections. In 1977, fourteen of them won election to the provincial assembly.[12]

A core of opposition activists thus gradually came to power within existing state institutions. The first non-KMT president of Taiwan, Chen Shui-bian, first rose to national fame as a defense lawyer for *dangwai* members arrested in the 1979 Kaohsiung Incident, and subsequently won office in 1981 as a member of the Taipei City Council. This

---

* Domestically, the political position of the KMT in Taiwan was never as absolute as that of mainland Chinese Communist authorities. Social forces ranging from Taiwanese entrepreneurs to the Presbyterian church remained somewhat outside their embrace. Internationally, the 1970s-era trend of countries throughout the world shifting diplomatic recognition from the Republic of China (i.e., Taiwan) to the People's Republic of China (Beijing) produced a deep sense of crisis among Nationalist authorities, and a desire to democratize to obtain greater legitimacy both on the world stage and in the eyes of their own citizens. Bruce Dickson, *Democratization in China and Taiwan: The Adaptability of Leninist Parties* (New York: Oxford University Press, 1997): 204–16.

meant that he, and others like him, gradually gained experience actually running a government and managing an organization—decades before he assumed the presidency in 2000.

During the 1980s, this group of opposition legislators was crucial in Taiwan's stable political transition. The waning years of Nationalist rule witnessed an upsurge in social movements—environmental, feminist, ethnic minority, consumer protection.[13] These were led by a younger generation of activists committed to the use of more confrontational tactics to push for political change. Across Taiwan, street protests multiplied—increasing tenfold between 1983 and 1988.[14] Many leaders of such movements rejected resort to the gradually opening legislative channels, viewing this as a disgraceful compromise with their hated Nationalist opponents. Taiwan could have degenerated into ungovernable chaos, with opposition forces struggling to manage an unstable and shifting array of demands emerging from the street, while Nationalist economic elites fled abroad in the face of an uncertain future. But, as Bruce Dickson notes, the existence of "a channel for the political opposition to participate in (local elections and supplemental elections for the Legislative Yuan and National Assembly) [meant] that political participation had a legitimate, if limited, outlet other than street protests and protracted social movements."[15]

Because of this, Taiwan took a different road. Political opposition to the Nationalist Party coalesced in a relatively stable institutional form. In 1986, radical activists and moderate legislators came together to form the Democratic Progressive Party. During the late 1980s, they pursued their activities in tandem. Protests erupted on the streets, while high-level negotiations with Nationalist authorities continued behind closed doors. But the increasingly open political environment (marked by the legalization of opposition parties and lifting of martial law in 1987) gradually steered discontent into regular electoral channels. The events of the late 1980s and early 1990s garnered the eye-catching news headlines—retraction of the talons of the authoritarian state, deep constitutional reform, and free and fair parliamentary and presidential elections. But these were merely the outgrowth of a gradual evolutionary process that had begun some fifteen years earlier.

Next, examine South Korea.

In the 1970s, South Korean civil society was significantly more organized, and its politics more contentious, than in Taiwan.[16] The spread of Christianity throughout South Korea in the late nineteenth century had given rise to a strong network of Protestant and Catholic churches. The early-twentieth-century anti-Japanese independence movement had left a heritage of organized political activism, particularly by labor and religious movements. Politically, the two decades after World War II saw a succession of unstable South Korean military regimes and weak democratic ones. This permitted the emergence of opposition political parties led by figures such as Kim Young-sam and Kim Dae-jung.[17]

These forces emerged as the primary opponents to the authoritarian rule of military strongman Park Chun-hee (1961–1979), particularly after 1972. That year, Park declared martial law and adopted a new constitution, dramatically expanding his control over the national legislature, and giving him the possibility of serving as president-for-life. Citizen protests surged, led by a combination of religious leaders, labor activists, and opposition politicians. While Taiwan in the late 1970s witnessed a gradual opening to the political opposition, South Korea went the other way. Park relied on emergency decrees and extensive repression to jail, detain, and torture thousands of dissidents. Opposition politicians were also targeted. In 1973, security forces kidnapped Kim Dae-jung from Japan, and were on the verge of executing him when he was saved at the last minute by U.S. intervention. In 1979, after supporting a series of labor protests, Kim Young-sam was expelled from the National Assembly and banned from politics.

This combination—hardline state policies plus a mobilized citizenry—meant that South Korea underwent a much more tumultuous and violent transition than Taiwan. In 1979, South Korea experienced a military coup after Park was assassinated by his intelligence chief. An escalating series of increasingly organized citizen protests against authoritarian rule followed. Demonstrations numbering in the tens (or hundreds) of thousands became a regular feature of Korean political life by the late 1980s.[18] Running street battles rocked major cities. Amid swirling clouds of tear gas, security forces battled protestors wielding Molotov cocktails. Internal chaos loomed as a real prospect.

However, as with Taiwan, South Korea managed a stable transition. And it did so for similar reasons. Despite harsh state repression, institutionalized channels of political participation continued to exist during the 1970s and 1980s. Semi-free elections funneled popular discontent toward national legislatures, opposition parties, and dissident leaders— even if distorted rules ensured that authoritarian rulers retained the upper hand.

This was key. First, it gave regime opponents hope that change could be achieved by political reform, rather than revolution. In the 1985 national legislative elections, opposition parties collectively achieved a higher popular vote than military-backed ones. This confirmed the legitimacy of opposition forces. It also prompted military authorities to begin negotiating an endgame strategy. Second, the existence of a highly organized political opposition made it possible to de-escalate away from the politics of the street. If protestors have a clear set of leaders whom they trust, you can negotiate, strike a deal, and get them off the street. That is exactly what happened in South Korea in 1987. After the military ruler attempted to anoint his successor, mass protests brought some 1 million students, workers, and citizens out in opposition. In response, the regime announced genuinely competitive elections and sweeping constitutional reform. A mere six months later, social pressures had been redirected into South Korea's first free and fair presidential contest. Third, the existence of experienced, established opposition leaders with broad national appeal cultivated over three decades helped ensure a stable transition. When Kim Young-sam (1993–1998) and Kim Dae-jung (1998–2003) ascended to the presidency, they gave the new South Korean state legitimacy in the eyes of regime opponents, while still managing to effectively govern the state bureaucracy.

The successful "East Asian Model" embodied by Taiwan and South Korea consequently consists of limited political liberalization at a relatively early stage—one at a much lower level of economic development than many observers have appreciated. Crucially, such liberalization steers opposition forces into seeking reform of existing institutions, rather than attempting to shatter them through revolutionary violence.

Of course, this dynamic isn't limited to East Asia. As autocratic regimes around the world face demands for greater political participation, whether from citizens seeking democracy, decolonization, or civil rights, they have different options. Totalitarian repression is one. Crush society under your boot. Grasp the economy with an iron fist. This has the advantage of breaking all resistance. However, it is hard to carry out in practice. It also torpedoes your economy. For that reason, this choice tends to be frowned on today, unless you are descended from a line of North Korean despots.

A second choice is authoritarian rule. Build a tough police state. Effectively bar formal political participation by your opponents. But allow civil society to develop in a semi-organized fashion outside the walls of your control. This is the story of a range of systems: from Communist Poland in the 1970s and 1980s, to apartheid-era South Africa, to a series of Egyptian military rulers.[19] In response, the Solidarity labor movement, African National Congress (ANC), and Muslim Brotherhood developed extensive networks within their respective societies. They became the primary competitors for power. Violence waxed and waned as authorities periodically moved to suppress them, and as these movements themselves confronted rival social forces. In 1980s and 1990s South Africa, for example, some of the bloodiest violence consisted of retaliatory violence between ANC supporters and those of competing opposition parties.

What does this mean for you as the outgoing authoritarian ruler? Well, at the end of the day, it creates the possibility for a negotiated accord. You find the well-organized opponent that you have been repressing can actually become a partner. You can sit down at a table, cut a deal, and enable a stable transition—one that holds society together and doesn't result in the mutilated bodies of your relatives being dragged through the streets. This is what occurred in Poland (1989) and South Africa (1990–1993). Of course, things can also go the other way. After a failed political accommodation following the 2011 Arab Spring, the Egyptian military toppled the newly elected president (a member of the Muslim Brotherhood) and launched a brutal crackdown to eradicate the movement. An escalating spiral of violence and terrorism has since followed.

Now, there is a third possibility. Faced with building social pressure for greater political participation, you could choose to be a reformist autocrat. You could gradually open channels to accommodate citizen demands. This is the Taiwan scenario.[†] It is also what has happened in many other countries that have experienced gradual transformations, such as Mexico. In the late twentieth century, some ninety years of authoritarian one-Party rule by the Institutional Revolutionary Party steadily gave way to opposition control of isolated municipal governments (pre-1980s), state governments (1989), the lower chamber of the national legislature (1997), and finally the Mexican presidency (2000).[20]

Or look at India. As the only nation rivaling China in population size, its experience merits particular attention.[21] In the nineteenth century, the British Empire attained the apex of control over India. But its rule was far from secure. The spread of modern transportation and print media fostered rising Indian nationalism, leading to demands for greater Indian participation in the tightly controlled imperial government.

British reactions varied. Harsh criminal sanctions and suspension of civil liberties were used to suppress citizen discontent.[22] Authorities sometimes resorted to outright violence. In 1919, faced with a peaceful citizen protest in the city of Amritsar, British officials ordered the military to open fire, leaving 370 dead and over 1,000 wounded.

But the primary response was gradual political liberalization. Late-nineteenth-century reforms charged local councils with handling issues such as education and public health. Early-twentieth-century reforms established unofficial Indian majorities in provincial legislatures and allowed indirect elections to select their membership. These "consultative" forms of government gradually gave way to real power. The authority of Indian-controlled legislative bodies steadily expanded. The

---

[†] South Korea falls somewhere between the second and third categories. Instead of a gradual process of political opening or a clearly negotiated transitional accord, Seoul's military leaders made a more-or-less unilateral announcement of free elections, which was followed by general acceptance by South Korea's highly organized opposition forces.

1935 Government of India Act, the last pre-independence constitution, increased the right to vote from some 7 million to 30 million people (roughly one-sixth of the adult population) and charged provincial Indian legislatures with oversight of most government functions.

As a result, the emerging political opposition took the form of reformists rather than revolutionaries. Pressure was channeled into—not out of—formal legal and political institutions. Founded in 1885, the Indian National Congress (Congress) evolved by the mid-twentieth century into the largest Indian nationalist organization. Yet for the first few decades, it did not even challenge British rule. Rather, it contented itself with calling for increased Indian participation in legislative bodies and the civil service. Even when Congress began to employ aggressive techniques of mass mobilization to contest British rule during the 1920s and 1930s, such as large-scale strikes and sit-ins, Congress leaders helped restrain popular passions. When a peasant mob burned to death twenty-two policemen in Chauri Chaura during the 1920–1922 non-cooperation campaign, Mahatma Gandhi called a halt to the entire effort. Further, as Congress politicians gradually assumed power, they did not call for the immediate overthrow of the imperial system. Instead, they cooperated with British governors in maintaining law and order, while exerting steady pressure for greater concessions in subsequent rounds of political bargaining. This "ritual 'dance' of the Congress and the Raj over so many years enforced compromise and taught each the limits of the possible in ways that facilitated not just a smooth transfer of power but a lasting commitment to a liberal society."[23]

This outcome was not foreordained. A turbulent wave of alternative social movements developed as political competitors to Congress. By the early twentieth century, emerging Hindu nationalist groups evolved into militant, quasi-fascist organizations willing to resort to terrorism, such as the Rashtriya Swayamsevak Sangh (RSS). Similarly, the 1920s witnessed a rise of radical peasant and labor movements. But seeing their interests best advanced by working through existing institutions, Congress remained firmly apart from such extreme movements.

Of course, political liberalization does not magically resolve all ills. As Ian Bremmer has argued in *The J Curve* (2006), it results in a transitional period of increased instability.[24] Immediately moving to nationwide free elections can be particularly polarizing. In the 1950s and 1960s, as Nigeria progressed from British colony to independent democracy, ethnic-based parties formed, quickly followed by inter-communal political competition, military coups, and civil war (1967–1970).[25] South Sudan has suffered similar problems since independence in 2011. Or take India itself. Political liberalization led to heightened distinctions between Hindus and Muslims, as activists manipulated religious identities for electoral advantage. The results: an expressly Muslim political party, followed by calls for a separate homeland, resulting in partition of the subcontinent between India and Pakistan at independence in 1947. Hundreds of thousands died in the resulting communal conflicts, while millions of Hindus and Muslims fled their ancestral homes in fear of violence.

But the benefits of gradual liberalization should not be underesti-mated. It can help create a stable opposition committed to working within the system for change. It can help promote the organic evolu-tion of institutions to handle political conflict. And it can help avoid violent revolution.

Comparing India with China drives home this point. During the early twentieth century, both transitioned away from autocratic impe-rial rule. As bloody as India's experience was, it was dwarfed by the decades of internal turmoil and civil war that wracked China follow-ing the collapse of the Qing dynasty (and discussed in more detail in Chapter 6). Also, India only had to do this once. China may yet repeat it.

CHINA: NONE OF THE ABOVE

China today is not following any of the three paths described above. Since the 1970s, it has abandoned North Korean–style totalitarian con-trol. But Chinese-style authoritarianism has been much tougher than that in South Africa or Poland. Chinese authorities have successfully blocked all efforts to openly organize coherent opposition to their rule, crushing all those who try—such as the New Democracy Party (1998), Falun Gong (1999), and New Citizens Movement (2013).

Beijing has also repeatedly backed away from the idea of gradual reform from within. Consider China's evolution over the past two decades. By the late 1990s, it had reached the same level of wealth (in per-capita GDP terms) as early 1970s-era Taiwan and South Korea—when those two experienced the first stirrings of internal tensions that would culminate in their political transitions.[26]

What has happened to China since? Well, every state reform that might put China on a path resembling that of Taiwan or South Korea has been aborted. It isn't that positive reforms don't occur. Rather, as discussed in Chapter 3, they are just are cut off at the knees whenever they appear on the verge of producing momentum toward deeper institutional reform. The 1990s village election movement? Aborted in 2000. Rule-of-law reforms? Curtailed after 2005. Microblogging as a political forum? Reversed in 2013.

Does this stop social discontent from arising? Of course not. It just means that it is not channeled into anything like the gradual institutionalization that the Taiwanese or South Korean opposition experienced during the 1970s and 1980s. So riots, protests, demonstrations, and mass petitions in China surged from 10,000 in 1994 to 74,000 in 2004.[27] But faced with implacable state opposition to any effort at political organizing, what happens to leaders of these protest activities? Do they learn to conduct PTA town hall meetings according to Robert's Rules of Order? No. They learn different skills. They move underground. They become radicalized. Participants lose confidence in the possibility of gradual reform to achieve their aims. They fragment. Religious figures, labor leaders, and village activists all pursue their activities independently of one another, rather than creating broad coalitions.

Of course, in the short term, this lack of an organized opposition gives state authorities a superficial sense of stability. But this is an illusion. It masks a steadily increasing risk of another type of political transition—a much less stable one.

AN ALTERNATIVE FUTURE

If China's political evolution differs from many countries, are there others that it does resemble? Yes. Try late-nineteenth-century Russia.[28]

Military humiliation at the hands of Western powers in the Crimean War of 1853–1856 had exposed Russia's technological inferiority. Late-nineteenth-century imperial Russia consequently confronted the same challenge that faced Deng Xiaoping in the late 1970s—how to catch up with vibrant Western (and Japanese) economies that were rapidly leaving them in the dust.

As with China, the imperial state initiated extensive economic and social reforms in response. Serfdom was abolished. Peasants received more rights. Massive domestic changes swept over Russia. Industrialization reworked the fabric of Russian life, bringing a tide of rural migrants to urban factories. Worker protests over conditions and pay began to erupt with increasing frequency. The new social media of the era—printed periodicals—permitted an educated elite to rapidly disseminate ideas throughout the country, often resorting to coded allusions to avoid imperial censors.

Like China today, late-nineteenth-century Tsarist Russia enjoyed decades of economic growth at rates that outpaced those of the United States and European nations, notwithstanding a bureaucratic-authoritarian political system that foreign observers saw as badly outdated. As the century drew to a close, speculation ran rampant as to when Russia might surpass Western powers in economic and military might.

Tsarist authorities launched sweeping reforms as well. They imported foreign legal institutions including models of legal education; a professional bar; Western-style courts and juries; and civil, commercial, and criminal codes. Excitement was palpable. "The slogans in the air in the 1860s were due process, open court proceedings, trial by jury and irremovable judges."[29] Officials even established local representative assemblies with limited powers of self-government.

Citizens took eagerly to these new channels. Reformers sought to use local assemblies to gradually push the imperial regime in a more liberal direction. Radical activists took advantage of legal novelties such as open court proceedings and independent judges. They turned trials into platforms calling for greater political change. In 1878, a young anarchist named Vera Zasulich became an instant media sensation when, after her arrest for trying to assassinate an imperial governor, the trial judge resisted government efforts to tamper with the case; her lawyer managed to turn the public proceedings into an indictment of police brutality. A jury of sympathetic citizens returned a verdict of "not guilty," and crowds erupted into public demonstrations upon her release.

Such developments caused serious worry among political elites. As in China today, rule-of-law institutions came under increasing suspicion from an authoritarian regime dead set against fundamental political reform—particularly after anarchists assassinated the reformist Tsar Alexander II in 1881. Russia entered its own counter-reform era. Under Alexander's successor, Russian authorities launched a two-decade-long rollback of liberal policies. They curtailed public trials, limited the rights of juries, asserted control over bar associations, removed political trials from the regular court system, and drastically reduced the powers of local assemblies.

Beginning in the late 1870s, imperial authorities also built up an extensive police state (one might call it "social stability maintenance with Russian characteristics"). They increasingly took responsibility for upholding law and order out of the hands of judges and gave it to the police, including the Okhrana (the Tsarist secret service). Agents of the latter enjoyed dramatically expanded powers that allowed them to detain and internally exile anyone even suspected of political crimes.

Of course, these measures did not succeed in stamping out all dissent. The existence of private property meant that there were limits on imperial power. Wealthy patrons continued to employ reformist intellectuals, despite state efforts to isolate them. Dissident authors continued to find markets for their works, notwithstanding official censorship.

The key result of the late-nineteenth-century Tsarist counter-reform era was to radicalize society. The imperial turn against law convinced moderates that gradual reform was impossible.[30] Decades of indiscriminate state repression collectively alienated the entire political spectrum—liberal constitutionalists, anarchist terrorists, religious nationalists, radical socialists, and ordinary citizens outraged by violations of their rights. It drove all of them to adopt ever more extreme political positions. Naturally, this produced an equal and opposite reaction within the ranks of Russian officials—fueling a growing paranoia about the risks of undertaking any reform whatsoever. As imperial rule entered its waning years, hardline policies also prevented the emergence of any organized and institutionalized political opposition. Like China today, imperial Russia during the counter-reform era had no Taiwanese *dangwai* movement, no South Korean opposition political parties, no Polish Solidarity trade union. It crushed any effort to organize these. This produced a surface veneer of political stability. But it also ensured that no coherent force existed to step into the void and pick up the power lying in the streets should the Tsarist state falter.

And that is precisely what happened. After an external shock weakened the regime—defeat in the 1904–1905 conflict with Japan—imperial authorities belatedly sought to implement deeper reforms. But by then, it was too little, too late. Institutions that might have helped channel popular input and bridge social divides, such as the new 1906 national legislature (Duma), were born weak and lacking in legitimacy. Both state and society had fractured too far. Historians still debate whether the 1911 assassination of prime minister Stolypin—Russia's last hope for institutional reform—represented a left-wing anarchist effort to undermine the regime in the name of revolution, or a plot by extreme right-wing forces within the imperial security services to eliminate a moderate voice for change that they viewed as a threat. But it did not matter. Any prospect for gradual reform was dead.

As Russia approached its ultimate test amid the wartime stresses of 1917, it was consequently torn between a brittle state resistant to change and a chaotic assortment of forces within society—military strongmen, popular mobs, radicalized intellectuals, and—detraining ominously at the Finland Station—committed underground revolutionaries hardened by decades of repression.

CONCLUSION

Stable liberal democracies are not created overnight. Instead, they are the result of decades-long evolutionary interactions between state and society.

But the path central leaders are pursuing is depriving China of precisely this kind of interaction—the kind that led to stable transitions elsewhere. China today is nowhere near the visions of authoritarian modernizers. But it is also far removed from the dreams of those in the democracy promotion camp. If the Chinese state crumbles, whether because of economic crisis or internal political struggles among Party leaders, stable democracy will not emerge from the ashes.

6

Possible Futures

EVERYONE WANTS A STORY with a happy ending. Particularly in the case of China. After a century of political turmoil and four decades of dizzying economic change, one just hopes things will—somehow—just work out.

This sentiment is pervasive in writing about China. Take Orville Schell and John Delury's recent work, *China's Search for Wealth and Power* (2013). They recount China's dramatic fall and rise since the nineteenth century through a series of mini-biographies of statesmen and intellectuals. Two are selected to represent post-1989 China. The first is Zhu Rongji, who as premier from 1998 to 2003 presided over the relatively liberal era that accompanied China's entry into the World Trade Organization in 2001. For the authors, he embodies state efforts at economic reform and technocratic modernization. The second is human rights activist (and 2010 Nobel Prize laureate) Liu Xiaobo, representing citizen demands for greater political participation. The authors conclude:

> In contemplating the future, it is always important to remember that, despite all its rigidities and infirmities, the Chinese Communist Party has repeatedly surprised the world with its ability to change course and prevail, including its most recent feat of steering China into the twenty-first century as a nascent superpower. . . . [T]hese two streams of thought [i.e., Zhu Rongji and Liu Xiaobo]—one in search of wealth and power, the other reaching for democracy—may

well converge in the future. . . . Of course, when and how this might
come to pass is still an unanswerable question.[1]

Two moderate forces—one represented by a reformist political insider,
the other by a peaceful opposition figure—somehow joining hands
after decades of antagonism to chart a new course for their country.
This is exactly how we Americans like to envisage political change. It is
tidy. And it creates a stirring narrative filled with sympathetic characters for the subsequent Hollywood adaptation of the story into a major
motion picture film.

But is that really what will happen? Is that where current trends in
China are taking us?

DEMISE OF THE LIBERAL DREAM

Schell and Delury are not unique. There is a deep belief that the complex back-and-forth between China's state and society has to lead to
something better. Either China's bureaucrats will themselves realize the
need for some kind of political reform. Or irresistible demands among
citizens for a more liberal society will be unleashed.

For James Mann, author of *The China Fantasy* (2006), this is the
Soothing Scenario—a slick self-serving story concocted by U.S. economic and foreign policy elites to sucker the American public into
deeper engagement and integration with China. When President Bill
Clinton lobbied Congress in 2000 to approve China's entry into the
World Trade Organization, a version of this narrative indeed did feature
in his efforts.[2] But a better description might be the *Liberal Dream*. It is
not simply a political tool. It regularly appears in academic and popular writing of all sorts—ranging from Bruce Gilley's *China's Democratic
Future* (2004) to the 2016 *Economist* report on China's rising middle
class.[3] A less cynical explanation would point to the near-genetic inability of Americans to conceive that steady evolution toward a more liberal
political order is anything other than the natural progression of history.

Why? True, China's internal problems are becoming more acute.
Tensions are rising. And yes, society is becoming more vocal and asser-
tive. But why take (relatively) sympathetic individuals such as Zhu
Rongji and Liu Xiaobo as archetypical representations of what these

trends are producing? One could just as easily select very different figures.

Take, for example, former security czar Zhou Yongkang, nationalist blogger Zhou Xiaoping, or Wei Yinyong, the disgruntled Guangxi quarry worker who detonated a series of parcel bombs in 2015, killing ten and injuring fifty-one. All of them are equally products of the complex interplay between China's state and society over the past two decades. The ruthless security chief who capitalizes on weak central leadership and Beijing's obsession with internal stability to build a mafia-like bureaucratic empire through black-box political maneuvering—only to be overthrown and have his turf seized by China's new top leader. The millennial activist who riles up public passions with his online anti-foreign rants and skyrockets to his fifteen minutes of national fame after being publicly praised by Xi Jinping himself for spreading "positive energy."[4] The aggrieved citizen who resorts to violent retribution rather than frozen legal or political channels to resolve disputes with his neighbors and business associates. This is the *other* China: between the proto-warlord, the anti-foreign nationalist, and the suicide bomber. And this is the side of the China story that all too often isn't examined—because it is frankly depressing, and because it doesn't fit in with how we like to think China "should" evolve.

The key question is: which will become more representative over time?

Back in late twentieth century, it was possible to hold out hope. The reform era was rich with possibility. But everything now points in exactly the wrong direction. China looks nothing like the hopeful East Asian transition stories of South Korea and Taiwan (see Chapter 5). Beijing is now steadily dismantling the political and ideological infrastructure of the 1980s and 1990s. Internal Party norms essential to the system's stability are being disassembled, brick by brick. Embryonic state institutions that might have helped facilitate China's slow evolution to an alternative political system have been strangled in the cradle by those fearful of what they might mature into.

Of course, figures like Zhu Rongji and Liu Xiaobo still exist. But as China's politics decay, as economic troubles worsen, and as society deforms under the molten heat of *weiwen* ("stability maintenance") policies, they are increasingly marginalized. Their voices are going quiet.

Look first within the Party elite. Back in 2012, the current premier Li Keqiang was the darling of Western and Chinese observers hoping for internal reform. With his Ph.D. in law, technocratic background in economics, and easy familiarity with foreign interlocutors, he could easily have served as a modern-day replacement for Zhu Rongji. Now, he is steadily being sidelined. Or examine society at large. Back in the heyday of China's social media platform Weibo in 2010, bad boy race car driver/blogger Han Han gained national notoriety with his penetrating criticism of China's social ills dispensed regularly to some 40 million followers. For many, he represented a new voice of social consciousness for the youth generation born since the 1980s. But since 2013, he has dropped from public view. And nationalist voices such as Zhou Xiaoping have surged to prominence.

This is the core of the problem facing China. It isn't merely that the two streams of thought identified by Schell and Delury are failing to come together. Rather, each is being steadily supplanted and outflanked by increasingly radical viewpoints and forces. One can certainly wish for a more liberal China. And observers can hold out the faint hope that it might somehow emerge. But objectively, it just looks increasingly unlikely.

CONTINUED AUTHORITARIAN RULE

Might China simply continue along under some form of authoritarian rule? In his recent book, *China's Future?* (2016), noted China scholar David Shambaugh leans toward this view, at least in the near-to-middle term. He ranks two scenarios as most probable: *Hard Authoritarianism* or *Soft Authoritarianism*. The former is a continuation of Beijing's existing hardline policies; the latter, a return to the more liberal ones of the early 2000s—relaxed media controls, more space for civil society, openness toward foreign concepts in the educational and cultural arenas, and so on. Viewing Xi Jinping as a deeply conservative leader, he assesses it more likely that *Hard Authoritarianism* will continue to dominate, but holds out a small possibility that Beijing might return to *Soft Authoritarianism* after the 19th Party Congress in 2017, if leadership changes should produce a coalition within the Politburo more amenable to political reform.[5]

There is much merit in Shambaugh's analysis. Beijing's existing policies do amount to a "terminal cancer" that "only [serve] to *accelerate* the Party's existing atrophy and decline."[6] And the likelihood of hardline policies continuing is indeed higher than that of more liberal ones returning, precisely because Beijing's rulers have convinced themselves that any experimentation with the latter risks triggering precisely the fundamental political transformation that they are determined to avoid. It is very easy to imagine Chinese politics devolving into a steady spiral of elite infighting, economic decline, ideological polarization, and rising social unrest—all under an atrophying, paranoid, and increasingly fragile authoritarian regime.

Where I disagree is in assessing the underlying reasons *why* this is all taking place. Shambaugh lays the responsibility at the feet of individual leaders. He identifies former senior leader Zeng Qinghong (a Jiang Zemin ally and a member of Politburo Standing Committee member from 2002 to 2007) as the "mastermind" behind the relatively liberal political atmosphere that characterized China around the turn of the millennium.[7] Similarly, he dates the beginning of China's current crackdown to 2009, after Zeng's retirement. He sees China today as undergoing but another stage in a political cycle of *fang* (relaxation) and *shou* (tightening) that have characterized China since the 1980s. But for him, things can change. Get the right leader in, dust off those temporarily shelved reform plans, and things can move in a different direction.[8]

This framework simply does not apply today. What is taking place in China now is not merely a short-term shift. It is not simply a version of, say, the three-month-long anti-bourgeois liberalization campaign in the winter of 1987. Nor is it simply the result of a shift in individual leaders. It runs much deeper. Across the board—in politics, economics, and ideology—the trends and practices that have sustained the engine of China's reform era have been steadily grinding down since the early 2000s. And in the absence of fundamental political reform, things are beginning to break loose. China is starting to slide.

To appreciate this, take a look at yet another potential track Shambaugh identifies for China, one he terms *Neo-Totalitarianism*:

> The reference point for such a scenario would be 1989–1992. It would
> involve the following: strict state controls over all major media and

social media; widespread detentions and arrests of intellectuals, students, lawyers, writers, and activists . . . termination of domestic and foreign NGOs; deployment of paramilitary PAP troops and stepped-up police patrols through Chinese cities; strict controls over foreign and internal travel for Chinese citizens; limited visas for foreigners and careful monitoring of Chinese interactions with them; xenophobic campaigns in the cultural and educational arenas; and other repressive measures.[9]

He does not see this as likely. For him, the private sector is too entrenched, the citizenry too resistant, and elements with the Party itself too committed to reform-era norms to permit such backsliding. In his words, "the genie is out of the bottle, and there is no going back."[10]

Now look deeper. Recognize that this is but a further extension of the existing top-down authoritarian controls described in his first two scenarios. Nor is it that difficult to imagine. Key elements are starting to materialize. As you read these words, public security officials are busy implementing China's draconian new foreign NGO law that entered into force January 1, 2017. Tough new political campaigns are winding their way through China's colleges. And state media regulators are cracking down on entertainment and news programs that "defile the classics" or promote "Western lifestyles."[11] This is a sign of how far the landscape has shifted. When one of America's top China experts wrote the above paragraph—back in the distant past of 2014–2015—it was regarded as a remote possibility. Now it is coming true. Within the framework of authoritarian rule, China is now steadily sliding in a yet more hardline direction.

POPULIST NATIONALISM

Shambaugh's final scenario has an additional flaw: he doesn't fully work through it. Despite invoking the term "totalitarianism," his proposed scenario lacks two key factors associated with it: pervasive resort to ideology and mass social mobilization. Both of those *did* characterize

Maoist China. But both were theoretically buried with the birth of the reform era. Could they return?

To distinguish the following from Shambaugh's own argument, let's call this the *Populist Nationalism* option.[12] Not only does it have echoes in China's own past, but strains of it are evident in many countries throughout the world today: in Venezuela, Russia, Turkey (after the failed 2016 coup), Thailand (after the successful 2014 coup), a range of far right-wing European parties, the United Kingdom (with the successful Brexit campaign to leave the European Union), and in the United States, with the 2016 election of Donald Trump as president.

How might China's variant play out? Surging unrest in the wake of an economic crash might prompt Beijing to play with returning to the Party's revolutionary roots in order to get ahead of rising popular discontent. A conflict in the South China Sea that spirals out of control might lead nationalist wildfires to spread uncontrollably in China's decaying, brittle Party apparatus and among an atomized, anxious society. Or a power struggle among China's elite might prompt a leader to play the populist card in an effort to circumvent his rivals. (Indeed, the widely popular leftist revival pursued by Bo Xilai in Chongqing from 2007 to 2012 might provide a ready-made model.) Whatever the proximate cause, the crucial point would be the following: politics would once again be fully in command, the final taboos of the reform era breached.

Resistance would be profound. America's established elites—professional politicians, East Coast intellectuals, global financiers—were horrified to see the rise of populist political challengers in the United States on both the left (Sanders) and right (Trump). So too would the vested beneficiaries of China's reform era correctly see this shift as their death knell. But if you are a Chinese leader seeking to pursue such policies, these elites are not your focus. You are throwing them overboard. Instead, your targets are those who perceive themselves left behind by the reform era boom. Underemployed college graduates. Low-income workers driven out of Beijing by grandiose urban redevelopment plans. Taxi drivers whose incomes are plummeting under the assault of the expanding Didi ride-sharing empire. Migrant parents who have scrimped and saved for years to afford the under-the-table fees for their children to attend the local urban school, only to look up to see the chauffeured Audis of their employers (and the local Party boss) speeding their children to English cram schools in preparation for study abroad. This is your audience. You seek populist policies to assuage their demands, nationalist rhetoric to stir their hearts, and convenient targets for their anger. Namely—away from you.

History offers guidance. The 1950s saw land reform (*tudi gaige*). Perhaps the 2020s require property reform (*fangdichan gaige*)—vacant investment properties seized or acquired at low prices by state authorities and redistributed to migrant workers and young office workers squeezed out of the housing market. Are well-off homeowners starting to squeal? Too bad. You have methods. Expand your anti-corruption campaign. Start looking into unpaid taxes. See who has failed to properly register their assets. Drag a few private businessmen in front of TV cameras to tearfully confess to how they illegally acquired wealth during the reform era. While you are at it, stage a few well-publicized appearances before cheering crowds of thousands of construction workers and retirees in Shanghai and Guangzhou. Swear that you will—*personally*—squeeze those rotten private developers and good-for-nothing local cadres, forcing them to cough up unpaid salaries and benefits.[13] Your goal, of course, is to firmly remind urban elites exactly how much worse things could get for them if they resist too much.

Nationalism is your ideological glue. Signal to patriotic citizens and grassroots Party activists your approval of their efforts against foreign countries that contest Beijing's claims of sovereignty in the East and South China Seas. Allow citizen boycotts of their products to spread nationwide. Launch torchlight processions on college campuses. Encourage students to read out the names of Han civilians killed in the most recent clashes in Xinjiang, or condemn the latest indignities visited on the motherland by "traitorous" Hong Kong localists. Sure, such policies have consequences. Foreign trade plummets. Reprisal killings rock ethnic areas of western China. But your image as the great leader—the only one who can save the nation—begins to crystallize in the eyes of the public. This proves useful when you turn against your residual opposition within the Party itself. Selectively leak names of certain officials with children and assets overseas to some of the more rabid nationalist bloggers.* Online fury mounts. Sporadic protests break out in front of government offices. As your purge gathers steam, the chants of your supporters mount outside your windows. . . .

Naturally, this would be exceptionally dangerous. It amounts to deliberately torching the entire social and political framework upon which the stability of China's reform era is based. Economic damage would be immense. It is unlikely that any existing Party leader would pursue anything remotely resembling such a scenario if they thought they had an alternative, precisely because setting such ideological fires would have real risks for them personally, as Stein Ringen has noted.[14] Beijing has demonstrated a nimble ability to steer more limited nation-alist protests to date.[15] But it is far from clear that any top leader who broke open the final sealed door of the reform era, and embraced mass movements, could successfully retain control. The flames of populist nationalism could easily be blown backward onto himself.

But is such a scenario inconceivable? Not at all. History suggests that China's leaders are more than capable of resorting to such measures when they view themselves facing an existential crisis, whether real or perceived. Precisely this dynamic is behind the tottering Qing dynasty's pivot to embrace the anti-foreign Boxer rebels in 1898. It also underlies Mao's decision to unleash the young Red Guard radicals upon the Party bureaucracy itself in 1966. At such crucial junctures, what was once inconceivable becomes all too possible.

THE DYNASTIC CYCLE: REDUX

Many have tried to imagine what China's future might hold. Something resembling the above framework is often used. Set out several scenarios. Invoke the metaphor of a "crossroads." Emphasize the crucial choice facing

---

* But didn't your own children study abroad? Wouldn't that be a problem for your own popular image? History can be malleable in the face of politics. After all, the son of Nationalist (and rabidly anti-communist) dictator Chiang Kai-shek not only spent twelve years in Stalinist Russia, but married a Soviet woman. Neither harmed his father's own political career. Nor did they impede the son's rise, first as head of the secret police, and later as Chiang's political successor (in Taiwan).

China's leaders. Conclude that their decision to select the correct path can help assure economic success, political stability, and a bright future.

This is a very top-down view. It inherently envisages a great man (or men) at the helm of China's ship of state, capably wielding a panoply of levers to steer the country. Such a framework is redolent with nostalgia for the late twentieth century—a handful of dark-suited leaders gathering around the windows of some central Party compound in Beijing to plan Nixon's 1972 visit to China, or hammer out the details of the 1978 plenum launching the reform era. With the shadow of the leader (Mao or Deng) in the background, consensus could be reached, the Party machinery kicked into effective operation, while favorable tailwinds (globalization, a young population) bore aloft their policies. Options abounded.

This is less true now. Internal tensions among the elite are worsening. Hard constraints—both economic and demographic—loom large. China's leaders are less and less in the driver's seat. They are finding themselves increasingly driven by events. Options are narrowing.

Now, there is an alternative framework to conceptualize things—one deeply rooted in China's own history. For generations, imperial scholars organized the regular ebb and flow of political power in China by invoking the idea of the *dynastic cycle*.

From the midst of chaos, a dynamic figure founds a new dynasty. Some are commoners who rise from nothing (such as the Han dynasty). Others are nobles who turn against their sovereigns (as with the Sui). Tight personal bonds tie the new leader together with a cohort of loyal supporters. Together, they overcome severe tests—fighting off internal enemies, defending against foreign challengers, and unifying the vast territory of China. (Think of the Manchu and Han bannermen who spearheaded the military steamroller of early Qing emperors in the seventeenth and eighteenth centuries.)

As the decades roll on, the charismatic founders pass away. Imperial rule institutionalizes. The examination system is re-established. Bureaucratic organs of the previous dynasty are revived and updated. Economic and social elites are once again drawn into a tight dance with political power. Central officials select and support an approved ideology. (Buddhism for the Tang, neo-Confucianism for the Ming.) Culture flourishes. Cities grow rich with trade. Strong and confident, China emerges as a major regional actor.

Then decay sets in. At first, the signs are slight. An aging emperor focuses his attentions on his favorite consort rather than matters of state. Lackadaisical paper-pushers multiply in minor provincial offices. But problems steadily worsen. Public works slowly suffer from inattention. Corruption spreads. Once-meritocratic structures are weakened by outright sale of official posts. The ideology that once bound the elite together becomes hidebound and resistant to change. Economic woes mount, requiring harsher financial burdens on peasants and merchants. Internal uprisings erupt with increasing frequency. Struggles within the imperial court intensify, weakening the ability of central officials to make decisions. (Take, for example, the 1898 palace coup that deposed the Guangxu emperor, after his launch of the abortive Hundred Days reform movement.) External conflicts drain the national treasury—whether expensive colonial expeditions in Korea and Vietnam (in the Tang), or desperate efforts to defend against Mongol assaults (Song) or European armies (Qing). Eventually, political erosion and mounting unrest fuse together in an explosive combination. Once-firm imperial structures give way; disorder descends across the land . . . at which point the whole cycle begins once again.

Such is the *longue durée* of Chinese history. It resembles the long-term political decay that has plagued other one-Party states and medieval empires alike.[16] And it shares similarities with the sclerosis that creeps into the joints of many large bureaucratic organizations as they age.[17] Sure, this hasn't been how we have thought of China over recent decades. But that is because we have been observing a brief snapshot of China at a specific moment in one particular cycle. After all, when Marco Polo encountered the full vigor of the Yuan dynasty in the thirteenth century, or Jesuit missionaries that of the early Qing empire in the 1700s, they were equally impressed. But fast-forward to a later point in history where institutional decay has fully set in, and attitudes—both inside and outside China—radically shift.

This point can be phrased yet more provocatively. Beijing's current rulers are toying with turning toward a "red dynastic" governance model—centralizing power in the hands of a few Party princelings, curbing the cultural openness that characterized the reform era, and so on (see Chapter 3). Why should they be able to escape their own history if they continue down this path? Rather than trying to engage in conceptual gymnastics to figure out if China today is more similar to 1970s Spain under Franco, or South Korea under Park, perhaps we should start seeing it for what it really is: a modernized, updated version of the traditional authoritarian-bureaucratic imperial system. China today is best understood as a version of *itself*, not of some tinpot authoritarian regime elsewhere in the world. And if Party leaders indeed succeed in fully realizing their goal of establishing (or re-establishing) governance with Chinese characteristics, shouldn't the historical consequences of that model follow as well?

China may not be at a crossroads. Rather, it may be in a downward spiral. *Soft Authoritarianism* could decay into steadily more intense versions of *Hard Authoritarianism*, possibly lurching into *Populist Nationalism*, with the specter of *Regime Collapse* looming in the background.

REGIME COLLAPSE

This is not to say that regime collapse is imminent or even likely. The Qing dynasty continued on for decades after its peak, even as problems of elite governance and social unrest steadily worsened. And other countries facing far worse challenges—say, Pakistan—somehow continue to struggle on.

Rather, the point is merely that China today is not the same as in the early reform era. Possibilities are narrowing. But ever since Gordon Chang infamously predicted the demise of the Communist Party in his *Coming Collapse of China* (2001) (unwisely doubling down on his prediction a decade later)† it has been more or less taboo in "serious" China circles to broach the subject. Not for fear of offending Beijing. But for sounding, well . . . kind of silly. This doesn't make sense. Even if one thinks it is a remote possibility, you at least have to sketch out what you think such a scenario would look like. After all, the unexpected collapse of long-established authoritarian regimes isn't exactly

---

† "I admit it: My prediction that the Communist Party would fall by 2011 was wrong. Still, I'm only off by a year." Gordon Chang, "The Coming Collapse of China: 2012 Edition," *Foreign Policy*, December 29, 2011, available at http://foreignpolicy.com/2011/12/29/the-coming-collapse-of-china-2012-edition/.v

an unknown event in recent world politics. Nor is it alien to China's own history.

Speculation on this front is inherently problematic, the potential variables too many to list. But a few things are clear. There is almost no chance of a stable, liberal democracy emerging in such a situation. All institutions outside the Party itself are weak, underdeveloped, and lack legitimacy. No alternative social forces or political movements of any size are waiting in the wings to pick up the pieces if the existing system should shatter. Put simply, China is not Taiwan or Poland of the 1980s (see Chapter 5). Nor is it even similar to China of the late 1940s, where the presence of Mao's well-organized guerrilla forces could impose a new political order as the corrupt Nationalist forces crumbled.

It is remotely possible to imagine China experiencing a fate paralleling that of Russia after the collapse of the Soviet Union in 1991—a sudden political decompression, a disorderly transition, followed in rapid order by the re-establishment of a military dictatorship or personalized authoritarian regime akin to Putin's. In short, either a revived *Hard Authoritarian* state or a *Populist Nationalist* one, albeit facing many of the same underlying problems as confront Beijing today. But even that is unlikely. Moscow moved from being a comprehensive one-Party Marxist-Leninist state to "Saudi Arabia with snow." Even after Soviet political structures failed, extensive natural resources and high oil prices permitted the emergence of a renewed Russian authoritarian petro-state run by a narrow elite, and possessing the cash to placate (or suppress) key sectors of the population.

China is different. China's reform era has produced what the Soviet Union lacked: a broad coalition of "winners"—urban residents, home-owners, SOE employees—whose comfortable lifestyles are intimately intertwined with the existing political system. Wealth is tied up in land and the real economy, not oil. And the divide between China's haves and have-nots is much deeper than in the Soviet Union in the late 1980s. On the one hand, this has contributed to national stability. The former recognize exactly how much they stand to lose if the system founders. But it also means that an actual political implosion would be much more disruptive, likely inseparable from a full-blown economic and social crash. It would represent a fundamental reshuffling of the cards.

Seriously trying to envisage this requires looking elsewhere—for example, the post-Arab Spring Middle East, early-twentieth-century Russia, or the fall of the Qing dynasty in 1912. A tough authoritarian regime that resists reform until the bitter end. Slow decline. Mounting internal tensions. A "black swan" event—a banking crisis, or the heavy-handed suppression of a mass citizen protest that spirals into wider unrest. Long-suppressed social and political fault lines open up, and the country lurches into the void.

What might this look like? In the heady early days, excitement grips the streets. Cheering masses gather in public squares. Symbols of the former regime are torn down. Particularly brutal local officials are paraded in front of crowds. Some are executed. Political prisoners are released from jail; returning dissidents greeted with fanfare. Meanwhile, some business elites quietly escalate efforts to move their wealth and families into second homes in Sydney or Los Angeles that they have prepared for precisely such an occasion. Others, emboldened by a sense of patriotism and historic destiny, join with liberal intellectuals and less-tainted former regime members to try to piece together a new order. (China's first, and most open, national legislative elections were held in 1912–1913.) Cameras click as they enter once-forbidden state compounds in Beijing to discuss China's future. But inside, tensions rise. Military elites and regional powerbrokers maneuver to protect their interests. Struggles for power escalate. Deadlock at the negotiating table devolves into heated public denunciations; denunciations slide into overt violence. Newborn structures rapidly give way. (After the assassination of one of the key opposition legislators in 1913, the reigning military strongman dissolved the embryonic parliament, and launched a failed effort to revive the imperial system, with himself as emperor.) Amid weak institutionalization, China simply dissolves.

Favorable geography and support of key army units ensure that the flat northern plain remains relatively unified under the rump state still nominally called the People's Republic of China. But an array of rogue military officers seize control over various southern provinces. Reconstituted as local warlords, they rule with the support of local business and urban elites, who rely on their forces to maintain order (and keep rural and migrant populations in check). Just as in the 1920s, bloody skirmishes regularly erupt as these new strongmen form and reform shifting alliances to unseat a rival, or protect their own seats of power. Some—say, those in Shanghai and Guangdong—seek foreign assistance as a means of propping up their own influence.[18] Within major population centers along the east coast (at least those in zones of relative security), urban life continues. But elsewhere, the situation is dire. Banditry stalks the countryside. Township militias spring up in response as citizens take the law into their own hands. Some of the worst violence occurs in minority areas, particularly in Xinjiang, where long-suppressed tensions erupt into brutal spasms of ethnic cleansing—on all sides.

This is the milieu in which the accumulated tensions that have built over the course of China's reform era come to a head. Long-suppressed struggles over religion, national identity, allocation of wealth, the desired relationship of state and society—all these begin to play themselves out not within the structures of an organized state, but rather in the ruins of a collapsed one. In Wuhan, university deans seek to ingratiate themselves with their local military patron. Flattering portraits of him appear in classrooms, while local bankers help organize unemployed youth into paramilitary security squads espousing a vague ideology fusing nationalism and Confucianism (and incorporating strangely popular ideas of racial superiority drawn from obscure American alt-right websites). Down in Sichuan, an idealistic young college-educated couple who spent years dabbling on the fringes of Chinese society in the organic farming movement (and searching for meaning in assorted communes) emerge as improbably effective firebrands. Passionately appealing to China's Maoist heritage, they mobilize the poor and oppressed into a secretive network that begins accumulating small caches of arms, allegedly for self-defense. Ideologies of all types spread like wildfire in the unsettled times. Messianic Christian and Buddhist prophets of all stripes gather throngs of supporters around them. Conspiracy theories regarding foreign influence abound. All appeal to a deep nationalist angst over the rising disorder. And just as in China and Europe in the early twentieth century (or Syria today), the widespread sense of insecurity fuels an inexorable slide toward extremism—increasing violence, eradication of rivals, organization of military forces, and the search for outside support. . . .

Loss of life could be extreme. At the outset of the Arab Spring, Syria's population numbered roughly 22 million. By 2016, some four years of civil war had left 11.5 percent of its citizens dead or injured. Over 10 million are currently displaced, either internally or as refugees abroad, contributing to the largest humanitarian crisis since World War II.[19] But even that would be dwarfed by a full-scale meltdown in China. The fall of previous dynasties unleashed cataclysmic, decades-long struggles for power marked by appalling death tolls. Roughly four decades passed between the collapse of the Ming (1644) and the Qing elimination of its last major internal rival (1681)—precisely the same length of time that elapsed between the fall of the Qing (1912) and the birth of the People's Republic of China (1949). Amid the resulting famines, civil wars, foreign invasions, and political violence, perhaps anywhere from a sixth to an eighth of the population perished in each period—some 25 million in the former, 40–50 million in the latter.[20] Extrapolate anything remotely similar to China today, with its 1.4 billion people, and you quickly arrive at the possibility for one of the greatest tragedies in human history.

CHINA IN THE WORLD

What might all this mean for China's relations with the rest of the world?

We have long been accustomed to thinking of Sino-U.S. relations (or with Germany, Australia, or Japan) as state-to-state issues. Teams of identically clad bureaucrats troop into a bland conference room, take their seats behind nameplates adorned with miniature national flags, and proceed to negotiate out a trade deal, cultural exchange, or code of engagement for naval encounters. Periodically, one country's leader makes a formal visit to the other. Observers probe details for signs of appropriate national respect (Was a red carpet extended to America's president on the airport tarmac? Was the correct Chinese flag used?), while newspapers analyze the content of their discussions with paragraphs that read "Beijing's position is . . ." or "Washington believes . . ."—as if those two inanimate metropolises themselves could hold opinions.

In the language of political scientists, this is a *realist* view of international relations. States (whether "China" or "Greece") are conceived of as billiard balls. They have boundaries and clear national interests. They bounce around the pool table of world politics with a mass and force reflecting their political or economic might. (Larger ones, like China or America, will send smaller ones spinning upon collision.) They also are controlled by leaders (or institutions) that can steer state policies in given directions.

Since 1978, China has clearly fit this mold. Party leaders in Beijing have been behaving pretty much as one would expect from a realist state. They have pursued territorial objectives—negotiating border accords with some neighbors (such as Russia or Kazakhstan), and strategically applying pressure on others (such as in the South China Sea). They have sought to strengthen the economy via trade accords (such as WTO entry) and national development plans. And they have sought to uphold social order within China's borders, both by carrots (expanding education and social services) and sticks (repressing dissent).

Now step back a moment. Consider how unusual that is. This is not how things work elsewhere in the world. As any casual reader of the morning newspaper is aware, there are many countries where the realist model does not apply. Some are shattered states (such as Somalia or Libya) lacking any semblance of effective central control. Others are fragile or weak states (such as Pakistan or the Democratic Republic of the Congo), where the official writ of the government extends only so far, and a wide range of subnational actors (ethnic groups, military factions, mining interests) can essentially pursue their own domestic and foreign policies with limited interference from their nominal government. Still others are entities that *look* like states (i.e., they have capitals and flags) but whose leaders (and many citizens) see themselves as representing interests broader than those contained within the simple boundaries laid out on a map. Take the former Soviet Union. Particularly back in the early years of the 1920s, it was an open question whether Soviet leaders saw themselves more as heads of a given state (the USSR) or the leaders of an international ideological movement (that of Marxist-Leninist revolution). Today, the same is true of Iran and Saudi Arabia. Leaders in both view themselves not merely as states, but (at least in part) as the physical manifestations of broader religious communities (Shia Islam for Tehran, Sunni Islam for Riyadh). Upholding "core interests" is not merely a question of defending national boundaries, but of mobilizing military, economic, and diplomatic resources to protect co-religionists abroad as well (such as in Syria, Iraq, or Yemen).

In the case of Saudi Arabia, it also includes spending tens of billions of dollars around the world promoting a specific ideology—Islamic fundamentalism (Wahhabism).[‡]

Nor does the realist model correspond with China as foreigners historically encountered it at different points over the past two centuries. Compare three different periods: the declining Qing empire of the mid-nineteenth century, the chaotic warlord era of the 1920s, and the zealous Maoist China of the late 1960s and early 1970s. In the first, Manchu emperors viewed themselves not leaders of a nation-state, but imperial dynastic rulers of a multi-ethnic empire.[21] During the second, there was simply no national government to speak of. As with Syria today, China was a shattered state. Last, the Cultural Revolution finds Beijing radicals viewing themselves not simply as heads of state, but as leaders of a worldwide revolutionary movement—competing with the Soviet Union for ideological influence in far-from-strategically-important Albania, using limited resources to build railroads in Southern Africa, and hosting the leader of America's Black Panther movement.

Why is this relevant? As of 2017, China is clearly a state. True. But as its domestic politics change, its external behavior will likely shift as well. Assumptions that have governed our understanding of China's foreign policy—based on decades of behavior observed since 1978—will begin to alter.

Let's examine this in detail. Assume Beijing slides toward increasingly tougher versions of *Hard Authoritarianism*. Once-easy assumptions of the reform era ("What is good for China is good for the Party, and vice versa") begin to give way to a cold new calculus. Increasingly, policies will be driven less by long-term considerations of "China's" interest, and more by pressing short-term demands of Party control. Costs—whether to long-term national interests or stable foreign relations—will be externalized (if possible) and simply absorbed (if not). Nor is this

---

[‡] Note that the United States is no stranger to this phenomenon. In American foreign policy, it finds its expression in the long-standing debate between realpolitik strategists and liberal idealists. The former view the United States as but one country among many, with its national interests defined in narrow strategic and economic terms. The latter perceive Washington as the leader (or at least a core member), of the free world, with a particular responsibility to promote and defend democratic values and human rights throughout the world.

mere speculation. It is actually happening. Look at Beijing's decision to continue pumping out massive, unprofitable quantities of steel and aluminum, sending worldwide commodity prices through the floor and generating escalating trade tensions with Europe and the United States, in order to prop up domestic employment. Or examine the new foreign NGO law, which inflicts massive collateral damage on four decades of people-to-people ties between China and the outside world, in the name of better controlling organizations that Party authorities deem a threat to their rule.

Keep going down that path, and Beijing steadily leaves behind the givens of the reform era. The technocratic sheen wears thin. Politically, up ahead looms the decision to curb numbers of students studying abroad, severing educational links with the outside world, and yet other echoes of China's own insular past. Yet further off in the distance, one can already start to see dim shadows of other authoritarian states (such as Zimbabwe and Burma) that chose to prioritize the narrow interests of a ruling elite over the nation at large. Militarily, this trajectory could witness a decision to aggressively push territorial claims in the East and South China Seas for the sake of rallying domestic support—even if objective evaluations of relevant costs and benefits might argue in favor of a slower, more steady approach to reach the same goals.

What if China slides toward rule by an even yet narrower elite? Or a personalized authoritarian regime—say, something akin to Putin? Bureaucratic decision-making authority would concentrate in the hands of a few. Both at home and abroad, channels of consultation atrophy. Economic policy becomes yet more erratic, foreign relations less predictable. Distinctions between state and leader become increasingly blurred. Beijing's cadres might increasingly behave less like bureaucrats and more like mafia chiefs—using state resources to settle their own rivalries, or send spectacular signals to those who offend them.[§] Should

---

[§] In 1984, Nationalist Chinese agents arranged the assassination in California of a Taiwanese author who had written a critical biography of President Chiang Ching-kuo. In 2006, Russian security forces did the same to a noted defector in a London restaurant via radioactive poisoning. Might the 2015–2016 kidnappings of Hong Kong booksellers (including one in Thailand) who had published salacious tabloid exposés on the private lives of top Chinese leaders be a sign of a similar trajectory?

their sense of insecurity increase, state institutions might be mobilized to move increasingly large amounts of national wealth into personal bank accounts abroad—such as the Shah of Iran in the 1970s, or Ferdinand Marcos of the Philippines in the 1980s. Indeed, China's own recent history has clear precedent for this. The late twentieth century saw Nationalist officials transfer massive assets into overseas holdings, making the Kuomintang one of the wealthiest political parties in the world—assets that Taiwanese authorities are only just now beginning to try to recover.[22]

Now consider what might happen if China were to move toward *Populist Nationalism*. Just as with populist movements in the Philippines, India, and America, this would likely witness a full-throated embrace of nativism and anti-globalization. Pressure on foreign firms would likely increase. State media exposés of their failings (such as the 2014 scandals affecting McDonald's and KFC) would multiply. Closed-door threats of regulatory action used to pressure Apple and Cisco to locate more of their R&D activities in China give way to more overt economic protectionism. China's new 2016 visa classification system is used to cull the numbers of foreigners.[23] Workers accustomed to simply "getting by" with a tourist visa—Filipino maids, Nigerian traders, and American English teachers (particularly those with religious affiliations)—find police aggressively enforcing the rules. Propaganda cartoons directed at female government employees warning them to avoid falling in love with "foreign spies" (and the 2016 arrest of a Swedish NGO activist) morphs into blatant anti-foreign incitement.[24] Play such trends out sufficiently far, and a broad range of foreigners in China might find themselves thinking about issues of physical safety in ways utterly alien to their experience over the reform era (but quite familiar to Japanese who have lived through various nationalist protests in China, Western expatriates in the Middle East, or the nineteenth-century Chinese immigrants to the American West who suffered through decades of nativist discrimination and exclusion).

There is an additional angle as well. If Beijing slips toward *Populist Nationalism*, attitudes toward the 50 million ethnic Chinese in the overseas diaspora could shift as well. Back in the 1950s, China's leaders such as Zhou Enlai largely abandoned the idea that Beijing had any special role to play in protecting their rights. In part, this reflected the political priorities of the day, such as the need to establish foreign relations with Southeast Asian countries (such as Indonesia) suspicious of their Chinese minority populations. But it also reflected the fact that consistent with a realist model of politics, Beijing's new rulers viewed themselves as heads of state, not as leaders of an international ethnic chauvinist movement.

Ideological shifts are starting to throw this into question. As discussed in Chapter 4, Beijing's leaders are steadily redefining the ideological basis for their rule in an ethno-nationalist narrative rooted in Chinese history, culture, and tradition. Domestically, this is already generating rising tensions with those who fit least well into this narrative—Muslim Uighurs, Chinese Christians, and Cantonese-speaking Hong Kongers. More aggressively promote *Populist Nationalism*, and difficult international questions present themselves as well. Does Beijing view itself as having a special claim over the Chinese diaspora abroad? If so, what is it? Merely establishing overseas Confucius Centers and promoting Chinese language education? Or might it see itself as having (or be driven by popular pressure to take) a special role in defending the legal interests of ethnic Chinese abroad? Tactically, might Beijing seek to stir up tensions between overseas Chinese communities and national governments—just as Moscow has attempted to mobilize nationalist sentiment among ethnic Russians in the "near abroad" of Ukraine and the Baltics?[25]

U.S. FOREIGN POLICY TOWARD CHINA

All the above is occurring as American foreign policy is entering massive flux.

Since 1979, America's China policy has followed regular and predictable lines. Cooperate on areas of common interest (1980s, countering the Soviet Union; 2010s, addressing climate change). Push back on areas of conflict (trade disputes). But do not allow tensions in particular areas (such as human rights) to overwhelm the broader bilateral relationship. Above all, focus on drawing China into the world. Entice Beijing to join international institutions and norms of global governance established by the United States and its allies in the wake of World War II.

Peruse works penned by American officials charged with handling Sino-U.S. relations and you find near-uniform commitment to these principles.[26] Sure, each proposes slightly tweaking the details. Downplay human rights yet further. Strengthen relationships with regional allies. Actively pursue freedom of navigation operations in the South China Sea. But each sees America's interests as deeply intertwined with upholding the broad parameters of the Sino-U.S. relationship established since 1979.

However, the foundations of this relationship are now cracking. Populist political uprisings in the West are undermining the existing international liberal order. America is now led by a president who openly denigrates core tenets that have governed Washington's global foreign policy since 1945—economic commitments to free trade, strategic guarantees to allies in NATO and East Asia, and ideological support for democratic governance worldwide. China is also re-examining its relationship with the existing international order. As the reform era ends, openness to outside influences—whether it be foreign investment, culture, or education—is no longer as attractive to Beijing. Nor does upholding existing international norms seem as necessary. China's leaders are steadily rewriting strategic facts on the ground with massive land reclamation projects in the disputed Spratly Islands. And they are toying with creating alternative multilateral institutions (such as the Asian Infrastructure Investment Bank) to replace American-dominated ones.

At time of writing (summer 2017), the entire post-1945 international order is at severe risk of going under—either from inattention or intent. This could easily suck four decades of Sino-U.S. relations along in the undertow. On the one hand, the first few months of President Donald Trump's administration have been marked by chaos, particularly in foreign policy. Large numbers of senior positions in the bureaucracy remain unfilled, key decision-making authority appears to be vested a small handful of family members and courtiers who fall in and out of presidential favor with distressing rapidity, while Trump's own early-morning Twitter pronouncements inject a perpetual sense of uncertainty as to what—if anything—American policy actually is. On the other, the administration flirts with a more dramatic break in U.S.-China relations. Threats of a trade war repeatedly resurface. And Trump has casually toyed with Beijing's red-button issue—Taiwan—as a card to obtain concessions from Beijing on trade and North Korea. Ahead lie entirely uncharted waters.

It is beyond this book's scope to try to outline a new American foreign policy for the twenty-first century. And any specific policy proposals related to China risk being dramatically out of date by time of publication (in spring 2018). Key agencies might very well not exist. The State Department faces massive proposed budget cuts of roughly 30 percent. The Bureau of Democracy, Human Rights, and Labor—responsible since 1977 for promoting democracy abroad and raising the cases of dissidents worldwide—could be gutted by an isolationist American administration uninterested in international human rights treaties and norms. Others could see their mandates dramatically altered. The Office of the United States Trade Representative now finds itself pivoting away from America's decades-long support for international free trade, and turning in a neo-mercantilist direction. Changing attitudes in Beijing will also undermine bastions of the Sino-U.S. relationship. For example, people-to-people ties will likely be collateral damage as a deepening chill renders a wide swath of foreign NGOs and colleges—many that have worked in China for decades—politically suspect.

Given such uncertainties, this section will confine itself to identifying several general principles to help to guide American policy as China's reform era ends.

• International engagement is in America's interest

Given the current popular mood (and the President's tweets), one can easily imagine America's foreign policy starting to slide dramatically. Citizen discontent with globalization (both free trade and immigration) fuses with latent suspicion of foreign interventionism (particularly in the wake of lengthy military interventions in Iraq and Afghanistan). Isolationism returns. Economically, high tariff barriers are erected to protect U.S. markets. Politically, Washington backs out of existing international commitments. NATO is fatally weakened as key allies lose confidence in America's reliability. The Monroe Doctrine is reasserted. Sphere of influences are tacitly recognized for Russia (in Eastern Europe) and China (in East Asia).

This would be very, very bad.

Start with a cold-blooded evaluation of core foreign policy interests. America's are twofold. First, a peaceful and stable international order. This protects the safety of the American homeland. It provides an environment where states can cooperate to build international institutions to ward off a range of collective non-state threats—whether terrorism, climate change, or infectious disease. It also protects against the rise of hegemonic state actors that might threaten the United States. Second, an open and fair global economic system. International trade has steadily risen as a proportion of the American economy over the past six decades, from 9 percent (1960) to 30 percent (2014).[27] Over 11 million jobs in the United States are supported by exports abroad.[28]

Retreat from the world, and bad things will happen. Foreign affairs aren't like those Las Vegas tourist ads. What happens overseas doesn't stay overseas. Eventually it comes back to bite you. It has happened before. In the decades after World War I, America abandoned the international architecture that the White House itself had helped create (the League of Nations) and implemented high tariff barriers (the 1930 Hawley-Smoot Tariff) to protect its own markets. The result? Global economic depression. Rise of radical ideologies—both at home and abroad. Worsening international tensions. Finally, a steady escalation in military conflicts abroad that ultimately endanger America's core interests, thereby sucking the United States into a global conflict.

Since 1945, America's engagement has helped avoid that fate in Asia. Pull back, and early-twenty-first-century East Asia starts to look a lot like early-twentieth-century Europe. Escalating strategic rivalries between powers such as China, Japan, and India. Rapid development of nuclear weapons by Japan and South Korea, with other nations likely to follow. Shifting alliances (and spreading proxy wars) as major nations seek to draw smaller powers to their sides. Think this impossible? Just look what is beginning to unfold in the Mideast as the region steadily devolves into a three-way struggle for influence between Iran, Turkey, and Saudi Arabia.

Strictly on strategic grounds alone, America has a deep interest in avoiding such an outcome in East Asia, the most populous region of the world and one with which our own economy is deeply tied. And in pursuing that goal, it is crucial to stay committed to the existing international architecture—the trade treaties, military alliances, and diplomatic relationships that have been at the center of America's Asia policy in the postwar era.

- **Regime change should not be U.S. policy . . .**

Coming years will likely see Sino-U.S. relations worsen dramatically over issues such as Taiwan and trade. Tensions will be exacerbated as China's domestic politics steadily degrade. Increasingly, some in Washington will be tempted to identify Beijing's rulers as the source of all problems. Calls will multiply for America to directly promote their overthrow, peacefully or otherwise. On the outskirts of the political spectrum, an assortment of groups committed to regime change in China will begin to coalesce, similar to those that emerged in prior decades focused on Cuba or Iran. Frustrated by decades of international neglect, some Chinese dissidents will lend their voices to the cause, seeing any hope of disrupting the increasing repression faced by their friends and family at home as better than none.

It would be a mistake for Washington policymakers to align themselves with such proposals. If the current regime in Beijing falls suddenly, it is likely to be replaced by something yet more radical. Think the emergence of ISIS from the rubble of collapsed authoritarian regimes in Iraq and Syria is a geopolitical problem from hell? Just wait until you are dealing with a parallel one in a country fifty times larger. Moreover, even the perception of direct U.S. involvement in promoting such a result is likely to ensure that the surging nationalist resentment that boils to the surface in the wake of a system-wide social and political collapse is focused directly at America itself.

Does this mean that American authorities should back away from public advocacy of democracy and human rights in China? Not at all. But they do need to seriously remember how decades of active efforts to engineer the overthrow of various regimes in Latin America and the Middle East fueled widespread anti-American sentiment in those regions that has percolated for decades.

• . . . but neither should support for the existing regime

But the flip side is also true. The United States should not simply slip into an easy embrace of authoritarian regimes abroad, whether in China or elsewhere.

This isn't driven by moral qualms, but rather hard realism. When the United States ties its destiny to a repressive regime abroad, it ends up ensuring that emerging popular discontent in that country ends up assuming an anti-American flair. Back Cuba's dictator Batista during the 1950s, and what do you get? Castro's revolution. Support the Shah in the 1960s and 1970s, and the militant youth of the Iranian Revolution end up targeting not just him, but the United States as well. The same story has played out in China as well. America's continued backing for Chiang Kai-shek's corrupt regime in the late 1940s—well past any sell-by date mandated by strategic wartime necessity—meant that rising domestic opposition to Chiang's Nationalist rule was highly likely to view the United States as a key part of the problem.

Today, the irony is that some of those who cut their teeth improving relations between the United States and China in the 1970s are at risk of repeating the same error. Just as American figures such as mid-twentieth-century publisher Henry Luce clung to a false equivalence between "China" and Chiang Kai-shek, so too do some American figures today seek to equate the Chinese Communist Party with "China." Particularly as China's reform era ends, as its leaders regress into a narrower, personalized authoritarian form of rule, and as unrest rises, the danger is that this myopic equivalence will render them incapable of perceiving rising social and pressures in China. Worse, it may render them open to political blowback.

This may seem difficult to believe. After all, isn't the United States currently one of the major *critics* of China's one-Party rule? But hit the fast-forward button on history for a moment. Examine the situation from a post-crisis perspective in which China's latent tensions have erupted. With China's elite having stashed their money in Los Angeles real estate, their children in American private schools, and having obtained green cards via investments in real estate projects run by companies owned by the families of top American officials, exactly how will China's discontented view the United States?

For the United States, this suggests the need to maintain a level of strategic distance from an authoritarian regime that is likely to experience internal problems. Pay close attention to China's changing domestic politics. Be aware that something else could come. And if does, remember to leave space at the international table for China, rather than shutting it out in the cold.

- **Liberalism at home**

Last, America must uphold its own liberal values at home. It must find ways to address its own pressing problems—political dysfunction and economic inequality—while holding firm to bedrock principles of democracy, free speech, and constitutional governance in the face of rising populist pressures.

This isn't merely a domestic issue. It is also a foreign policy one. America's strength is not measured simply by the size of its GDP, nor by how many carrier battle groups it deploys. Historically, the United States has enjoyed enormous soft power as a result of its liberal values. Ideals of freedom and liberty hold immense attraction around the world. Despite violating these ideals at home (segregation) and abroad (support for Latin American dictators during the Cold War), America has traditionally represented an alternative (sometimes imagined, often real) to the ethnic oppression and crony capitalism plaguing many corners of the globe. This has given the United States an outsized ability to rally allies to its side in times of crisis, promote international standards, and attract the best and brightest immigrants from around the world. America's openness also gives it a worldwide appeal enjoyed by few other countries. Others might be as wealthy (Japan), militarily advanced (Russia), or provide better social services to their citizens (Sweden). But it is American films that are consumed by a global audience and American colleges to which many around the world aspire. Abandon America's own liberal values and principles, and we throw away one of our strongest diplomatic tools. We weaken ourselves at home. And we erode our influence abroad.

In particular, the United States must remain an open, tolerant society. A swing back toward anti-immigrant nativism would be exceptionally bad. America has largely managed to avoid the balkanization that has troubled European or Southeast Asian politics—where various immigrant communities (and their descendants) are never fully accepted (or view themselves) as part of mainstream society. Historically, that has simply not been the long-term trajectory in the United States, precisely because immigrants and their children see themselves as fully American, with a future in this country. Drop that, and all of those assumptions go out the window. If America itself slips away from its liberal ideals into a more narrowly tribal self-definition, it could suddenly find that the strident ethno-nationalist propaganda being peddled by external actors—whether by Russia, China, or various extremist Islamic groups—starts to find an increasingly receptive audience among communities within the United States. Play that out far enough, and America's own social fabric starts to tear apart.

CONCLUSION

As horrible as it might be to contemplate, one also now needs to start seriously thinking about worst-case scenarios. Suppose some or all of the above principles are breached on the American side—either because of a willful desire to break the status quo, or as a result of a protracted period of haphazard American foreign policy. Simultaneously, China's own domestic politics continue to spiral downhill, with escalating levels of internal repression and unrest. What could happen?

Quite likely: a radicalization of viewpoints in *both* China and America. Extreme nationalist views would begin to crowd out moderate ones. Within China, foreign-educated officials would be subjected to tight political controls. Blacklists would spread. Scholars and entrepreneurs with overseas connections would be made the target of nationalist attacks in the press. In the United States, "China" or "Chinese" would start to replace "immigrants" or "Muslims" as bogeymen in populist right-wing social media. Ordinary educational exchanges would come under suspicion; some lambasted as unpatriotic. Hate crimes against Americans of Chinese ancestry would surge.

Of course, this is not unprecedented. Both the nineteenth and twentieth centuries saw outbreaks of rampant nativist sentiment sweep both the United States (Chinese Exclusion Act, McCarthyism) and China (Boxer Rebellion, Cultural Revolution). As John Pomfret details in his recent work *The Beautiful Country and the Middle Kingdom* (2016), such episodes have regularly marred the 250-year-long relationship between China and the United States, which has swung between infatuation and deep disdain on both sides.

The United States and China might now be entering yet another decades-long slide into nativism and mutual distrust. If that is the case, it is imperative for the "moderate middle" in both countries—those who do not succumb to the knee-jerk tendency to demonize the other—to start thinking through how to best preserve some residual level of mutual understanding between the two countries and peoples amid what is likely to be a very long and bitterly cold diplomatic winter. For it is these efforts that will plant the seeds for our children and grandchildren to in time rebuild the Sino-American relationship on the ashes of the current one.

CONCLUSION

古之 . . . 欲治其国者，先齐其家；欲齐其家者，先修其身

The ancients . . . wishing to govern their states well, first set their families in order; wishing to set their families in order, they first cultivated their persons.

—大学 (The Book of Great Learning, ca. 500 BC)

The passage above, taken from one of China's classics, is deeply familiar to generations of imperial scholars. It embodies the core of Confucian governance. Instill virtue in the ruler, and it will radiate out progressively to set things right in society at large.

Now try repeating that to your friends and family. If they are like many Americans, they will just think it odd. Some will perceive it as pre-industrial moralizing totally unsuited to the twenty-first century. (Did the successes and failures of President Obama's administration really hinge on his relationship with his wife?) Others will read it as an amorphous call for top-down authoritarian rule, with vague remonstrations about proper behavior replacing meaningful checks on official power.

But it is possible to interpret it in another way—one entirely consistent with our own cultural biases and understanding of how states work in the world of today. A nation's governance is not isolated from the society around it. It is built upon deep-seated patterns and practices developed through billions of interactions between citizens themselves and with local authorities. When that newly elected councilwoman takes office in your city, she isn't a blank slate. She is drawing on norms of behavior (how to chair a meeting, deal with dissent, and push her plans through) that she acquired previously serving (for example) as head of your local Parent-Teachers Association (PTA). And when that group of gangly, red-faced high-school students stands in front of that PTA to make their first public presentation in their lives (say, regarding a planned bake sale to fund their spring class excursion), that isn't coming out of the blue. It is the reflection of yet earlier dynamics—the encouragement of a parent, the inspiration of a teacher, the support of their youth pastor—who helped them realize their potential and channel their energies toward appropriate forms of civic participation.

Behind their neoclassical facades, these are the core foundations on which all of Washington's grand institutions of governance are built. The fate of a nation's political system is inextricably intertwined with what is happening in society generally. Still doubt this? Take the steady erosion of America's civil society and social capital since the mid-twentieth century, outlined in Robert Putnam's work *Bowling Alone* (2000). Add in three decades of stagnant real wages for most American workers, and the resulting toll that has exacted on their families and children. What do you get? The rise of Trumpist populism—subverting mainstream political channels of participation in favor of mass rallies and late-night Twitter rants—as a challenge to existing U.S. political institutions.[*]

The tie between governance and society exists worldwide. Governments in Beijing, Paris, and Tehran are similarly rooted in deep-seated norms and practices arising out of their own societies. And as the reform era ends, the core problem China faces is bubbling to the

---

[*] Indeed, to the extent that President Trump's administration is a heavily family affair, relying greatly on his children and their spouses, perhaps the Confucian adage cited above has even more direct relevance to American governance than one might think at first glance!

surface: weak levels of institutionalization extending throughout society and state alike.

External manifestations of control are not in question. One cannot open a drawer in the office of a Chinese Party committee without being deluged by documents from higher-level authorities. Set up new evaluation mechanisms for officials. Warn Internet service providers to take down articles. Merge bureaucratic organs. Study the most recent speeches by Politburo leaders. For Stein Ringen, these amount to a *controlocracy*—an elaborate dictatorship unprecedented in size and complexity in human history.

But look behind the shiny nameplates and imposing government buildings. For all of China's surface stability, there is a deep absence of institutionalized norms. Sit in a Beijing café and watch overburdened parents try to deal with an upset child. Observe teachers struggle how to motivate students. Follow official reactions to a mass petition by farmers angered by the perceived failure of state officials to provide adequate compensation for seizure of their lands. All too often, the response is one of two things: resort to top-down control, or simple concession. Instruct local authorities to cave in and buy off the most vocal protestors, regardless of the underlying merit of their complaints. Send in security forces to bludgeon others into subservience. Steer students back toward mechanical rote memorization of the required answers for the *gaokao*. Hand the child off to an indulgent nanny (or ship them off to a boarding school abroad) to gratify his or her every whim. Yes, stability is maintained. But at what cost? What are the lessons learned? Pro-forma compliance with rules. Deep cynicism toward structures of governance that, after all, one has had little input in creating. If China is a controlocracy, it is one whose foundations are sunk into the shifting sands of a chaotic, deinstitutionalized society.

Building real institutions is not a question of a Party secretary (or parent) pounding his desk to mandate better systems of control. Nor is it a matter of issuing more bombastic exhortations of belief. Rather, it requires repeated practice on the part of the child, the student, and the citizen. It requires *agency*—a regular back-and-forth between ruled and ruler alike through organized channels of governance (whether democratic or otherwise) that build popular faith in them as channels to resolve grievances and manage social tensions. The reform era was

China's golden opportunity to slowly construct such institutions. It failed to do so. Gradualist reforms that Chinese officials and citizens themselves had pursued—both inside and outside the existing Party-state—were slowly choked by an increasingly toxic atmosphere. And the consequences of that will steadily play themselves out over the decades to come.

One hates to end on a depressing note. And since some will undoubtedly attempt to frame this book as calling for the "Westernization" of China, one final word is in order.

The Introduction invoked the Three Gorges Dam as an analogy for Beijing's late reform-era response to escalating social and political pressures: steadily constructing increasingly massive top-down bulwarks.

Now, there is an alternative choice.[1] Just outside the bustling provincial capital of Chengdu lies one of the oldest and most unique water diversion and irrigation projects in the world. Dujiangyan both tames the Min tributary of the Yangtze river and diverts its waters into a complex set of channels that irrigate the fertile fields of the humid Sichuan basin. Completed around 256 BC, Dujiangyan halted the regular floods that had ravaged the region. The regular supply of water for agriculture laid the foundation for the economic and strategic expansion of state power into southwestern China.

The project's most unique engineering aspect is the lack of any dams. It instead relies entirely on natural gravitational forces and the local topography to divert water into an elegantly constructed set of channels. Unlike the Three Gorges Dam or the levees along the Yellow River, which rely on the overwhelming force and weight of massive man-made barriers to restrain surging floodwaters, Dujiangyan channels them instead into a cascading network of canals, streams, and ditches to water the rice fields that feed China.[2]

What Dujiangyan represents—both practically and metaphorically—is an alternative model of Chinese governance. It represents the possibility of constructing institutions that channel building pressures (whether hydrological or social), rather than leading them to accumulate dangerously. It is authentically Chinese. And it is also more stable. Despite being at the epicenter of the massive 2008 Wenchuan earthquake, Dujiangyan waterworks survived undamaged, with little flooding to nearby residents.[3] In contrast, the Three Gorges Dam (and the weight of the water behind it) appears to actually itself be *altering* the seismic profile of the surrounding land, producing an upsurge in earthquakes and landslides.

All too often, China's future is posed as a choice between "domestic" versus "foreign" models. It is not. Instead, the question for its leaders and citizens alike is, What version of "China" do they wish to pursue? The Three Gorges Dam or Dujiangyan? The open, cosmopolitan empire of Tang, or the closed, ethnocentric one of the Ming? The gradualist reformers of the late twentieth (and nineteenth) centuries, or the fiery radicals who emerge when those are frustrated?

Over the coming decades, China will struggle mightily with these choices. And as it does, many will look back at their own history for answers. When they do, hopefully they will examine that of the reform era, in search of lessons from paths not taken.

EPILOGUE

After finishing the original manuscript in 2016, I hesitated on the title—*End of an Era*. Edgy and provocative? Sure. But arguing that China's reform era was over…was that perhaps too much? In 2019, it has now become conventional wisdom.

Not just among foreigners. In late 2017, Xi Jinping enshrined himself by name in the charter of the Chinese Communist Party (CCP). Doing so was a major sign in itself. Only Deng and Mao had been similarly commemorated.[1] In translation, the phrase Xi selected to designate his ideology as a new guiding principle for CCP rule sounds stilted and odd. "Xi Jinping Thought on Socialism with Chinese Characteristics for a New Era?" What does that really mean? But recognize how carefully chosen that is. That language—now engraved in the state constitution, recited faithfully in the state media and regurgitated in every mandatory political study session for Party cadres—emphasizes that China is entering a "new era" (*xin shidai*). The signal is utterly clear. Mao founded the People's Republic of China. Deng launched the reform era. And now Xi is in charge.

I had mentally prepared myself to be pelted with brickbats from academic colleagues who disagreed with me. What I had not expected was for China's top leader to publicly announce that, Yes, the reform era is over, and we are moving on to something new.

All of the major trends flagged in Chapters 2-4 are deepening.[2]

Economically, China is slowing down. Official figures show GDP growth unerringly attaining (or slightly exceeding) state-mandated targets (6.5% in 2018, downgraded to a band between 6.0% and 6.5% in 2019). But independent estimates show a more significant decline, with some finding the growth rate falling below 5% since 2015. Domestic woes were exacerbated in 2018 as Sino-U.S. trade tensions spiraled towards an all-out trade war. The Trump administration imposed tariffs on $250 billion worth of Chinese exports to the United States (and threatened hundreds of more), while Beijing responded in a tit-for-tat manner. By winter 2018-19, this had contributed to the sense of a more dramatic slowdown. Car sales plunged for the first time in two decades, resulting in widespread job losses in auto manufacturing. Waves of lay-offs washed over China's once-dynamic tech sector.

Demographically, China's fundamentals are worsening. Birth rates briefly rose after Beijing relaxed population planning policies in 2015, allowing families to have two children. But they have since plummeted. As in other countries, high housing costs and an uncertain future have prompted Chinese millennials to reconsider plans to start families. In 2018, China recorded 15.23 million births—a drop of two million compared with just the year before, and the lowest figure in over half a century. Such numbers amplify the long-term challenges (labor markets, stability of pension funds) that China will confront as it rapidly ages over the coming decades.

There is now a deeper recognition of the U-turn in China's economic policy. Back in 2016, some still placed hope in Beijing's repeated promises for deeper market reforms. Few do now. Leading economists such as Nicholas Lardy have gone from writing books such as *Markets Over Mao: The Rise of Private Business in China* (2014) to *The State Strikes Back: The End of Economic Reform in China?* (2019). Xi's commitment to national industrial policy and an expanded role for state-owned enterprises (SOEs) have come into sharper focus. And the resulting policies—such as a massive increase in the share of bank lending going to SOEs—are slowly asphyxiating China's private sector.

So China's era of rapid growth is fading into the past, and Beijing is steadily departing from reform-era policies. Does this mean a crisis is imminent? No. Beijing still has levers it can pull to ward off immediate problems. And it is. Early 2019 saw central officials flood China's economy with yet another boost of fiscal spending. Growth picked up. Markets rose. But the effectiveness of such short-term measures is increasingly declining with each use. And they amount to merely kicking longer-term problems (rising debt levels, steadily deteriorating performance of SOEs) down the road. Sooner or later, the bill will come due.

Ideologically, China is closing up. What limited space had emerged in culture, media, and civil society during the reform era continues to shrink. This is directly linked to Xi's effort to reassert the absolute primacy of the Party in state and society alike (memorably inscribed into the official CCP charter in 2017 as "the Party leads everything").

Pressure has intensified in colleges. In summer 2018, authorities launched a "patriotic education" campaign at intellectuals, aimed at ensuring their loyalty. Mandatory ideological courses for students are multiplying, university centers devoted to the study of "Xi Jinping Thought" proliferating. Professors who once casually commented on China's social or legal problems in their classrooms are falling silent, fearful of both the video cameras newly installed in lecture halls and the official encouragement for students to report on teachers with "negative" attitudes. Controls are tightening on even those institutions that had once prided themselves on enjoying a somewhat looser touch. In one particularly clear signal, central authorities parachuted an official from the Ministry of State Security (China's version of the KGB or FBI) in the fall of 2018 to run China's top college, Peking University.

Controls over spiritual belief are also tightening. Since the 2016 national work conference noted in Chapter 4, "sinicization" of religion has emerged as a top Party priority. A flurry of activities has followed. Mandatory flag-raising ceremonies at Buddhist and Daoist temples. The 2018 provisional accord with the Vatican (with the Holy See apparently conceding some power over the nomination of bishops). And a dramatic escalation of pressure on faiths viewed as "foreign"—particularly Christianity and Islam. This book noted the 2013-16 crackdown on churches in Zhejiang. That indeed seems to have been the precursor for a national campaign. Major unregistered churches in Guangzhou, Beijing, and Chongqing were shuttered in the fall of 2018, with pastors and worshippers spirited off and held incommunicado for lengthy periods of time. And Beijing has signaled it will go yet further. State religious officials are now calling for Protestant churches to rid themselves of "foreign influences" and incorporate aspects of "traditional Chinese culture" into their liturgy, music, and architecture. A re-translation of the Bible is even in the works—with the aim of ensuring that the core teachings of Christianity itself are consistent with Party ideology. All of this raises the very real likelihood that space for religious belief could deteriorate yet further. This is particularly true given developments in western China, where Party authorities have escalated repression of Islam to a magnitude comparable to (or even exceeding) the Cultural Revolution (see below).

Even in private companies, Beijing has begun reviving once-moribund Party cells, pressuring foreign joint ventures to formally confirm their role in operations and management. Demands for yet more extreme moves have begun circulating. In 2018, radical leftist voices in academia and social media seized on Beijing's renewed support for SOEs and called for private entrepreneurs to retire from the stage. Amid viral online debate, one of China's richest men did just that. In September 2018, Jack Ma (discussed in Chapter 2) announced he was stepping down as the head of China's top tech firm Alibaba to focus on philanthropic endeavors. Many saw a clear omen. After all, who better to read the political tea leaves of a Party increasingly jealous of any and all players—and select a propitious moment to exit—than an immensely wealthy businessman with a rock star-like following among youth?[3] Deep uncertainty echoed in the ranks of China's private sector. Facing rising U.S.-China trade tensions and an increasingly uncertain economic outlook, Beijing decided to try to temporarily quell rising fears, with Xi issuing a series of soothing words in November regarding the place of private enterprise in China's development, even as he continued to affirm the crucial role of state companies.

Superficially, China's leaders continue to ritually gesture toward their socialist ideological roots. Party leaders greeted the 200th anniversary of Marx's birth in 2018 with elaborate fanfare. Officials were required to reread the Communist Manifesto. For children, a new animated cartoon series sought to bring to life Marx's life as a youth.

But Beijing's nominally Communist leaders today aren't remotely interested in class revolution. They certainly do not want workers rising up. Indeed, fears of unrest are partially behind the ongoing mass evictions targeting migrant laborers in the capital, resulting in Beijing's population actually shrinking since 2016—the first time in decades. One irony of China today is that the worst fear of its Communist rulers today is that there actually might be a labor leader somewhere out there capable of organizing the proletariat to take action. That is precisely why Chinese officials aggressively moved in the summer and fall of 2018 to crush a string of wildcat Marxist student groups in Chinese colleges who had started to take some of those required political readings just a little *too* seriously and actually reach out to provide aid groups of disaffected workers with labor grievances. Party leaders remember their own history, and they are determined not to let anyone else repeat it.

That raises a key question. What exactly does the Party stand for? What does it represent ideologically? And as Chapter 4 notes, this is still in flux. Underneath those hoary Marxist slogans regularly trotted out in official media, it is slowly pivoting back to a more narrowly ethno-nationalist definition of self under the rubric of "traditional culture" [*chuantong wenhua*]. Quotations from Confucius proliferate in both official speeches and mandatory ideological classes for students. And just as in the Maoist era, the Party's ideology looks to be increasingly inseparable from the personality of the top leader himself—with the *Xuexi Qiangguo* smartphone app featuring Xi's speeches and thoughts as a 21st century stand-in for those 1960s-era little red books filled with quotations from Mao.[4]

Politically, the partially institutionalized norms of the reform era continue to erode. As predicted, China is steadily sliding back toward a more personalized authoritarian regime, with power highly concentrated in the hands of a single ruler.

Thanks to editorial tolerance for last-minute edits, Chapter 3 highlighted a crucial step in this process: the 19th Party Congress in fall 2017. Party leaders avoided naming a political successor to Xi as he entered his second (and theoretically final) five-year term as Party general secretary. As noted above, they also simultaneously elevated his place in the Party's ideological pantheon, vaulting him well ahead of his immediate predecessors in importance, with phrasing that resonated with terms once reserved for Mao alone.

Such moves paved the way for the 2018 constitutional amendments removing the two-term limit on Xi's role as state president. Adopted in 1982, that limit had been an explicit reform-era norm supported by figures such as Deng to steer China away from the lifetime single-man rule of the Maoist era. Removal has cleared the way for its resumption. Other shifts have similarly strengthened Xi's other two roles as Party chief and military head (and correspondingly weakened any remaining norms of collective leadership), such as requiring Politburo members to make regular work reports to Xi himself (in his role of CCP General Secretary).

Since the book's release, two other crucial norms have visibly crumbled.

The first is a shift within the middle levels of the Chinese state: the "re-Partyization" of the bureaucracy. Remember that the reform era saw Beijing back away from the radical Maoist years in which slogan-spouting Party cadres were charged with absolute leadership at every level of government. The 1980s saw responsibility for day-to-day management of state affairs—in fields ranging from agriculture to law—steadily turned over to technocrats within the bureaucracy. This is now eroding as well.

Take the government reorganization plan launched in 2018. It eliminated a wide swath of state bureaus and fused them with Party organs. For example, the state civil service commission was folded into the Party Organization bureau; the State Administration of Religious Affairs merged into the Party's United Front Work department. Or examine closely the 2018 constitutional amendments creating a new national supervisory commission. This established a new body—effectively the Party's disciplinary inspection committee in new form—as an oversight organ for all state employees, rather than merely Party members.

On first glance, these might seem but mundane tweaks to boring organization charts. Who cares what happens to some mid-level paper-pushers? But this misses the point. This is how the partial distinction between Party and state that gradually emerged over the course of China's reform era steadily collapses back into a tighter unity. It is how government technocrats whose currency lies in their technical expertise steadily lose ground to Party political hacks attuned to whatever prevailing political line happens to emerge from Beijing. Naturally, such shifts deeply reflect Xi's drive to return the Party to the driver's seat everywhere in state and society.

Why does this matter? Those who recall China's past readily see danger. They can think back to the Anti-Rightist campaign to see how Beijing's current move to widen the sweep of Party discipline inspectors, coupled with their increased emphasis on targeting "political deviation," will shut down the remaining space within universities for any real discussion of the problems facing the country. And they can remember yet more radical periods such as the Cultural Revolution in which experts or intellectuals were totally marginalized by political toadies willing to spout whatever nonsense happened to catch the eyes of their superiors, with disastrous consequences for the nation at large.

Even those unfamiliar with China can appreciate the risks. Bad things happen when your politics start dissolving your core institutions of governance. Policymaking becomes erratic. Decisions increasingly depend on the whims of individual leaders. And the ability of officials to identify and respond to crises steadily degrades. Take the United States. Sure, the machinery of American government is far more institutionalized than in China. But reflect on the turmoil that envelops one federal agency after another as President Trump regularly purges officials deemed disloyal. Look at discussions (in spring 2019) over who should run the Federal Reserve (the U.S. central bank). Actual financial experts? Or nakedly partisan political loyalists whose priorities include ensuring Trump's reelection? Examine ongoing struggles over what should guide the actions of American immigration officials. Settled court decisions? Or the dictates of whatever 30-year-old political advisor happens to have the president's ear on a given Tuesday? Suddenly, all those vicious ideological struggles that wracked 1950s China over whether officials should be "red" (having the correct political ideology) versus "expert" (technical knowledge) suddenly seem a lot less arcane. Indeed, they acquire ominous overtones for your own system. You don't even have to change the color coding.

The second crucial shift is the intensification of repression in China's arid western region of Xinjiang. Of course, fears of ethnic unrest among Xinjiang's largely minority population have meant that Beijing has always wielded a heavier hand there. And as the hardback version of this book noted, police controls escalated significantly after an explosion of interethnic rioting between Muslim Uighur and Han Chinese residents in 2009.

But since 2017, there has been yet another qualitative leap in repression. Specifically, Beijing has constructed a web of political re-education camps into which some 10% of the Uighur population—estimates range from hundreds of thousands to up to 1.5 million people—have been pre-emptively disappeared. State efforts to eradicate Uighur identity and religion are escalating. Mosques are being shuttered, Han "volunteers" organized to physically live in Uighur homes to observe and report on their internal family practices. (Does the son have a beard? Is pork served at dinner?).

Naturally, this is a major international human rights issue. It raises frightening parallels with other cases of mass ethnic detention elsewhere in the world—ranging from the U.S. internment of Japanese-Americans during World War II to early-stage Nazi concentration camps in the 1930s. And it has begun to attract global attention. Once limited to Western human rights groups and United Nations officials, condemnation of China has begun to rise from new directions, including the Turkish foreign ministry and Indonesian Islamist political movements.

But Beijing's radical intensification of hardline policies in Xinjiang also represents the disintegration of yet another crucial domestic political norm. Remember how social politicization operated in pre-reform China. Mao sought to exploit cracks in Chinese society. He fanned the flames of internal division to strengthen his own personal power and that of the Party. Broad swaths of the population were preemptively labeled for having "bad" class backgrounds, or for having family ties overseas. Not only were they regularly denied benefits such as college education, but they were periodically dragged out to be savaged in public—convenient internal enemies who could both be scapegoated for social ills and rallied against in the name of national unity.

That largely ended with the reform era. Leaders such as Deng Xiaoping sought to paper over the cracks in Chinese society in the name of stability and economic development. Sure, Beijing still came down like a hammer on individual dissidents in the 1980s and 1990s. But the practice of labeling large swathes of the population as politically "unreliable" faded. No longer were groups—say, the children of landless peasants against those from landlord families—pitted against one another in an us-versus-them, life-or-death struggle.

But in China today, not only can you see specific Maoist tools (political re-education camps, public confessions) actually re-materialize before your eyes, but you can also now easily envision some of the broader policies (social politicization, manipulation of internal divisions) returning and steadily engulfing wider and wider segments of society. Indeed, reports indicate some of these practices are starting to migrate out of Xinjiang and to neighboring provinces that also have heavily Muslim, but not Uighur populations. And once you see that, it is quite easy to envision how some within the Party bureaucracy could start to adopt some of the same mentality (if not necessarily exactly the same practices) to other groups deemed a potential problem—say, the large Christian population. And things just start to spin from there. . . .

Chapter 1 specifically flagged two reform-era norms that remained yet unbroken. The first: no resort to bottom-up mobilization. As of spring 2019, that still holds. There is zero indication that Xi or other top leaders have any desire to call people out into the streets. That lesson of the Cultural Revolution, at least, still runs deep. The second was "the ideological redefinition of China remains embryonic. . . . [S]tate television continues to promote interethnic harmony rather than rank appeals to majority-group chauvinism." Technically, that is still true. Chinese state media outlets still mouth the same tired platitudes of interethnic harmony, presenting developments in Xinjiang as but the establishment of vocational institutes directed at reintegrating a few bad elements back into society.

But look at Beijing's new policies in western China. And watch some of the more unsavory corners of China's internet as nationalism, Islamophobia, and conspiracy theories morph and merge under the tacit gaze of Beijing's censors. That second point is beginning to give way. The embryo is growing into a fetus.

So what does this all mean? I stick by the framework in Chapter 6. In the short term, China will continue to slide toward an increasingly hardline, increasingly personalized authoritarian regime. Elements of China's totalitarian Maoist past will steadily re-emerge. But this will not be an unending progression toward a dystopian Orwellian future of perfect—and permanent—control. In the long term, this is a recipe for the revival of the kind of internal political instability that many observers had thought was dead and buried since the beginning of the reform era.

Any time authors make such statements, it is important to ask them to back them up with predictions. That also helps keep us honest over time. So let me set out a number of developments I expect to see in the short term.

ECONOMICS

Rising Internal Stress. China is exiting an era marked by an ever-expanding economic pie. This will severely test Beijing. Hard budget constraints—and difficult tradeoffs—loom in the near future. Guns or butter? Faced with an impending tsunami of elderly baby boomers, do you cut back on those cushy pensions promised to retirees? Revamp your plans for increased military spending? Curb the massive flow of funds into domestic security operations in Xinjiang and elsewhere? Short term or long term? Continue relying on adrenaline bursts of debt-fueled stimulus spending to maintain growth levels and keep property prices high? Or risk immediate pain in order to set the economy on a sounder foundation for the future?

IDEOLOGY

Steady Redefinition. Party ideology will continue to mutate. Increasingly, authorities will clothe their Leninist one-Party system in the ideological garb of classical China and the rhetoric of Confucianism. Marxism will not disappear overnight. But its core—a class-based revolutionary discourse with Western roots (and a bearded German face)—is just too incongruous with Beijing's current direction. The CCP today is not a revolutionary force. It is a reactionary one striving to preserve the status quo at all costs. Expect the reddish tones of Marxism to steadily fade into the yellow hues of imperial China.

Revived Scope. China's reform era saw widespread de-politicization of society. In culture, academia, and media alike, the ideological controls of the Maoist era receded. But now the tides have turned. One by one, fields once regarded as marginal are being submerged by intensifying demands for Party control and ideological correctness. To date, this has primarily involved areas of *public* endeavor—such as law or journalism—driven by Beijing's omnipresent fear of social unrest. But as such trends continue, expect these pressures to increasingly lap up against the *private* lives of citizens. Choices once regarded as mundane—say, the decision of low-level civil servants to send their children to international high schools in preparation for college abroad—might start to be regarded in a more politicized light.

Particularly watch Party attitudes toward the role of women in society. Faced with declining birth rates and an increasing neo-conservative ideology, it is all too easy to imagine how a steady drip of recent events (local Party notices encouraging members to take the lead in having two children, speed dating events for singles run by the CCP Youth League, a lecture by a self-proclaimed Confucian master on "female morality" organized by a Wuhan college) could steadily crystalize into a much more comprehensive political platform aimed at remodeling society and promoting pro-natalist and patriarchal values.

POLITICS

Continued Erosion. Expect deeper erosion of reform-era norms. Take one concrete example. Now that term limits have been removed for the top Party post, it is difficult to see why implicit age and term limits for Politburo and Central Committee members might not suffer a similar fate.

Keep an eye out for any sign that Party institutions themselves are being marginalized. Since 1978, we have become accustomed to China's leaders exercising power through more regularized channels—say, the national Party Congresses held every five years. But think back to the Maoist era. Remember those long stretches of time in which nominally authoritative Party organs simply faded into the reflected glory of Mao himself. And then start double-checking dates of recent Party conferences, and whether they actually took place.[5]

Bureaucratic Decay. Technocratic rule will wobble yet further as China slides back towards single-man rule. Expect the stultifying atmosphere within the bureaucracy to worsen. Party cadres will increasingly fear rivals using charges of "political deviation" to knock them out of the corner office. Local officials will eschew innovative governance reforms in favor of *pro forma* recitations of higher-level speeches. Channels that once permitted limited input into the state planning of law and regulation (say, from university academics) will atrophy. Further up the hierarchy, mid-level cadres will increasingly compete for central attention by striving to outdo each other in carrying out pet projects of their superiors. ("Quick—he's coming to visit next month. How much of the transportation budget can we divert to build some soccer fields?") At the very top, the repeated public oaths of fealty to Xi by elites will intensify in volume. But behind the scenes, expect brutal Machiavellian infighting as the next generation of Party leaders jockey for a pole position (and seek to eliminate likely rivals) in preparation for an eventual leadership succession—one marked by the near-total absence of any clear norms or procedures.

Steadily Worsening Climate for Minorities and Foreigners. The rising nativist tides currently battering China's religious and ethnic minorities will steadily engulf a wider swath of the foreign community as well. Major warning signs include Beijing's fall 2018 detention of two Canadians on national security grounds following Ottawa's arrest of a Chinese tech executive and the opening skirmishes of the U.S.-China visa wars (in spring 2019). As tensions rise both between (and within) China and America, expect nationalist sentiment in both countries to ignite and spread outside of the fields such as military strategy and economic policy, and begin burning through a range of other cultural and person-to-person ties (such as academic exchanges).

Looking yet further ahead, it is also important to watch for signals that longer-term risks of domestic instability are beginning to materialize. These include:

Economics. Sudden shifts affecting widely shared interests. For example, rapid declines in urban housing prices or waves of corporate bankruptcies (coupled with widespread layoffs).

Ideology. Signs that the us-versus-them strand of Party propaganda is crystallizing into a clearer and more public call for immediate action against internal enemies.[6]

Politics. Indications that elite power struggles are deepening, such as changes in the numbers and ranks of those targeted in Party purges, or an escalation in the severity of charges leveled against them (such as a shift from allegations of mere corruption to political deviation or plotting the overthrow of Party rule). And above all: calls by top leaders for people to take to the streets in any form.

To those, of course, one has to add the unforeseen, such as the sudden death of a top leader or a routine military exercise in the South China Sea gone awry. Any of those could easily be the kind of unexpected trigger that detonates latent social and political tensions, tipping the flow of China's history from an era of incremental change measured in years to one of rapid, kinetic transformation marked in hours.

For outsiders, the once-controversial idea that China's reform era is over is now widely accepted. Some are considering the implications of this in a rational and reasoned manner. Are domestic political shifts in Beijing altering its strategic posture in the South China Sea? If so, what is the best response to take in conjunction with our allies? What specific trade policies disadvantage American manufacturers? What steps can be taken to defend U.S. interests? Those are the right questions to be asking.

Yet others are responding very differently. Just as predicted in Chapter 6, there is now a radicalization of viewpoints in *both* Beijing and Washington. Extremist voices are rising. Rational economic and strategic concerns are fusing with deep-seated national insecurities and virulent domestic identity politics in a toxic combination. Right-wing figures—many with an eye to whipping up populist outrage for domestic political gain—now openly cast U.S.-China relations as a new Cold War, seeking revival of institutions such as the Committee on the Present Danger and the House Un-American Activities Committee. And some within America's halls of power are beginning to flirt with truly dangerous and disturbing concepts—ones sharing more in common with those sometimes peddled in dark corners of Moscow or Beijing than with decades of principled U.S. foreign policy. When I hear top State Department officials muse publicly about "civilizational challenges" posed by China and make off-hand comments about ethnicity or race,

I frankly start so see some of my nightmare scenarios take a step closer to reality.

For Americans, we have to fix our own system. We have to stay true to our own liberal democratic values. We must remain an open and tolerant society. Precisely because Cold War analogies will be twisted by many over the coming years for political gain, it is useful to conclude with one of the seminal documents from that period—the 1946 Long Telegram by American diplomat George Kennan. After comprehensively analyzing both the internal weaknesses of the Soviet Union and the foreign policy challenges it presented for the United States, he concluded:

"Finally, we must have courage and self-confidence to cling to our own methods and conceptions of human society. After all, the greatest danger that can befall us . . . is that we shall allow ourselves to become like those with whom we are coping."

Carl Minzner
New York
April 2019

NOTES

⟫⟪

Preface

1. United States, *Daily Consular and Trade Reports* (Washington, DC: Department of Commerce and Labor, Bureau of Manufactures, February 18, 1913), 873. https://books.google.com/books?id=IWZJAQA AMAAJ&lpg=PA873&dq=%22Shanghai%20to%20Peking%22%20day s&pg=PA865#v=onepage&q=%22Shanghai%20to%20Peking%22%20 days&f=false

2. For a more detailed examination of early-twentieth-century legal reform efforts in China, and foreign involvement, see Amy Epstein Gadsden, "Building the Rule of Law in Early Twentieth-Century China (1905– 1926)" (dissertation, University of Pennsylvania, 2005) http://repository. upenn.edu/dissertations/AAI3165677; Jeremiah Jenne, "The Perils of Advising the Empire: Yuan Shikai and Frank Goodnow," *Chinafile*, December 30, 2015, http://www.chinafile.com/reporting-opinion/ viewpoint/perils-advising-empire; Jedidiah J. Kroncke, *The Futility of Law and Development: China and the Dangers of Exporting American Law* (Oxford University Press, 2016); and Jedidiah J. Kroncke, "An Early Tragedy of Comparative Constitutionalism: Frank Goodnow and the Chinese Republic," *Pacific Rim Law & Policy Journal* 21, no. 3 (2012): 533.

3. Donald Trump, *Time to Get Tough: Making America Great Again* (Washington, DC: Regnery Publishing, 2011), 3.

   Barry Naughton, "Economic Rebalancing," in *China's Challenges*, eds. Avery Goldstein and Jacques Delisle (Philadelphia: University of Pennsylvania Press, 2015), 108–9.

4.   Kevin O'Brien, "Studying Chinese Politics in an Age of Specialization," *Journal of Contemporary China* 20, no. 71 (2011): 535.

5.   Stephen Walt, "The Cult of Irrelevance," *Foreign Policy*, April 15, 2009, http://foreignpolicy.com/2009/04/15/the-cult-of-irrelevance/.

6.   I specifically hope more historians add their voices to the mix. A survey of more than two hundred national security officials revealed that they rated qualitative evidence and arguments drawn from history and case studies most useful to their decision-making. Conversely, quantitative research, formal modeling, and game theory ranked low. Paul Avey and Michael Desch, "What Do Policymakers Want from Us? Results from a Survey of Current and Former Senior National Security Decision Makers," *International Studies Quarterly* 58, no. 4 (2014): 227–46.

Introduction

1.   Sui-Lee Wee, "Thousands Being Moved from China's Three Gorges – Again," *Reuters,* August 22, 2012, accessed March 24, 2014, http://www.reuters.com/article/2012/08/22/us-china-threegorges-idUSBRE87L0ZW20120822. Some language in this introduction is adapted from the author's earlier work, Carl Minzner, "China at the Tipping Point? The Turn Against Legal Reform," *Journal of Democracy* 24, no. 1 (2013): 65–72.

2.   "孔子曰：'夫君者舟也，人者水也。水可载舟，亦可覆舟。君以此思危，则可知也。" Wang Su, *Kongzi Jiayu Yu Yizhu* [Annotated Sayings of Confucius] (Guilin: Guangxi Normal University Press, 1998), 53.

3.   Michael Wines, "China Admits Problems with Three Gorges Dam," *New York Times,* May 19, 2011, accessed March 24, 2014, http://www.nytimes.com/2011/05/20/world/asia/20gorges.html.

4.   Evan Osnos, "Boss Rail," *New Yorker,* October 22, 2012, accessed March 24, 2014, http://www.newyorker.com/reporting/2012/10/22/121022fa_fact_osnos?currentPage=all.

5.   Jonathan Kaiman, "Liu Zhijun, China's Ex-Railway Minister, Sentenced to Death for Corruption," *Guardian,* July 8, 2013, accessed March 24, 2014, https://www.theguardian.com/world/2013/jul/08/liu-zhijun-sentenced-death-corruption.

6.   J Capital Research, J Triage Report, "Year of the (White) Elephant," February 29, 2012, accessed March 24, 2014, http://www.economia.unam.mx/deschimex/cechimex/chmxExtras/documentos/catedra/catedra2013/cursointensivo/Programacion/Materialapoyo/YearoftheWhiteElephant.pdf.

7.   Patrick Chovanec, "China's High-Speed Rail Dilemma," *An American Perspective from China,* January 14, 2011, accessed March 24, 2014, http://chovanec.wordpress.com/2011/01/14/chinas-high-speed-rail-dilemma/.

8.   Ashley Feinberg, "China's Replica of Paris Is Now an Eerily Depressing Ghost Town," *Gizmodo,* August 7,

2013, accessed March 24, 2014, http://gizmodo.com/
chinas-replica-of-paris-is-now-an-eerily-depressing-gh-1055641763.

9. Jonathan Kaiman, "Chinese Protest at Planned Chemical Plant
over Pollution Fears," *Guardian,* May 16, 2013, accessed March
24, 2014, http://www.theguardian.com/world/2013/may/16/
china-protest-chemical-plant-kunming-px.

10. Zhu Zue, "Gangsters Instigated '08 Riot in Guizhou," *China Daily,*
March 16, 2010, accessed March 24, 2014, http://www.chinadaily.com.cn/
china/2010-03/16/content_9593995.htm; Joseph Fewsmith, "An 'Anger-
Venting' Mass Incident Catches the Attention of China's Leadership,"
China Leadership Monitor, issue 26 (2008), http://media.hoover.org/sites/
default/files/documents/CLM26JF.pdf.

11. Sui-Lee Wee and Maxim Duncan, "Jailing of Wheelchair-Bound
Beijing Airport Bomber Sparks Anger," *Reuters,* October 15, 2013,
accessed March 24, 2014, http://www.reuters.com/article/2013/10/15/
us-china-explosion-idUSBRE99E02F20131015.

12. Bloomberg News, "China's Second-Richest Man Recovers after Knife
Attack," *Bloomberg,* September 18, 2013, accessed March 24, 2014, http://
www.bloomberg.com/news/2013-09-18/china-s-2nd-richest-man-zong-
returns-from-knife-wound.html.

13. Liu Dong, "Petitioner Identified as Xiamen Bus Arsonist," *Global Times,*
June 9, 2013, accessed March 24, 2014, http://www.globaltimes.cn/
DesktopModules/DnnForge%20-%20NewsArticles/Print.aspx?tabid=9
9&tabmoduleid=94&articleId=787924&moduleId=405&PortalID=0;
Edward Wong, "Chinese Link 47 Deaths in Bus Blast to a Suicide,"
New York Times, June 8, 2013, accessed March 24, 2014, http://www.
nytimes.com/2013/06/09/world/asia/chinese-link-bus-blast-to-jobless-
mans-suicide.html.

14. Zong Shengli, Li Guozhong, 2005 年社会治安形势 [The Situation of
Social Order in 2005], in Ru Xin, Lu Xueyi, and Li Peilin, eds., 2006
年:中国社会形势分析与预测 [Analysis and Forecast on China's
Social Development (2006)] (Beijing: Social Sciences Academic Press,
2006), 151.

15. Clifford Coonan, "Has China Lost Its Humanity," *Independent*, October
21, 2011, http://www.independent.co.uk/news/world/asia/has-china-lost-
its-humanity-2374293.html; "China's Hit-Run Scandal: Yue Yue Dies,"
Sydney Morning Herald, October 21, 2011, http://www.smh.com.au/world/
chinas-hitrun-scandal-yue-yue-dies-20111021-1mbpc.html.

16. Ian Johnson, "In China, Video of Deadly Accident Reignites Debate over
Lack of Trust," *New York Times*, June 9, 2017, accessed June 26, 2017,
https://www.nytimes.com/2017/06/09/world/asia/china-woman-run-
over-video.html.

17. Benjamin Kang Lim and Ben Blanchard, "Xi Jinping Hopes Traditional
Faiths Can Fill Moral Void in China: Sources," *Reuters,* September 29,

2013, accessed March 24, 2014, http://www.reuters.com/article/2013/09/29/us-china-politics-vacuum-idUSBRE98S0GS20130929.

18. Andrew Jacobs, "Confucius Statue Vanishes Near Tiananmen Square," *New York Times,* April 22, 2011, accessed March 24, 2014, http://www.nytimes.com/2011/04/23/world/asia/23confucius.html?_r=0.

19. Yasheng Huang, *Capitalism with Chinese Characteristics* (New York: Cambridge University Press, 2008).

20. James T. Areddy, "Defying Mao, Rich Chinese Crash the Communist Party," *Wall Street Journal,* December 29, 2012, accessed March 24, 2014, http://online.wsj.com/news/articles/SB10001424127887323723104578187360101389762.

21. Bloomberg News, "China's Billionaire People's Congress Makes Capitol Hill Look like Pauper," *Bloomberg,* February 27, 2012, accessed March 24, 2014, http://www.bloomberg.com/news/2012-02-26/china-s-billionaire-lawmakers-make-u-s-peers-look-like-paupers.html.

22. Benjamin Kang Lim and Ben Blanchard, "China Puts Former Security Chief Under House Arrest – Sources," *Reuters,* December 11, 2013, accessed March 24, 2014, http://www.reuters.com/article/2013/12/11/us-china-politics-zhou-idUSBRE9BA0C420131211.

23. Compare Andrew Nathan's article "China's Changing of the Guard: Authoritarian Resilience," *Journal of Democracy* 14 (January 2003), with the one appearing a decade later, "China at the Tipping Point: Foreseeing the Unforeseeable," *Journal of Democracy* 20 (January 2013).

24. Edward Wong and Jonathan Ansfield, "Many Urge China's Next Leader to Liberalize," *New York Times,* October 21, 2012, accessed March 24, 2014, http://www.nytimes.com/2012/10/22/world/asia/many-urge-chinas-next-leader-to-enact-reform.html?pagewanted=all&_r=1&.

25. Clare Baldwin, "Luxury in China Loses Luster as Wealthy Flee," *Reuters,* January 16, 2014, accessed March 24, 2014, http://www.reuters.com/article/2014/01/16/us-china-luxury-hurun-idUSBREA0F0H320140116.

26. Nicholas D. Kristof, "Looking for a Jump-Start in China," *New York Times,* January 5, 2013, accessed March 24, 2014, http://www.nytimes.com/2013/01/06/opinion/sunday/kristof-looking-for-a-jump-start-in-china.html.

27. "Xi Jinping Becomes 'Core' Leader of China," *Guardian,* October 27, 2016, https://www.theguardian.com/world/2016/oct/27/xi-jinping-becomes-core-leader-of-china.

28. Nicholas Kristof, Twitter post, January 20, 2014, 7:21 A.M., https://twitter.com/NickKristof.

29. Closing statement by Xu Zhiyong at his trial, January 22, 2014, accessed May 18, 2015, translation available at http://chinachange.org/2014/01/23/for-freedom-justice-and-love-my-closing-statement-to-the-court/.

Chapter 1

1. This chapter is adapted from the author's previous article, Carl Minzner, "China after the Reform Era," *Journal of Democracy* 26, no. 3 (June 2015): 129–43.

2. Larry Diamond, "Facing Up to the Democratic Recession," *Journal of Democracy* 26, no. 1 (January 2015): 141–55.

3. Francis Fukuyama, "Why Is Democracy Performing So Poorly?" *Journal of Democracy* 26, no. 1 (January 2015): 11–20.

4. Deng Xiaoping, "Emancipate the Mind, Seek Truth from Facts, and Unite as One in Looking to the Future" (speech, Third Plenary Session of the Eleventh Central Committee of the Chinese Communist Party, Beijing, China, December 13, 1978), http://en.people.cn/dengxp/vol2/text/b1260.html.

5. Yasheng Huang, *Capitalism with Chinese Characteristics* (New York: Cambridge University Press, 2008), 83.

6. "Zhonggong zhongyang, guowuyuan guanyu jiaqiang shehui zhi'an zonghe zhili de jueding" (CCP Central Committee, State Council decision regarding strengthening the comprehensive management of public security), February 2, 1991.

7. Suisheng Zhao, "A State-Led Nationalism: The Patriotic Education Campaign in Post-Tiananmen China," *Communist and Post-Communist Studies* 31, no. 3 (1998): 287–302.

8. Some material is paraphrased or transposed directly from Carl Minzner, "China at the Tipping Point: The Turn against Legal Reform," *Journal of Democracy* 24, no. 1 (January 2013): 65–72.

9. Bruce J. Dickson, *Red Capitalists in China: The Party, Private Entrepreneurs, and Prospects for Political Change* (New York: Cambridge University Press, 2003).

10. "Guojia gongwuyuan kaoshi 20 nian baokao renshu zhang 344 bei" (In 20 years, civil-service applicants increased by a factor of 344), *Beijing News,* November 7, 2013, http://epaper.bjnews.com.cn/html/2013-11/07/content_476317.htm.

11. Kam Wing Chan, "Migration and Development in China: Trends, Geography, and Current Issues," *Migration and Development* 1, no. 2 (December 2012): 190.

12. Minxin Pei, *China's Trapped Transition: The Limits of Developmental Autocracy* (Cambridge: Harvard University Press, 2006).

13. Joel Wuthnow and Phillip C. Saunders, "Chinese Military Reforms in the Age of Xi Jinping: Drivers, Challenges, and Implications," Center for the Study of Chinese Military Affairs, National Defense University Press, March 2017, http://ndupress.ndu.edu/Portals/68/Documents/stratperspective/china/ChinaPerspectives-10.pdf?ver=2017-03-21-152018-430.

14. See Michael C. Davis, "Hong Kong's Umbrella Movement: Beijing's Broken Promises," and Victoria Tin-bor Hui, "Hong Kong's Umbrella Movement: The Protests and Beyond," *Journal of Democracy* 26, no. 2 (April 2015): 101–21.

15. Andrew J. Nathan, "China's Changing of the Guard: Authoritarian Resilience," *Journal of Democracy* 14, no. 1 (January 2003): 6–17; David Shambaugh, *China's Communist Party: Atrophy and Adaptation* (Washington, DC: Woodrow Wilson Center Press, 2008), 105; Kellee Tsai, "Cause or Consequence? Private-Sector Development and Communist Resilience in China," in *Why Communism Did Not Collapse*, ed. Martin Dimitrov (Cambridge: Cambridge University Press, 2013), 205–34.

16. Carl Minzner, "Legal Reform in the Xi Jinping Era," *Asia Policy* 20 (July 2015): 4–9.

17. David Shambaugh, "The Coming Chinese Crackup," *Wall Street Journal*, March 6, 2015.

18. Willy Lam, "Xi Jinping Forever," *Foreign Policy*, April 1, 2015.

Chapter 2

1. Chen Hui, "Faxue shuoshi yingpin canting fuwuyuan" [Graduate with Masters Degree in Law Seeks Position as Cafeteria Worker], *Chutian Jinbao*, May 14, 2012, http://ctjb.cnhubei.com/html/ctjb/20120514/ctjb1733469.html. Parts of this chapter (including Chart 1) are adapted from the author's previous article, Carl Minzner, "The Rise and Fall of Chinese Legal Education," *Fordham International Law Journal* 36, no. 2 (2013): 335–96.

2. Xinhua, "China Has 282 Million Rural Migrant Workers by End of 2016," March 14, 2017, http://news.xinhuanet.com/english/2017-03/14/c_136128403.htm.

3. Such narratives continue to have modern resonance, with both mainland Chinese authorities and their political opponents seeking to appropriate them. See, e.g., Wang Ping, "Fan Zhongyan," *CCTV.com*, April 6, 2004, http://www.cctv.com/program/civilization/20040406/101759.shtml; David Wu, "Historical Figures: Fan Zhongyan, Advocating the Nation's Fate Before Comfort," *Epoch Times*, December 2, 2014, http://www.theepochtimes.com/n3/1117985-historical-figures-fan-zhongyan-advocating-the-nations-fate-before-comfort/.

4. Gregory Clark et al., "Surnames: A New Source for the History of Social Mobility," *Explorations in Economic History* 55 (2015): 3–24.

5. Zhu Suli, "Jingying zhengzhi yu zhengzhi canyu" [Elite Politics and Political Participation], *Zhongguo Faxue* [China's Jurisprudence] 5 (2013).

6. Timothy Brook, *The Troubled Empire: China in the Yuan and Ming Dynasties* (Cambridge, MA: Harvard University Press, 2010), 36.

7. Jonathan Spence, *The Search for Modern China* (New York: W. W. Norton: 1990), 58–64.
8. David Lague, "1977 Exam Opened Escape Route into China's Elite," *New York Times*, January 6, 2008, http://www.nytimes.com/2008/01/06/world/asia/06china.html.
9. He Weifang, in discussion with the author, Beijing, August 2, 2011.
10. Huo Xiandan, "Faxue jiaoyu yu falü zhiye de biange" [Changes in Legal Education and the Legal Profession], in *Zhongguo Zouxiang Fazhi 30 Nian 1978–2008* [China's Journey Toward the Rule of Law: 1978–2008], eds. Cai Dingjiang and Wang Chenguang (Beijing, Social Science Academic Press, 2008), 161, 164.
11. John Knight, Terry Sicular, and Yue Ximing, "Educational Inequality in China: The Intergenerational Dimension," in *Rising Inequality in China: Challenges to a Harmonious Society*, eds. Shi Li, Hiroshi Sato, and Terry Sicular (New York: Cambridge University Press, 2013), 151, 153.
12. Sun Xiaoli, "Beida deng mingxiao nongcunwa suo zhan bili yuanhe yuelaiyue shao" [Why Is the Percentage of Rural Children in Beijing University and Other Top Schools Steadily Declining?], *Guangzhou Ribao* [Guangzhou Daily], October 16, 2013, http://edu.china.com.cn/henan/2013-10/16/content_30308642.htm.
13. Pan Xiaoling, Chen Qianrong, Xia Qianliu, Xing Heqian, "Qiong haizi meiyou chuntian? Hanmenzidi weihe li yixian gaoxiao yuelaiyueyuan?" [Is There No Spring for Poor Children? Why Are Top Colleges Further and Further Away for Impoverished, Talented Youth?]" *Southern Weekend*, August 5, 2011, http://www.infzm.com/content/61888.
14. In 2012, only 20.8 percent of Beijing college students at elite "985" colleges (such as Peking, Qinghua, Renmin Universities) came from rural backgrounds. Ironically, even a school such as China Agricultural University has witnessed declining numbers of rural students, sinking from 34.66 percent (2002) to 24.34 percent (2013). Sun Xiaoli, "Beida deng mingxiao nongcunwa."
15. Emily Hannum et al., "Education in the Reform Era," in *China's Great Economic Transformation*, eds. Loren Brandt and Thomas G. Rawski (Cambridge: Cambridge University Press, 2007), 221–22.
16. Jing Lin, "Education Stratification and the New Middle Class," in *Education and Social Change in China: Inequality in a Market Economy*, ed. Gerard A. Postiglione (Armonk, NY: M. E. Sharpe, 2006), 190.
17. Hongbin Li et al., "Unequal Access to College in China: How Far Have Poor, Rural Students Been Left Behind?" *China Quarterly* 221 (2015): 198–99.
18. See the comments of the director of the Population and Labor Economics Research Institute of the Chinese Academy of Social Science, Cai Fang, "Zhenzheng de chengshi hua ying shixian nongmingong shiminhua" [Cai Fang: Real Urbanization Requires Achieving the 'Citizen-ation' of Rural

Migrant Laborers], *Caijing*, February 18, 2013, http://comments.caijing.com.cn/2013-02-18/112510633.html.

19. Kam Wing Chan, "Crossing the 50 Percent Population Rubicon: Can China Urbanize to Prosperity?," *Eurasian Geography and Economics* 53, no. 1 (2012): 69.

20. Fang Lai et al., "The Education of China's Migrant Children: The Missing Link in China's Education System," *International Journal of Educational Development* 37 (2014): 68–77.

21. See, e.g., Zhao Han, "Rule Change Forces Migrants' Children Out of Beijing for School," *Caixin*, February 16, 2015, http://english.caixin.com/2015-02-16/100784599.html.

22. Huang Chen, "Home Alone," *Caixin*, June 3, 2014, http://english.caixin.com/2014-06-03/100685459.html. For an excellent, if heart-rending, depiction of this reality, see *Last Train Home*, directed by Lixin Fan (2009; New York, NY: Zeitgeist Films, 2011), DVD.

23. Tania Branigan, "China Struggles with Mental Health Problems of 'Left-Behind' Children," *Guardian*, August 30, 2014, https://www.theguardian.com/world/2014/aug/30/china-left-behind-children-mental-health.

24. Xiaogang Wu and Zhuoni Zhang, "Changes in Educational Inequality in China, 1990–2005: Evidence from the Population Census Data," *Research in the Sociology of Education* 17 (2010): 145.

25. Yiqin Fu, "China's Unfair College Admissions System," *The Atlantic*, June 19, 2013, https://www.theatlantic.com/china/archive/2013/06/chinas-unfair-college-admissions-system/276995/. Underlying data available here: https://docs.google.com/spreadsheets/d/1XgT5uoO31m5gPnPXRpAQfc26LIlJHDCrhsl6asgm-WM/edit#gid=2.

26. Fei-Ling Wang, *Organizing through Division and Exclusion: China's Hukou System* (Stanford: Stanford University Press, 2005), 142–43.

27. See, e.g., "Bi gongzi: 69 percent daxuesheng qixin diyu nongmingong" [Comparing Wages: Starting Salaries for 69 Percent of University Graduates Are Lower than Migrant Workers], *Xinhua*, May 28, 2013, http://zgws.xinhuanet.com/themeinfo.aspx?id=2317.

28. See Ministry of Education statistics, *Quanguo linian canjia gaokao renshu he luquren tongji* [Historical Statistics on Numbers of Gaokao Test-Takers Compared with those Who Passed], People's Daily Website, http://edu.people.com.cn/n/2013/0503/c116076-21359059.html.

29. Yang Dongping, "Gaodeng jiaoyu gonggong zhengce de yanbian" [Changes in Higher Education Policy], in *Zhongguo Jiaoyu Fazhan Yu Zhengce 30 Nian* [China's Education Development and Policy 1978–2008], ed. Zhang Xiulan (Beijing, Social Science Academic Press, 2008), 251, 262–62.

30. Zhao Litao and Sheng Sixin, "China's 'Great Leap' in Higher Education," EAI Background Brief No. 394 (Singapore: East Asian Institute,

National University of Singapore, 2008), 8, http://www.eai.nus.edu.sg/publications/files/BB394.pdf.

31. Minzner, "Chinese Legal Education," 346–47.

32. For comprehensive data on numbers of Chinese college students since the late 1990s, see the statistical section of China's Ministry of Education, http://www.moe.edu.cn/publicfiles/business/htmlfiles/moe/s4958/list.html, or the corresponding material on the website of the Ministry of Statistics, http://www.stats.gov.cn/.

33. Data are compiled from the annual Statistical Yearbooks of China (for data from 1949 to the mid-1990s), published by China's Ministry of Statistics, and from the corresponding website (for more recent years), where they are reported as *gaodengxuexiao putong benzhuanke biyesheng shu*. These numbers include both *benke* (university) and *zhuanke* (junior college) students—categories not broken out separately in earlier data. These data do not include technical high schools, adult education, or other educational programs. Rather, these statistics give a rough idea of the number of Chinese students studying in a tertiary education setting most closely approximating a college degree.

34. Fiona Tam, "Scandals Hit Educators in Hubei," *South China Morning Post*, October 13, 2009, http://www.scmp.com/article/695189/scandals-hit-educators-hubei; Zheng Caixiong, "College Head Detained for Corruption," *China Daily*, October 13, 2009, http://www.chinadaily.com.cn/cndy/2009-10/13/content_8783690.htm.

35. "Looks Good on Paper," *Economist*, September 28, 2013, http://www.economist.com/news/china/21586845-flawed-system-judging-research-leading-academic-fraud-looks-good-paper.

36. Ibid.; Yong Zhao, *Who's Afraid of the Big Bad Dragon? Why China Has the Best (and Worst) Education System in the World* (San Francisco: Jossey-Bass, 2014), 93–118.

37. Charles Seife, "For Sale: 'Your Name Here' in a Prestigious Science Journal," *Scientific American*, December 17, 2014, http://www.scientificamerican.com/article/for-sale-your-name-here-in-a-prestigious-science-journal/.

38. Interview with university professor, Beijing, China, July 15, 2011.

39. Interview with university professor, Kunming, China, Aug 12, 2011.

40. Terence Tse and Mark Esposito, "Youth Unemployment in China: A Crisis in the Making," *CNBC*, February 20, 2014, http://www.cnbc.com/id/101433696.

41. Keith Bradsher, "Chinese Graduates Say No Thanks to Factory Jobs," *New York Times*, January 23, 2013, http://www.nytimes.com/2013/01/25/business/as-graduates-rise-in-china-office-jobs-fail-to-keep-up.html.

42. "Wages for China's Newest College Grads Are Plunging," *Bloomberg*, June 1, 2017, https://www.bloomberg.com/news/articles/2017-06-01/china-s-graduate-salary-slump-is-new-economy-s-competitive-edge

43. China Labour Bulletin, "Wages and Employment," http://www.clb.org.
     hk/content/wages-and-employment. Note that this trend may be on the
     verge of reversing. As of 2017, average nominal wage growth for migrant
     workers appears to be slowing. Tom Hancock, "Migrant Workers Feel
     Pinch as Beijing Pulls Back on Wages," Financial Times, September 4,
     2017, https://www.ft.com/content/0383433e-8ca0-11e7-a352-e46f43c5825d.

44. Indeed, data suggest some truth behind this perception. The average
     national entry-level salaries for recent college graduates (4,014 yuan,
     or $590, per month) appear to be roughly the same as newly hired
     elevator mechanics in Shanghai (4,000 yuan per month). "Wages for
     China's Newest College Grads Are Plunging," Bloomberg; Fu Danni,
     "Shanghai's Vocational Schools Open Doors for Rural Students,"
     Sixth Tone, April 27, 2017, http://www.sixthtone.com/news/1000074/
     shanghais-vocational-schools-open-doors-for-rural-students.

45. According to a 2012 report by China's Industrial Bank, of some
     "2.7 million Chinese citizens who made over US$960,000, . . . 85 percent
     intended to send their children abroad for education." Andrew Ross,
     "How the Children of China's Elite Learned to (By)pass the Gaokao,"
     China Economic Review, July 11, 2015, http://www.chinaeconomicreview.
     com/how-children-chinas-elite-learned-bypass-gaokao.

46. "Open Doors Fact Sheet: China," Institute of International Education,
     2015, http://www.iie.org/Research-and-Publications/Open-Doors/Data/
     Fact-Sheets-by-Country/2015#.WAfqmJMrK8U. Note that in addition
     to students pursuing undergraduate and graduate degrees, it also
     includes small numbers of students pursuing Optional Practical Training,
     temporary employment related to their field of study. But it does not
     capture the increasing numbers of mainland Chinese students who are
     enrolling directly in America elementary or secondary schools.

47. University of Washington, "Enrollment Data for Autumn 2016 New
     Undergraduate Students," November 20, 2016, https://www.washington.
     edu/regents/files/2016/11/2016-11-A-7.pdf; Tamar Lewin, "Taking More
     Seats on Campus, Foreigners Also Pay the Freight," New York Times,
     February 4, 2012, http://www.nytimes.com/2012/02/05/education/
     international-students-pay-top-dollar-at-us-colleges.html. Tuition data for
     the 2016–2017 school year at the University of Washington are available
     at "Total Cost of Attendance: International Students," University of
     Washington, accessed June 14, 2017, https://admit.washington.edu/costs-
     and-financial-aid/total-cost-of-attendance#international.

48. For relevant survey data, see Xiaobing Wang et al., "College Is a Rich,
     Han, Urban, Male Club: Research Notes from a Census Survey of Four
     Tier One Colleges in China," China Quarterly 214 (2013): 456–70.

49. Tim Higgins, "Chinese Students Major in Luxury Cars," Bloomberg,
     December 20, 2013, http://www.bloomberg.com/bw/articles/2013-12-19/
     chinese-students-in-u-dot-s-dot-boost-luxury-car-sales.

50. "China's Stalled Social Mobility," *China Story*, accessed November 8, 2016, https://www.thechinastory.org/key-article/chinas-stalled-social-mobility/.

51. Daniel Bell, *The China Model: Political Meritocracy and the Limits of Democracy* (Princeton: Princeton University Press, 2015).

52. Yasheng Huang, *Capitalism with Chinese Characteristics: Entrepreneurship and the State* (New York: Cambridge University Press, 2008), 112.

53. Calculations indicate that the levels of income equality seen in the mid-1980s are the lowest in the history of the People's Republic of China. Chen Zongsheng and Zhou Yunbo, "The Urban/Rural Gap and Its Impacts on Income Inequality of Chinese Residents," in *Rural Development Issues*, eds. Arnold V. Burlingham and Wesley N. Townsand (New York: Nova Science, 2008), 107, 111.

54. The chart here is reproduced from Terry Sicular, "The Challenge of High Inequality in China," *Inequality in Focus* 2, no. 2 (August 2013): 1, http://www.worldbank.org/content/dam/Worldbank/document/Poverty%20documents/Inequality-In-Focus-0813.pdf.

55. Ibid. Other Chinese researchers reach similar, if slightly higher, figures. In 2015, for example, Beijing University scholars calculated China's 2012 Gini coefficient to be 0.49. Wang Ling, "Zhongguo shehui bu pingdeng qushi kuoda: 1 percent de jiating zhan san fen zhi yi de caichan" [Inequality in Chinese society continues to worsen: 1 percent of families control a third of all wealth], *Yicai.com*, January 13, 2015, http://www.yicai.com/news/2016/01/4738424.html.

56. Lily Kuo, "China Is Hiding How Bad Income Inequality Is in the Country," *Quartz*, April 29, 2014, http://qz.com/204180/china-is-hiding-how-bad-income-inequality-is-in-the-country/.

57. Yu Xie and Xiang Zhou, "Income Inequality in Today's China," *Proceedings of the National Academy of Sciences* 111, no. 19 (2014): 6928, http://www.pnas.org/content/111/19/6928.full.

58. Shen Hu, "China's Gini Index at 0.61, University Report Says," *Caixin*, December 10, 2012, http://english.caixin.com/2012-12-10/100470648.html. New research suggests even higher rates of income concentration among China's wealthiest than previously realized. See Thomas Piketty, Li Yang, and Gabriel Zucman, "Capital Accumulation, Private Property, and Rising Inequality in China, 1978–2015," National Bureau of Economic Research Working Paper 23368, April 2017, http://www.nber.org/papers/w23368#fromrss, figures 11–12, producing significantly higher estimates of the total national income share controlled by the top 10 percent and 1 percent, respectively, over the course of the reform era.

59. K. S. Jomo, "Growth with Equity in East Asia?" DESA Working Paper No. 33, United Nations Department of Economic and Social Affairs, September 2006, 5, http://www.un.org/esa/desa/papers/2006/wp33_2006.pdf.

60. See data available on the World Bank website, at "GINI Index," World Bank, accessed November 8, 2016, http://data.worldbank.org/indicator/SI.POV.GINI.

61. Historical data are available in Francisco H. G. Ferreira, Phillippe G. Leite, and Julie A. Litchfield, "The Rise and Fall of Brazilian Inequality: 1981–2004," *Macroeconomic Dynamics* 12, no. 2 (September 2008): 199. Recent data are available on the World Bank website. See note 55 above.

62. Sicular, "Challenge in China," 2.

63. Yasheng Huang, "Policy Model and Inequality: Some Potential Connections," in *China's Challenges*, eds. Avery Goldstein and Jacques Delisle (Philadelphia: University of Pennsylvania Press, 2014), 83–104.

64. Shenggen Fan, Linxiu Zhang, and Xiaobo Zhang, "Reforms, Investment, and Poverty in Rural China," *Economic Development and Cultural Change* 52, no. 2 (January 2004): 395, 396–98.

65. Huang, *Capitalism with Chinese Characteristics*, 112.

66. Albert Park and Bruce Johnston, "Rural Development and Dynamic Externalities in Taiwan's Structural Transformation," *Economic Development and Cultural Change* 44, no. 1 (October 1995): 181.

67. Huang, *Capitalism with Chinese Characteristics*, 118–25.

68. Andrew Walder and Xiaobin He, "Public Housing into Private Assets: Wealth Creation in Urban China," *Social Science Research* 46 (2014): 85, 88.

69. Ibid., 93.

70. Janet Koech and Jian Wang, "China's Sputtering Housing Boom Poses Broad Economic Challenge," Federal Reserve Bank of Dallas, *Economic Letter* 9, no. 9 (2014), https://www.dallasfed.org/assets/documents/research/eclett/2014/el1409.pdf; Hanming Fang et al., "Demystifying the Chinese Housing Boom," NBER Working Paper No. 21112, National Bureau of Economic Research, Cambridge, MA, April 2015, http://www.nber.org/papers/w21112.pdf.

71. Matt Clinch, "China 'Tulip Fever' Sees House Prices Skyrocket 76 percent to Close In on San Jose," *CNBC*, September 15, 2016, http://www.cnbc.com/2016/09/15/china-tulip-fever-sees-house-prices-skyrocket-76-to-close-in-on-san-jose.html.

72. Thomas Piketty, Li Yang, and Gabriel Zucman, "Capital Accumulation, Private Property and Rising Inequality in China, 1978–2015"; Niu Weikun, "1 percent Jiating zhanyou quanguo sanfen zhiyi yishang caichan" [1 percent of Households Control over 1/3 of National Assets], *Beijing Wanbao*, July 26, 2014, http://bjwb.bjd.com.cn/html/2014-07/26/content_200825.htm; Christina Larson, "China's 1 Percent vs. America's 1 Percent," *Bloomberg*, July 28, 2014, http://www.bloomberg.com/bw/articles/2014-07-28/chinas-one-percent-vs-dot-americas-one-percent.

73. Emmanuel Saez and Gabriel Zucman, "Wealth Inequality in the United States since 1913: Evidence from Capitalized Income Tax Data," NBER Working Paper No. 2062, National Bureau of Economic Research, Cambridge, MA, October 2014, http://www.nber.org/papers/w20625; Emmanuel Saez, "Striking It Richer: The Evolution of Top Incomes in the United States" (unpublished manuscript, June 25, 2015), http://eml.berkeley.edu/~saez/saez-UStopincomes-2014.pdf.

74. Anthony B. Atkinson, *Inequality, What Can Be Done?* (Cambridge: Harvard University Press, 2015); Joseph E. Stiglitz, *The Great Divide: Unequal Societies and What We Can Do about Them* (New York: W. W. Norton, 2015); Robert D. Putnam, *Our Kids: The American Dream in Crisis* (New York: Simon and Schuster, 2015).

75. Jaycee Lui, "China's Disaffected Diaosi Tribe," *gbtimes*, February 3, 2015, http://gbtimes.com/life/chinas-disaffected-diaosi-tribe.

76. See, e.g., Maureen Fan, "Confessed Police Killer Lionized by Thousands in China," *Washington Post*, November 14, 2008, http://www.washingtonpost.com/wp-dyn/content/article/2008/11/13/AR2008111304384.html; Michael Wines, "Civic-Minded Chinese Find a Voice Online," *New York Times*, June 16, 2009, http://www.nytimes.com/2009/06/17/world/asia/17china.html.

77. For an extensive analysis of the abuses associated with the chengguan, see "'Beat Him, Take Everything Away': Abuses by China's Chengguan Para-Police," Human Rights Watch, May 23, 2012, https://www.hrw.org/report/2012/05/23/beat-him-take-everything-away/abuses-chinas-chengguan-para-police.

78. Li Chengpeng, "Li Chengpeng's Essay Translated: Watermelon Vendor Died Pursuing the Chinese Dream," trans. Helen Gao, *Telegraph*, July 19, 2013, http://www.telegraph.co.uk/news/worldnews/asia/china/10190914/Li-Chengpengs-essay-translated-watermelon-vendor-died-pursuing-the-Chinese-dream.html.

79. Alex Stevens, "Rioting Crowd Severely Beats 5 Chengguan for Killing Civilian," *Shanghaiist*, April 21, 2013, http://shanghaiist.com/2014/04/21/rioting-crowd-beats-5-chengguan-for-killing-civillian.php (warning, highly graphic photos).

80. Christopher Carothers, "Chengguan Killer Gets Public Sympathy," *Wall Street Journal*, July 2, 2010, http://blogs.wsj.com/chinarealtime/2010/07/02/chengguan-killer-gets-public-sympathy/; Sam Canpadee, "Villager Attacks 19 Chengguan with Sulfuric Acid in Xianmen," *Shanghaiist*, October 21, 2013, http://shanghaiist.com/2013/10/21/villager-attacks-chengguan-with-sulfuric-acid.php.

81. Martin Whyte, in his 2010 work, concluded that "we do not see many signs in the 2004 national survey data that a large portion of Chinese adults feel that the social order in which they live is unjust (with some exceptions, particularly involving the injustice of pervasive discrimination

against Chinese citizens with rural household registration),” while noting that “even if we can be confident that no social volcano was looming in 2004, we cannot be quite so certain that the level of acceptance of inequalities and optimism about future opportunities that we observed then is the dominant mood today.” Martin King Whyte, *Myth of the Social Volcano: Perceptions of Inequality and Distributive Injustice in Contemporary China* (Stanford: Stanford University Press, 2010), 68, 199.

82.   As Joshua Rosenzweig has noted, such tensions represent a form of populist discontent that can be steered in a variety of different directions. Joshua Rosenzweig, “Public Opinion, Criminal Justice, and Incipient Popular Liberalism in China,” *China Story*, March 17, 2014, https://www. thechinastory.org/2014/03/public-opinion-criminal-justice-and-incipient-popular-liberalism-in-china/.

83.   See, e.g., China Labour Bulletin, “Strike Map,” http://strikemap.clb.org. hk/strikes/en. For a discussion of “protest bargaining,” see Ching Kwan Lee and Yonghong Zhang, “The Power of Instability: Unraveling the Microfoundations of Bargained Authoritarianism in China,” *American Journal of Sociology* 118, no. 6 (May 2013): 1475–1508.

84.   Yu Jianrong, “Emerging Trends in Violent Riots,” *China Security* 4, no. 3 (2008): 76–77.

85.   Wire Staff, “Kindergarten Knife Attacker Executed in China,” *CNN*, May 29, 2010, http://www.cnn.com/2010/WORLD/asiapcf/05/29/china.knife. attacker.death/; Edward Wong, “Fifth Deadly Attack on a School Haunts China,” *New York Times*, May 12, 2010, http://www.nytimes.com/2010/ 05/13/world/asia/13china.html.

86.   Javier Hernandez and Iris Zhao, “At Kindergarten Blast in China, ‘The World Didn’t Seem Real,’ ” *New York Times*, June 16, 2017, https://www. nytimes.com/2017/06/16/world/asia/china-kindergarten-explosion-jiangsu-suspect.html.

87.   For the details of two recent examples, see Zhou Qijun, “Arsonist Posted Complaint about Pay Dispute Just before Attack on Public Bus,” *Caixin*, January 6, 2016, http://english.caixin.com/2016-01-06/100896711.html (arson attack on public bus by contractor embroiled in dispute over back wages kills seventeen); Te-Ping Chen, “China Blast Suspect Dead, State Media Says,” *Wall Street Journal*, Oct. 2, 2015, http://www.wsj.com/ articles/china-blast-suspect-dead-state-media-says-1443785566 (quarry worker engaged in disputes with neighbors and local officials launches bombing campaign against malls, hospitals, government buildings, killing ten).

88.   Josh Chin, “China’s Communist Party Tells Kids Being a Loser Is Nothing to Be Proud of,” *Wall Street Journal*, December 3, 2014, http:// blogs.wsj.com/chinarealtime/2014/12/03/communist-party-paper-warns-youth-on-dangers-of-self-deprecation/.

89.   See, for example, the censorship instructions by state authorities ordering deletion of relevant Internet content. Anne Henochowicz, “Ministry of

Truth: Merchant Killed by Chengguan," *China Digital Times*, July 19, 2013, http://chinadigitaltimes.net/2013/07/ministry-of-truth-merchant-killed-by-chengguan/.

90. Amy Qin, "Li Chengpeng's Social Media and Blog Accounts Suspended," *New York Times*, July 9, 2014, http://sinosphere.blogs.nytimes.com/2014/07/09/li-chengpengs-social-media-and-blog-accounts-suspended/.

91. Li Shi, Hiroshi Sato, and Terry Sicular, "Rising Inequality in China: Key Issues and Findings," in Li, Sato, and Sicular, *Rising Inequality in China*, 1–43.

92. For a comprehensive analysis of the limits associated with two of China's major social welfare policies, see Qin Gao, *Welfare, Work, and Poverty: Social Assistance in China* (New York: Oxford University Press, 2017), and Mark Frazier, *Socialist Insecurity: Pensions and the Politics of Uneven Development in China* (Ithaca, NY: Cornell University Press, 2010).

93. Jim Yardley, "China Plans to Cut School Fees for Its Poorest Rural Students," *New York Times*, March 13, 2005, http://www.nytimes.com/2005/03/13/world/asia/china-plans-to-cut-school-fees-for-its-poorest-rural-students.html.

94. "Elite Unis to Reserve 50,000 Places for Rural Students," *Xinhua*, April 3, 2015, http://news.xinhuanet.com/english/2015-04/03/c_134123709.htm; Ellis Liang, "Top Beijing Universities to Enroll Fewer Local Students, Report Says," *South China Morning Post*, June 15, 2015, http://www.scmp.com/news/china/society/article/1822708/top-beijing-universities-enrol-fewer-local-students-report-says.

95. Global Times, *Jingji renshi kangyi yidi gaokao: yanzhong yingxiang bendiren quanyi* [Beijing Hukou Holders Protest Allowing Non-Locals to Sit for the Gaokao: Serious Effects on the Interests of Local (Beijing) Residents], October 19, 2012, http://edu.163.com/12/1019/14/8E6G3ET000294JD0.html.

96. He Huifeng, "Thousands of Chinese Parents Take to the Streets to Protest University Admissions Quotas," *South China Morning Post*, May 15, 2016, http://www.scmp.com/news/china/policies-politics/article/1945104/thousands-chinese-parents-take-streets-protest. As of fall 2016, the details of the plan were still available on the website of the Ministry of Education. A Google cached version of the *2016 nian bufen diqu kuashengyuan jihua tiaokong fang'an* is available here: http://webcache.googleusercontent.com/search?q=cache:olmttoVdrYYJ:www.moe.gov.cn/srcsite/A03/s180/s3011/201605/W020160504363945237428.xls+&cd=1&hl=en&ct=clnk&gl=us.

97. Zhou Tian, "Local Officials Have Little Love for National Hukou Reform," *Caixin*, February 25, 2015, http://english.caixin.com/2015-02-25/100785562.html.

98. Sheng Menglu and Li You, "Push to Widen College Access Suffers Setback," *Caixin*, June 14, 2016, http://english.caixin.com/2016-06-14/100954553.html.

99. Pei-chia Lan, "Segmented Incorporation: The Second Generation of Rural Migrants in Shanghai," *China Quarterly* 217 (2014): 243.
100. Ibid., 248–52.
101. Guo Kai, "Beijing's Five-Year Plan: Cut Population, Boost Infrastructure," *China Daily*, May 6, 2016, http://www.chinadaily.com.cn/china/2016-05/06/content_25108950.htm.
102. Lucy Hornby, "Beijing Migrants No Longer Welcome as City Caps Population," *Financial Times*, April 19, 2017, https://www.ft.com/content/822e982c-1b40-11e7-bcac-6d03d067f81f?mhq5j=e1.
103. Shi Rui and Li Shiyun, "Revival, Resistance for National Pension Push," *Caixin*, July 27, 2016, http://english.caixin.com/2016-07-27/100971396.html.
104. See, e.g., Joseph Kahn, "China to Drop Urbanite-Peasant Legal Differences," *New York Times*, November 3, 2005, http://www.nytimes.com/2005/11/03/world/asia/china-to-drop-urbanitepeasant-legal-differences.html. For an excellent analysis of the reality behind such reports, see Kam Wing Chan and Will Buckingham, "Is China Abolishing the *Hukou* System?," *China Quarterly* 195 (2008): 582–606.
105. For example, compare the content of central reforms, "Guowuyuan fabu 'Guanyu jinyibu tuijin huji zhidu gaige de yijian'" [State Council Issues "Opinion on Further Promoting Hukou Reform"], *People's Daily*, July 30, 2014, http://politics.people.com.cn/n/2014/0730/c70731-25369521.html, with a survey of prior government hukou reforms through end of 2004, "Recent Chinese Hukou Reforms," Congressional-Executive Commission on China, http://www.cecc.gov/recent-chinese-hukou-reforms.
106. Cheang Ming, "Single's Day: Alibaba Smashes Records at World's Largest Shopping Event," *CNBC*, November 11, 2016, http://www.cnbc.com/2016/11/11/singles-day-news-alibaba-poised-to-smash-records-at-worlds-largest-online-shopping-event.html; Brian Deagon, "Cyber Monday, Black Friday Set Online Sales Records," *Investor's Business Daily*, November 29, 2016, http://www.investors.com/news/technology/cyber-monday-black-friday-set-online-sales-record/.
107. James Quinn, "Alibaba Can Become Bigger than Walmart, Says Founder," *Telegraph*, January 23, 2015, http://www.telegraph.co.uk/finance/financetopics/davos/11365479/Alibaba-can-become-bigger-than-Walmart-says-founder.html.
108. Stephen Letts, "China's Economic Growth of 6.7pc Shows 'Uncanny Stability,'" *Australian Broadcasting Company News*, October 18, 2016, http://www.abc.net.au/news/2016-10-19/china-gdp-economic-data/7946492.
109. Victor Reklaitis, "China's GDP at 6.9 percent? Try 3%: Analysts React to Latest Growth Figures," *MarketWatch*, October 19, 2015, http://www.marketwatch.com/story/chinas-gdp-at-69-try-3-analysts-react-to-latest-growth-figures-2015-10-19. Confidence in official

statistics took a further hit in early 2017, with the life sentence of the former head of the national statistics bureau for corruption, and the public confirmation that officials in multiple provinces had been engaged faking economic data for prior years. "Two Chinese Provinces Faked Economic Data, Inspectors Say," *Bloomberg,* June 11, 2017, https://www.bloomberg.com/news/articles/2017-06-12/ two-chinese-provinces-falsified-economic-data-inspectors-say.

110. Dexter Roberts, "Layoffs Loom in China as Growth Slows," *Bloomberg,* January 14, 2016, http://www.bloomberg.com/news/articles/2016-01-14/ layoffs-loom-in-china-as-growth-slows.

111. Dexter Roberts and Lulu Yilun Chen, "China's Hunt for Growth in the Countryside," *Bloomberg,* August 7, 2015, http://www.bloomberg.com/ news/articles/2015-08-27/china-s-hunt-for-growth-in-the-countryside.

112. See, e.g., "Guowuyuan ban'gongting guanyu zhichi nongmingongdengrenyuan fanxiang chuangye de yijian" [Opinion of the General Office of the State Council Regarding Supporting Migrant Workers and Others to Return to the Countryside to Start Businesses], issued June 17, 2015, http://www.gov.cn/zhengce/content/2015-06/21/ content_9960.htm; "Zhonggong zhongyang guowuyuan guanyu jiada gaige chuangxin lidu jiakuai nongye xiandaihua jianshe de ruogan yijian" [Joint Opinion of the Central Committee and State Council regarding Expanding Innovation in Reform and Accelerating Agricultural Modernization], *Xinhua,* February 1, 2015, http://www.gov.cn/zhengce/ 2015-02/01/content_2813034.htm.

113. Zhang Yue, "High-Tech Enterprise Startups Supported," *China Daily,* January 14, 2016, http://usa.chinadaily.com.cn/business/2016-01/14/ content_23083472.htm.

114. "Guowuyuan bangongting guanyu shenhua gaodeng xuexiao chuangye jiaoyu gaige de shishi yijian" [Implementing Opinion of the State Council Regarding Deepening Reform of Education on Entrepreneurship in Institutions of Higher Education, issued May 4, 2015, http://www.gov.cn/ zhengce/content/2015-05/13/content_9740.htm

115. Li Xiaojuan and Liu Zhui, "Jiaoyu bu: yunxu daxuesheng baoliu xueji xiuxue chuangye" [Ministry of Education to Allow University Students to Retain Student Status and Stop Out of School to Found Start-Ups], *Beijing Chenbao,* May 15, 2015, http://politics.people.com.cn/n/2015/0515/ c70731-27003476.html.

116. An Lu, "Premier Li Calls for Developing Vocational Education," *Xinhua,* May 10, 2015, http://news.xinhuanet.com/english/2015-05/10/c_ 134226715.htm.

117. Stephen Roach, "China's Services Sector Is Growing, but Far Too Few Chinese Are Spending," *South China Morning Post,* November 27, 2015, http://www.scmp.com/comment/insight-opinion/article/ 1884050/chinas-services-sector-growing-far-too-few-chinese-are; Barry

Ritholtz, "Stephen Roach's Pivot to China," *Bloomberg*, December 22, 2015, http://www.bloombergview.com/articles/2015-12-22/ stephen-roach-s-pivot-to-china.

118.   David Pierson, "Apple Beats Earnings Estimates, Nearly Doubles Revenue in China," *Los Angeles Times*, October 27, 2015, http://www. latimes.com/business/technology/la-fi-tn-apple-earnings-20151027-story. html.

119.   Laurie Burkitt, "Starbucks to Add Thousands of Stores in China," *Wall Street Journal*, January 12, 2016, http://www.wsj.com/articles/ starbucks-plans-thousands-of-new-stores-in-china-1452580905.

120.   Tom Mitchell, "The Ugly Subtext Beneath China's Two-Track Economy Tale," *Financial Times*, January 17, 2016, http://www.ft.com/intl/cms/s/2/ bb494388-bb9b-11e5-bf7e-8a339b6f2164.html.

121.   Eva Dou, "Didi, China's Uber, Navigates Rough Regulatory Road," *Wall Street Journal*, October 11, 2016, http://www.wsj.com/articles/ didi-chinas-uber-navigates-rough-regulatory-road-1476105950.

122.   Alex Webb, "Apple's China Problem Is That Local Phones Are Good—and Cheap," *Bloomberg*, July 24, 2016, https://www.bloomberg.com/news/articles/2016-07-24/ apple-s-china-problem-is-that-local-phones-are-good-and-cheap.

123.   Amie Tsang and Sui-Lee Wee, "McDonald's China Operations to Be Sold to Locally Led Consortium," *New York Times*, January 9, 2017, https:// www.nytimes.com/2017/01/09/business/dealbook/mcdonalds-china-citic- carlyle.html

124.   Peter Ford, "For Chinese Leader Xi Jinping, It's All About the Communist Party," *Christian Science Monitor*, November 20, 2015, http://www.csmonitor.com/World/Asia-Pacific/2015/1130/ For-Chinese-leader-Xi-Jinping-it-s-all-about-the-Communist-Party-video.

125.   Gwynn Guilford, "Two-Thirds of New Investors in China's Stock Market Mega-Rally Didn't Finish High School," *Quartz*, March 27, 2015, http:// qz.com/371412/two-thirds-of-new-investors-in-chinas-stock-market-mega- rally-didnt-finish-high-school/.

126.   Gabriel Wildau, "China's Hunt for Short-Seller Tests Legal Boundaries," *Financial Times*, July 19, 2015, https://www.ft.com/content/88280be8- 2b85-11e5-8613-e7aedbb7bdb7; "Crackdown on 'Malicious' Short-Selling," *China Daily*, July 17, 2015, http://usa.chinadaily.com.cn/epaper/2015-07/ 17/content_21312451.htm.

127.   The image of the *Economist*'s January 16, 2016, front cover is available at http://www.economist.com/printedition/covers/2016-01-14/ap-la-na.

128.   Barry Naughton, "Economic Rebalancing," in Goldstein and Delisle, *China's Challenges*, 108–9.

129.   "China Forex Reserves Fall $512.66 Billion in 2015, Biggest Drop on Record," *Reuters*, January 7, 2016, http://www.reuters.com/article/ us-china-economy-forex-reserves-idUSKBN0UL13W20160107.

Chapter 3

1. A similar tone of disquiet is evident in the writings of other prominent democracy theorists. See, e.g., Larry Diamond, "Democracy in Decline," *Foreign Affairs*, July/August 2016, 151–59.

2. Francis Fukuyama, *Political Order and Political Decay* (New York: Farrar, Straus and Giroux, 2014), 370–71, 378.

3. Ibid., 372–85.

4. Ibid.

5. Some language in this chapter has been adapted from Carl Minzner, "Back and Forth from Beijing," *International Herald Tribune*, May 29, 2009, http://www.nytimes.com/2009/05/30/opinion/30iht-edminzner. html.

6. Jenny Jarvie, "Atlanta Schools Cheating Scandal: 11 Educators Convicted of Racketeering," *Los Angeles Times*, April 1, 2015, http://www.latimes. com/nation/la-na-atlanta-school-cheating-convictions-20150401-story. html. The full report by Georgia state investigators is available at Office of the Governor, State of Georgia, *Special Investigation to Probe Allegations of Test Tempering and Related Matters in the Atlanta Public School System (APS)*, June 30, 2011, https://assets.documentcloud.org/documents/ 215260/georgia-investigation.pdf.

7. "China's GDP Is 'Man-Made,' Unreliable: Top Leader," *Reuters*, December 6, 2010, http://www.reuters.com/article/us-china-economy-wikileaks-idUSTRE6B527D20101206. Nor is this an isolated example; see Jeremy Wallace, "Here's Why It Matters That China Is Admitting That Its Statistics Are 'Unreliable,'" *Washington Post*, December 28, 2015, https:// www.washingtonpost.com/news/monkey-cage/wp/2015/12/28/heres-why-it-matters-that-china-is-admitting-that-its-statistics-are-unreliable/; Lyu Changjiang, et al., "GDP Management to Meet or Beat Growth Targets" (working paper, 2015), http://ssrn.com/abstract=2579824.

8. Principal-agent problems in the Chinese bureaucracy have been the subject of extensive academic study in recent years. For one comprehensive recent work, see Yongshun Cai, *State and Agents in China: Disciplining Government Officials* (Stanford: Stanford University Press, 2015).

9. Some material in this chapter is adapted from the author's earlier work, Carl Minzner, "Riots and Coverups: Counterproductive Control of Local Agents in China," *University of Pennsylvania Journal of International Law* 31, no. 1 (Fall 2009): 53, 61–63.

10. Lawrence J. R. Herson, "China's Imperial Bureaucracy: Its Direction and Control," *Public Administration Review* 17, no. 1 (1957): 44, 48.

11. Ibid.; Jonathan K. Ocko, "I'll Take It All the Way to Beijing: Capital Appeals in the Qing," *Journal of Asian Studies* 47, no. 2 (1988): 296.

12. Frederick Teiwes, *Politics at Mao's Court: Gao Gang and Party Factionalism in the Early 1950s* (Armonk, NY: M. E. Sharpe, 1990).

13. Ibid.; Kevin J. O'Brien and Lianjiang Li, "Selective Policy Implementation in Rural China," *Comparative Politics* 31 (1999): 172; Harry Harding, *Organizing China: The Problem of Bureaucracy, 1948–1976* (Stanford: Stanford University Press, 1981), 165–77, 277.

14. Ezra F. Vogel, *Deng Xiaoping and the Transformation of China* (Cambridge, MA: Harvard University Press, 2011), 50.

15. Susan H. Whiting, "The Cadre Evaluation System at the Grass Roots: The Paradox of Party Rule," in *Holding China Together*, eds. Barry J. Naughton and Dali L. Yang (Cambridge: Cambridge University Press, 2004), 101–15.

16. Minzner, "Riots and Coverups," 66.

17. Deng Xiaoping, "Emancipate the Mind, Seek Truth from Facts and Unite as One in Looking to the Future" (speech, Central Working Conference, December 13, 1978), http://en.people.cn/dengxp/vol2/text/b1260.html.

18. Kevin O'Brien, *Reform without Liberalization: China's National People's Congress and the Politics of Institutional Change* (New York: Cambridge University Press, 1991), 125–56.

19. Zhonghua gongheguo cunmin weiyuanhui zuzhifa (shixing) [Organic Law on Villagers Committees (experimental)], issued November 24, 1987.

20. Yang Dongping, "Chinese Higher Education during the Past Thirty Years: The Transformation of Public Policy," in *China's Education Development and Policy, 1978–2008*, ed. Zhang Xiulan (Leiden, Netherlands: Brill, 2011), 325.

21. Yuhua Wang and Carl Minzner, "The Rise of the Chinese Security State," *China Quarterly* 222 (2015): 348. Some of the material in this chapter has been adapted from this article.

22. Qiao Shi, *Qiao Shi tan minzhu yu fazhi* (Qiao Shi on Democracy and Rule of Law) (Beijing: People's University Press, 2012), 92.

23. Kevin O'Brien and Li Lianjiang, "Suing the Local State: Administrative Litigation in Rural China," *China Journal* 51 (2004): 96, table 1.

24. Material in this section is adapted from the author's earlier work, Carl Minzner, "The Turn against Legal Reform," *Journal of Democracy* 24 (2013): 66. See also Carl Minzner, "China's Turn against Law," *American Journal of Comparative Law* 59, no. 4 (Fall 2011): 935, 941–42.

25. See Kevin O'Brien and Lianjiang Li, "Accommodating 'Democracy' in a One- Party State: Introducing Village Elections in China," in *Elections and Democracy in Greater China*, eds. Larry Diamond and Ramon H. Myers (Oxford: Oxford University Press, 2001), 101–25.

26. For an excellent book-length treatment of Peng Zhen's views, see Pittman Potter, *From Leninist Discipline to Socialist Legalism: Peng Zhen on Law and Political Authority in the PRC* (Stanford: Stanford University Press, 2003).

27. O'Brien and Li, *Accommodating Democracy*, 110–11.

28. Li Fung Cho, "The Emergence of China's Watchdog Journalism," in *Investigative Journalism in China: Eight Cases in Chinese Watchdog Journalism*, eds. David Bandurski and Martin Hala (Hong Kong: Hong Kong University Press, 2010), 166–70; Ying Chan, "The Journalism Tradition," in Bandurski and Hala, *Journalism in China*, 8.

29. Joseph Fewsmith, *The Logic and Limits of Political Reform in China* (New York: Cambridge University Press, 2013), 69, 93–94. Fewsmith translates "dangnei minzhu" as "inner-party democracy."

30. For an excellent analysis of the Sun Zhigang case—the high-water mark of early 2000s legal activism—see Keith Hand, "Using Law for a Righteous Purpose: The Sun Zhigang Incident and Evolving Forms of Citizen Action in the People's Republic of China," *Columbia Journal of Transnational Law* 45 (2006): 114–95.

31. Fewsmith, *Logic and Limits of Political Reform*, 68–97; Linda Jakobsen, "Local Governance: Village and Township Direct Elections," in *Governance in China*, ed. Jude Howell (Lanham, MD: Rowman and Littlefield, 2004), 97, 108–10.

32. Ethan Leib and Baogang He, "Editor's Introduction," in *Search for Deliberative Democracy in China*, eds. Ethan Leib and Baogang He (New York: Palgrave Macmillan, 2006), 7.

33. Duncan Hewitt, "Weibo Brings Change to China," *BBC News*, August 1, 2012, http://www.bbc.com/news/magazine-18887804; Michael Wines and Sharon LaFraniere, "In Baring Facts of Train Crash, Blogs Erode China Censorship," *New York Times*, July 28, 2011, http://www.nytimes.com/2011/07/29/world/asia/29china.html.

34. Fewsmith, *Logic and Limits of Political Reform*, 106.

35. See generally Minzner, *China's Turn against Law*.

36. Decision of the Central Committee of the Chinese Communist Party on Deepening Reform of Cultural Institutions [Zhonggong zhongyang guanyu shenhua wenhua tizhi gaige tuidong shehui zhuyi wenhua da fazhan da fanrong ruogan da wentu de jueding], issued October 18, 2011, http://news.xinhuanet.com/politics/2011-10/25/c_122197737.htm.

37. Damon Yi and Amy Qin, "Appointment at Chinese Journalism School Highlights Growing Party Role," *New York Times*, August 25, 2014, http://sinosphere.blogs.nytimes.com/2014/08/25/appointment-at-chinese-journalism-school-highlights-growing-party-influence/.

38. Maria Repnikova and Kechang Fang, "Behind the Fall of China's Greatest Newspaper," *Foreign Policy*, January 29, 2015, http://foreignpolicy.com/2015/01/29/southern-weekly-china-media-censorship/.

39. Notwithstanding the "fragmented authoritarianism" of post-Mao China, scholars in the 1980s could still speak of the Party as a unified, coherent actor, intertwined with society, but removed from specific interest groups. Susan Shirk, "The Chinese Political System and the Political Strategy of Economic Reform," in *Bureaucracy, Politics, and Decision-Making*

in Post-Mao China, eds. Kenneth Lieberthal and David Lampton (Berkeley: University of California Press, 1992), 60–68.

40. Sebastian Heilmann, "Regulatory Innovation by Leninist Means: Communist Party Supervision in China's Financial Industry," *China Quarterly* 181 (2005): 1, 6.

41. Carl Walter and Fraser Howie, *Red Capitalism: The Fragile Financial Foundation of China's Extraordinary Rise* (Singapore: John Wiley and Sons, 2012), 185–214.

42. Andrew Wedeman, "The Intensification of Corruption in China," *China Quarterly* 180 (2004): 895.

43. Andrew Wedeman, *Double Paradox: Rapid Growth and Rising Corruption in China* (Ithaca, NY: Cornell University Press, 2012), 100.

44. "King Coal's Misrule," *Economist*, November 28, 2015, http://www.economist.com/news/china/ 21679263-rise-and-fall-corrupt-coal-fuelled-economy-king-coals-misrule.

45. See, e.g., David Barboza, "Billions in Hidden Riches for Family of Chinese Leader," *New York Times*, October 25, 2012, http://www.nytimes. com/2012/10/26/business/global/family-of-wen-jiabao-holds-a-hidden-fortune-in-china.html.

46. Wedeman, *Double Paradox*, 1–4.

47. Minxin Pei, *Crony Capitalism: The Dynamics of Regime Decay* (Cambridge, MA: Harvard University Press, 2016), 78–115.

48. Minxin Pei, "China's War on Corruption Could Hasten Communist Party's Decline," *Nikkei Asian Review*, May 19, 2015.

49. "Xi Warns of Party 'Cabals and Cliques,'" *Xinhua*, May 3, 2016, http:// news.xinhuanet.com/english/2016-05/03/c_135331500.htm.

50. Walter and Howie, *Red Capitalism*, 14–21.

51. "China Puts Coal Production Capacity on the Chopping Block," Bloomberg, February 5, 2016, http://www.bloomberg.com/news/articles/ 2016-02-05/china-puts-1-billion-tons-of-coal-capacity-on-chopping-block.

52. Arthur Kroeber, *China's Economy: What Everyone Needs to Know* (New York: Oxford University Press, 2016), 109–110.

53. "Why China's $1 Trillion Merger Makeover Could Fail," Bloomberg, September 7, 2016, http://www.bloomberg.com/news/articles/2016-09-07/china-s-1-trillion-makeover-of-bloated-soes-attracts-skeptics.

54. Michael Shuman, "A Steel Mill Lives Again, in a Setback for China," *New York Times*, June 9, 2016, http://www.nytimes.com/2016/06/10/ business/international/a-steel-mill-lives-again-in-a-setback-for-china. html.

55. "China's Anonymous Economic Orable Signals Shift from Debt," *Bloomberg*, May 9, 2016, http://www.bloomberg.com/news/articles/2016-05-09/china-s-anonymous-economic-oracle-signals-shift-from-debt-binge.

56. Gwynn Guilford, "China Has Collected $1.3 Billions from One-Child Policy Violators So Far This Week, *Quartz*, December 4, 2013, http://

qz.com/154079/china-has-collected-3-1-billion-from-one-child-policy-violators-so-far-this-year/; Mei Fong, *One Child: The Story of China's Most Radical Experiment* (New York: Houghton Mifflin Harcourt, 2016), 75, 78.

57.   Stanley Lubman, "After the One-Child Policy: What Happens to China's Family-Planning Bureaucracy?," *Wall Street Journal*, November 12, 2015, http://blogs.wsj.com/chinarealtime/2015/11/12/after-the-one-child-policy-what-happens-to-chinas-family-planning-bureaucracy/.

58.   Mei Fong, *One Child*; Laurie Burkitt, "In Rural China, One-Child Policy Enforcers Push a New Message," *Wall Street Journal*, May 12, 2016, http://www.wsj.com/articles/in-rural-china-one-child-policy-enforcers-push-a-new-message-1463012457.

59.   Medha Rajagopalan and Koh Gui Qing, "China Ends 1-Child Birth Policy, but It May Be Too Little, Too Late," *Scientific American*, October 30, 2015, http://www.scientificamerican.com/article/china-ends-1-child-birth-policy-but-it-may-be-too-little-too-late/.

60.   Notably, China entered into its demographic transition to an aging society at a much earlier stage of economic growth than other developing countries. Feng Wang, "The Future of a Demographic Overachiever: Long-Term Implications of the Demographic Transition in China," *Population and Development Review* 37 (2011): 173–90, https://www.brookings.edu/wp-content/uploads/2016/06/03_demographics_china_wang.pdf; Wenmeng Feng, "The Silver and White Economy: The Chinese Demographic Challenge," in *Fostering Resilient Economies: Demographic Transition in Local Labour Markets* (OECD Local Economic and Employment Development, forthcoming), https://www.oecd.org/employment/leed/OECD-China-report-Final.pdf. As a result, unlike other East Asian countries such as Japan and South Korea, it will grow old well before it grows rich.

61.   United Nations Economic and Social Commission for Asia and the Pacific (ESCAP), "In China, the Proportion of Elderly within the National Population Will Triple by 2050," accessed October 30, 2016, http://www.unescap.org/ageing-asia/did-you-know/366/china-proportion-elderly-within-national-population-will-triple-2050; Feng Wang, "Racing towards the Precipice," *Brookings Institution*, June 1, 2012, http://www.brookings.edu/research/articles/2012/06/china-demographics-wang.

62.   Wang Feng, Yong Cai, and Baochang Gu, "Population, Policy, and Politics: How Will History Judge China's One-Child Policy?," *Population and Development Review* 38 (2010): 126. Alternative policies, such as the non-coercive population control mechanisms that China had already implemented in the 1970s or a two-child policy with spacing between births, "would not only have achieved China's population control goal, but would also have produced more favorable social and demographic conditions." Ibid., 123.

63. Elizabeth Economy, *The River Runs Black: The Environmental Challenge to China's Future* (Ithaca, NY: Cornell University Press, 2004), 96, 101–2.

64. Alex Wang, "The Search for Sustainable Legitimacy: Environmental Law and Bureaucracy in China," *Harvard Environmental Law Review* 37 (2013): 365, 387–90.

65. Ibid., 390–92.

66. Ibid., 399–409.

67. Li Jing, "80 Per Cent of Groundwater in China's Major River Basins Is Unsafe for Humans, Study Reveals," *South China Morning Post*, April 11, 2016, http://www.scmp.com/news/china/policies-politics/article/1935314/80-cent-groundwater-chinas-major-river-basins-unsafe; Shan Juan, "Asthma on the Rise over Past Decade," *China Daily*, January 7, 2015, http://www.chinadaily.com.cn/china/2015-01/07/content_19255667.htm.

68. Alex Wang, "Chinese State Capitalism and the Environment," in *Regulating the Visible Hand? The Institutional Implications of Chinese State Capitalism*, eds. Bengamin L. Liebman and Curtis J. Milhaupt (New York: Oxford University Press, 2015), 251–82.

69. Lingling Wei, "China Presses Economists to Brighten Their Outlooks," *Wall Street Journal*, May 3, 2016, http://www.wsj.com/articles/china-presses-economists-to-brighten-their-outlooks-1462292316.

70. Some material in this chapter is adapted from the author's earlier work, Carl Minzner, *China's Turn against Law*, 974–75.

71. Some material in this chapter is adapted from the author's earlier work, Carl Minzner, "Xinfang: An Alternative to Formal Chinese Legal Institutions," *Stanford Journal of International Law* 42 (2006): 103, 148–51.

72. Indeed, the provincial work team's conclusions could be applied to a wide array of governance failures in China, both at the local and national levels.

73. Xi Chen, *Social Protest and Contentious Authoritarianism in China* (New York: Cambridge University Press, 2011), 27; Murray Scot Tanner, "China Rethinks Unrest," *Washington Quarterly* 27, no. 3 (Summer 2004): 137–56.

74. Tom Orlik, "Unrest Grows as Economy Booms," *Wall Street Journal*, September 26, 2011, http://www.wsj.com/articles/SB10001424053111903703604576587070600504108.

75. Didi Kristen Tatlow, "Chinese Man's Death in Custody Prompts Suspicion of Police Brutality," *New York Times*, May 12, 2016, http://www.nytimes.com/2016/05/13/world/asia/china-lei-yang-police-death.html.

76. "Gastric Contents in Respiratory Tract Make Lei Die of Suffocation, Autopsy Confirms," *People's Daily Online*, June 30, 2016, http://en.people.cn/n3/2016/0630/c98649-9079920.html.

77. Echo Huang and Josh Horwitz, "The Death of a Young Man in Police Custody Is Rattling the Trust of China's Middle Class," *Quartz*, January 3, 2017, https://qz.com/876828/

the-death-of-a-young-man-in-police-custody-is-rattling-the-trust-of-chinas-middle-class/; Zhang Shuai, "Beijing Police Officers Punished over Man's Death," *China Radio International English*, December 29, 2016, http://english.cri.cn/12394/2016/12/29/3821s948487.htm.

78. Brian Fung, "Wukan Revisited: No, China's Village Experiment in Democracy Isn't Over," *Atlantic*, September 23, 2012, http://www.theatlantic.com/international/archive/2012/09/wukan-revisited-no-chinas-village-experiment-in-democracy-isnt-over/262734/.

79. Emily Rauhala and Xu Yangjingjing, "Wukan Symbolized Hope for Chinese Democracy: A New Crackdown May Change That," *Washington Post*, June 21, 2016, https://www.washingtonpost.com/news/worldviews/wp/2016/06/21/wukan-symbolized-hope-for-chinese-democracy-a-new-crackdown-may-change-that/.

80. Liz Carter, *Let 100 Voices Speak: How the Internet Is Transforming China and Changing Everything* (London: I. B. Tauris, 2015).

81. Minzner, *Xinfang*, 105.

82. Guangyuan Zhou, "Illusion and Reality in the Law of the Late Qing," *Modern China* 19, no. 4 (1993): 430–36.

83. Ho-fung Hung, *Protest with Chinese Characteristics: Demonstrations, Riots, and Petitions in the Mid-Qing Dynasty* (New York: Columbia University Press, 2011), 83–84.

84. Philip Huang, *Chinese Civil Justice, Past and Present* (Lanham, MD: Rowman and Littlefield, 2010), 194.

85. Andrew Jacobs and Chris Buckley, "China Targeting Rights Lawyers in a Crackdown," *New York Times*, July 22, 2015, http://www.nytimes.com/2015/07/23/world/asia/china-crackdown-human-rights-lawyers.html; Javier C. Hernandez, "Zhou Shifeng, Chinese Lawyer, Is Sentenced to 7 Years for Subversion," *New York Times*, August 4, 2016, http://www.nytimes.com/2016/08/05/world/asia/china-zhou-shifeng-sentence.html.

86. Those with money or connections (such as a relative in the local government) are more likely to have better access to legal channels. Ethan Michelson, "Climbing the Dispute Pagoda: Grievances and Appeals to the Official Justice System in Rural China," *American Sociological Review* 72 (2007): 461n3, 466.

87. Thomas F. Remington and Xiao Wen Cui, "The Impact of the 2008 Labor Contract Law on Labor Disputes in China," *Journal of East Asian Studies* 15, no. 2 (2015): 271–83; Mary Gallagher et al., "China's 2008 Labor Contract Law: Implementation and Implications for China's Workers," *Human Relations* 68, no. 2 (February 2015): 198, 205–6.

88. Aaron Halegua, *Who Will Represent China's Workers? Lawyers, Legal Aid, and the Enforcement of Labor Rights*, U.S.-China Law Institute, New York University (2016), 23, fig. 5, http://usali.org/chinasworkers/.

89. Mary E. Gallagher, *Authoritarian Legality: Law, Workers, and the State in Contemporary China* (New York: Cambridge University Press, 2017), 89,

chart 3.6 (reproduced in the original). Naturally, as such figures can only capture disputes actually filed, they necessarily exclude those in which aggrieved parties do not approach state organs.

90. Many workers go to court without a lawyer by their side. Even in relatively well-off Beijing, only 55 percent of workers involved in labor cases in 2014–2015 were represented by counsel. Halegua, *Who Will Repreent China's Workers*, 40.

91. As in many other countries, even if they get into court, China's less well-off generally find the deck stacked against them. A 2013 survey of Shanghai court opinions found "dismal" chances of success for the have-nots, such as farmers and migrant workers, while government agencies and state-owned enterprises enjoyed "enormous advantages." Success rates by the former against the latter: 0 percent. Xin He and Yang Su, "Do the 'Haves' Come Out Ahead in Shanghai Courts?" *Journal of Empirical Legal Studies* 10 (2013): 132, http://onlinelibrary.wiley.com/doi/10.1111/jels.12005/ full. Naturally, this picture can vary depending on the jurisdiction and venue. Halegua, *Who Will Represent China's Workers*, 11–18.

92. China's authoritarian controls limit the ability of workers to collectively organize to pursue legal or political remedies for poor working conditions or back pay. The one authorized labor union—the All-China Federation of Trade Unions—is a Party-dominated entity focused on preventing, rather than facilitating, worker activism. See generally Eli Friedman, *Insurgency Trap: Labor Politics in Postsocialist China* (Ithaca, NY, and London: Cornell University Press/ILR Press, 2014); Ching Kwan Lee, "Precarization or Empowerment? Reflections on Recent Labor Unrest in China," *Journal of Asian Studies* 75, no. 2 (2016): 317–33.

93. Despite official controls, a range of civil society organizations had sprung up in recent years to assist workers in challenging local labor abuses. Many of these have gone under as China's broader political atmosphere has worsened. In late 2015, Chinese authorities conducted a broad sweep of leading labor activists in China's manufacturing center of Guangdong. Mimi Lau, "State Media Accuses Detained Labour Activists of Litany of Offences," *South China Morning Post*, December 25, 2015, http://www.scmp.com/news/china/policies-politics/article/1893988/ state-media-accuses-detained-labour-activists-litany.

94. See generally Minzner, "Riots and Coverups."

95. Nectar Gan, "Chinese Taxi Drivers Attempt Mass Suicide in Beijing during Vehicle Leasing Protest," *South China Morning Post*, April 4, 2015, http://www.scmp.com/news/china/article/1756065/ suicide-bid-more-30-chinese-taxi-drivers-beijing-protest-over-vehicle.

96. Malcolm Moore, " 'Mass Suicide' Protest at Apple Manufacturer Foxconn Factory," *Telegraph*, January 11, 2012, http://www.telegraph.co.uk/ news/worldnews/asia/china/9006988/Mass-suicide-protest-at-Apple-manufacturer-Foxconn-factory.html.

97. Mary E. Gallagher and Yuhua Wang, "Users and Non-Users: Legal Experience and Its Effect on Legal Consciousness," in *Chinese Justice: Civil Dispute Resolution in China*, eds. Margaret Y. K. Woo and Mary E. Gallagher (New York: Cambridge University Press, 2011), 204.

98. Gallagher, *Authoritarian Legality*, 180.

99. Fukuyama, *Political Order and Political Decay*, 381.

100. Yu Jianrong, "Xinfang zhidu diaocha ji gaige silu" [A Survey of the Xinfang System and Thoughts on Reform], in *2005 Nian: Shehui Xing Shi Fenxi Yu Yuce* [2005 Analysis and Forecast on China's Social Development] (Beijing: Social Sciences Academic Press, 2005), 212, 214–15.

101. Tania Granigan, "Chen Guangcheng: How China Tried to Lock Down a Blind Man," *Guardian*, April 27, 2012, https://www.theguardian.com/world/2012/apr/27/chen-guangcheng-china-lockdown; Andrew Jacobs, "Taking Big Risks to See a Chinese Dissident under House Arrest," New York Times, October 28, 2011, http://www.nytimes.com/2011/10/19/world/asia/despite-violence-chinese-dissidents-emboldened-supporters-stream-to-see-him.html.

102. Yang Su and Xin He, "Street as Courtroom: State Accommodation of Labor Protest in South China," *Law & Society Review* 44 (2010): 157–174.

103. Benjamin L. Liebman, "A Populist Threat to China's Courts?," in *Chinese Justice: Civil Dispute Resolution in Contemporary China*, eds. Margaret Y. K. Woo and Mary E. Gallagher (New York: Cambridge University Press, 2011).

104. Benjamin L. Liebman, "Malpractice Mobs: Medical Dispute Resolution in China," *Columbia Law Review* 113 (2013): 181, 186.

105. Ibid., 233

106. Ibid., 181.

107. Xu's memoir provides an excellent window into how his views evolved over two decades of activism. Xu Zhiyong, *To Build a Free China: A Citizen's Journey*, translated by Joshua Rosenzweig and Yaxue Cao (Boulder, CO: Lynne Rienner Publishers, 2017).

108. Fu Hualing and Richard Cullen, "Climbing the *Weiquan* Ladder: A Radicalizing Process for Rights-Protection Lawyers," *China Quarterly* 205 (2011): 42.

109. Teng Biao, "The Attack on China's Rights Defense Lawyers and Implications for the Legal Profession" (speech, Leitner Center for International Law and Justice, New York, NY, September 15, 2015).

110. Kevin O'Brien, *Rightful Resistance in Rural China* (New York: Cambridge University Press, 2006), 135–38.

111. *Access to Justice in China: Roundtable Before the Congressional-Executive Commission on China*, 118th Cong. 32 (2004) (prepared statement of Kevin O'Brien, professor of political science, University of California, Berkeley), http://www.cecc.gov/sites/chinacommission.house.gov/files/

documents/roundtables/2004/CECC%20Roundtable%20Testimony%20-
%20Kevin%20O'Brien%20-%207.12.04.pdf. For a list of tactics employed
in one Chinese city between 1992 and 2002, see Xi Chen, *Social Protest
and Contentious Authoritarianism in China*, 170.

112. Kevin J. O'Brien and Yanhua Deng, "Repression Backfires: Tactical
Radicalization and Protest Spectacle in Rural China," *Journal of
Contemporary China* 24, no. 93 (2015): 457–70, http://papers.ssrn.com/
sol3/papers.cfm?abstract_id=2367997; Jonathan Watts, "Chinese Village
Protest Turns Into Riots of Thousands," *Guardian*, April 12, 2005, https://
www.theguardian.com/world/2005/apr/12/china.jonathanwatts.

113. Edward Wong, "China Goes Quiet on Rise of Local Security
Budgets," *New York Times*, March 6, 2014, http://sinosphere.blogs.
nytimes.com/2014/03/06/beijing-goes-quiet-on-rise-of-local-security-
budgets/. In 2014, Beijing ceased releasing relevant figures. Michael
Martina, "China Withholds Full Domestic-Security Spending
Figure," *Reuters*, March 4, 2014, http://www.reuters.com/article/
us-china-parliament-security-idUSBREA240B720140305.

114. Feng Chen and Yi Kang nailed the issue precisely in their 2016 article,
when they stated, "Party-directed institution[s] of conflict management
[do] not amount to the institutionalization of dispute resolution. In fact,
[Committees for the Comprehensive Management of Public Security]
rely heavily on ad hoc measures to operate, despite their stated working
rules and procedures. This is largely forced upon them by the nature of
disorganized contention, whose dispersal and unexpectedness require
quick, flexible and niche-targeting responses. The Party's increasing
discretionary power further encourages ad hoc-ism, which undermines
the institutionalization of conflict resolution." Feng Chen and Yi Kang,
"Disorganized Popular Contention and Local Institutional Building in
China: A Case Study in Guangdong," *Journal of Contemporary China* 25,
no. 100 (2016): 610.

115. Naturally, this is not without parallel. America's early-twenty-first-century
"war on terror" steadily led to an ever-expanding array of U.S. foreign
policy concerns—economic development, information collection,
and monitoring—to be regarded as challenges to be comprehensively
managed through a national security lens.

116. Lingling Wei, "A Rare Look inside China's Central Bank Shows
Slackening Resolve to Revamp Yuan," *Wall Street Journal*, May 23, 2016,
http://www.wsj.com/articles/china-preferring-stability-to-free-markets-
loses-resolve-to-revamp-currency-1464022378; Shanghai housing authority
tweaks property policy following protest, *Reuters*, June 13, 2017, http://
www.nasdaq.com/article/shanghai-housing-authority-tweaks-property-
policy-following-protest-20170612-00678.

117. Yanhua Deng and Kevin J. O'Brien, "Relational Repression in
China: Using Social Ties to Demobilize Protesters," *China Quarterly* 215

(2013): 533–52, http://polisci.berkeley.edu/sites/default/files/people/u3854/ CQ13.pdf. Such policies are taking a toll on many of those charged with enforcing them. Kevin J. O'Brien, "China's Disaffected Insiders," 28 *Journal of Democracy* (2017): 5-13.

118. Patrick Boehler, "Local Government Threatens Severe Punishments for Families of Tibetan Self-Immolators," *South China Morning Post*, February 14, 2014, http://www.scmp.com/news/china-insider/article/1427690/ sichuan-county-sets-down-years-long-punishments-families-tibetan.

119. Agence France-Presse, "Tibetan Monks Shy Away from Self-Immolation as Families Threatened by Chinese Police," *South China Morning Post*, December 22, 2015, http://www.scmp.com/news/china/policies-politics/ article/1893884/tibetan-monks-shy-away-self-immolation-families. The coming years will undoubtedly see such control mechanisms refined yet further. For example, Beijing is currently engaged in an ambitious effort to build a nationwide "social credit" monitoring system by 2020 that ties together government and corporate databases - criminal records, credit histories, videogame habits, social media histories – to rank the trustworthiness of each citizen. One one hand, this would be a useful tool to curb bad loans to deadbeats. But it could also be deployed to cleanly and silently apply pressure on dissident voices – limiting the investigative journalist who has published one-to-many problematic stories from accessing online ride-sharing services, or blocking a given activist from renting an apartment (or using online payment services) anywhere other than his designated city of residence.

120. For a comprehensive discussion of CCP regime strategies aimed at maintaining popular support, see Bruce Dickson, *The Dictator's Dilemma* (New York: Oxford University Press, 2016). See pp 117–120 for a specific discussion of NIMBY protests.

121. Jason Todd, "China's Rigid Stability—Yu Jianrong 于建嵘 Analyses a Predicament," *China Story*, January 27, 2013, https://www.thechinastory.org/2013/01/ chinas-rigid-stability-an-analysis-of-a-predicament-by-yu-jianrong.

122. Material in this section is adapted from two earlier works of the author. First, an essay originally published as "Legal Reform in the Xi Jinping Era," in the roundtable "The Future of 'Rule According to Law' in China," *Asia Policy* 20 (2015): 4–9. *Asia Policy* is a journal published by The National Bureau of Asian Research (NBR). Reprinted with the permission of the publisher. Second, an essay originally published as "Is China's Authoritarianism Decaying into Personalised Rule," in the *East Asian Forum*, 24 April 2016, http://www.eastasiaforum.org/2016/04/24/ is-chinas-authoritarianism-decaying-into-personalised-rule/.

123. Teng Biao, "China's Irrepressible Lawyers," *Washington Post*, July 19, 2015, https://www.washingtonpost.com/opinions/chinas-irrepressible-lawyers/ 2015/07/19/81d0a04e-2a7b-11e5-a250-42bd812efc09_story.html.

124. See, e.g., Paul Gewirtz, "What China Means by 'Rule of Law,'"
     New York Times, October 19, 2014, http://www.nytimes.com/2014/10/20/
     opinion/what-china-means-by-rule-of-law.html; Fu Hualing, "China's
     Striking Anti-Corruption Adventure: A Political Journey towards the
     Rule of Law," in *The Beijing Consensus? How China Has Changed the
     Western Ideas of Law and Economic Development*, ed. Weitseng Chen
     (New York: Cambridge University Press, 2017).
125. Stein Ringen, *The Perfect Dictatorship: China in the 21st Century* (Hong
     Kong: Hong Kong University Press, 2016), viii; David Shambaugh,
     China's Future (Cambridge, UK: Polity, 2016), 2.
126. Zheng Yongnian, "How to Square Xi's 'Rule of Law' Campaign with
     China's Crackdown on Lawyers," *Huffington Post*, February 16, 2016,
     http://www.huffingtonpost.com/zheng-yongnian/rule-of-law-china-
     crackdown-lawyers_b_9238644.html.
127. "Zhongyang dangxiao zuzhi bianxie 'Xiang dang zhongyang kan qi'
     chuban" ["Look to the Party Center," organized and edited by the
     Central Party School, is Published], *Xinhua*, May 24, 2016, http://news.
     xinhuanet.com/book/2016-05/24/c_129011949.htm.
128. Zhongong zhongyang bangong ting, guowuyuan yinfa "Guanyutuixing
     lvshi guwen zhidu he gongzhi lvshi gongsi lvshi zhidu de yijian" [Offices
     of the Central Party Committee and State Council Publish "Opinion
     on Promoting Systems of Legal Counsel, Professional Lawyers, and
     Corporate Lawyers in Public Companies"], *Xinhua*, June 16, 2016, http://
     www.gov.cn/zhengce/2016-06/16/content_5082884.htm.
129. Imperial rulers enacted extensive criminal codes, for example, but
     exempted their own officials from their full sweep. Klaus Mühlhahn,
     Criminal Justice in China: A History (Cambridge, MA: Harvard University
     Press, 2009), 47.
130. Minzner, *China's Turn against Law*, 935.
131. Indeed, as China's government bureaus drop out of official U.S.-China
     rule-of-law dialogues amid a rapidly chilling atmosphere, the Supreme
     People's Court is increasingly serving as the lead counterpart in state-to-
     state discussions.
132. Mimi Lau, "Hundreds of Chinese Judges Quitting over Low Pay and
     'Bureaucratic Intervention,'" *South China Morning Post*, May 21, 2015,
     http://www.scmp.com/news/china/policies-politics/article/1814291/
     chinese-judges-quitting-due-low-pay-and-bureaucratic.
133. Samuel Huntington, *Political Order in Changing Society* (New Haven,
     CT: Yale University Press, 1968), 12.
134. *Economist*, "To Rule China, Xi Jinping Relies on a Shadowy Web of
     Committees," June 10, 2017, http://www.economist.com/news/china/
     21723127-it-system-he-exploits-deftly-rule-china-xi-jinping-relies-
     shadowy-web-committees.

135. Of course, the Party political-legal apparatus has continued to have its own head, Meng Jianzhu, who is but an ordinary Politburo member—unlike Zhou Yongkang, who was a standing committee member. (See Chart 3.4) Some have interpreted this as a move to "downgrade" or marginalize the security apparatus. But this overlooks the extent to which—contrary to prior practice—the general Party Secretary Xi Jinping has emerged as the sole Standing Committee member supervising Meng. What this actually reflects is an unusual concentration of power in the hands of China's top leader. Yuhua Wang and Carl Minzner, "The Rise of the Chinese Security State," *China Quarterly* 222 (2015): 355.

136. David Lampton, "Xi Jinping and the National Security Commission: Policy Coordination and Political Power," *Journal of Contemporary China* 24 (2015): 769, 776.

137. Li Ling, "The Rise of the Discipline and Inspection Commission, 1927–2012: Anticorruption Investigation and Decision-Making in the Chinese Communist Party," *Modern China* 42, no. 5 (2016): 447–82; Wedemen, *Double Paradox*, 80–109.

138. Chun Han Wong, "China's Xi Jinping Puts Loyalty to the Test at Congress," *Wall Street Journal*, March 1, 2016, http://www.wsj.com/articles/chinas-xi-jinping-puts-loyalty-to-the-test-at-congress-1456853257.

139. Ouyang Haoya, "Bu zuowei beihou bufa 'lan' zuosui" [Underneath the failure to act, there is no lack of "sloth"], *China Discipline and Supervision Daily*, June 15, 2015, http://fanfu.people.com.cn/n/2015/0615/c64371-27156099.html.

140. "Head of the Central Disciplinary Inspection Team Stationed in the Ministry of Education: Increase Supervision of Inappropriate Speech by College Professors" [Zhong jiwei zhu jiaoyu bu jijian zuzhang: jiaqiang jiandu gaoxiao jiaoshou bu dang yanlun], *People's Daily*, January 20, 2016, http://politics.people.com.cn/n1/2016/0120/c1001-28070616.html.

141. "China Starts New Inspections over State Organs, Firms," *Xinhua*, July 2, 2015, http://news.xinhuanet.com/english/2015-07/02/c_134376956.htm.

142. "Xi Jinping weihe fanfu qiangdiao guiju yishi" [Why Xi Jinping Repeatedly Emphasizes the Need to Strengthen Rules Consciousness], *Xinhua*, March 2, 2016, http://news.xinhuanet.com/politics/2016-03/02/c_1118150779.htm.

143. Willy Lam, "President Xi Lays Down His Own 'Political Rules,'" *China Brief* 15, no. 16 (2015): 4–7, https://jamestown.org/program/president-xi-lays-down-his-own-political-rules/.

144. Kevin Yao and Ben Blanchard, "Fearing Graft Probes, Chinese Officials Shun Spotlight, Seek Retirement," *Reuters*, July 8, 2014, http://www.reuters.com/article/us-china-corruption-idUSKBN0FD2GV20140708; "Former Shenzhen Deputy Mayor Falls to Death, 54 Cadres Have Experienced Unnatural Deaths," Shenzhen fu shizhang Chen Yingchun

zhuilou shenwang, 54 ming guanyuan fei zhangchang siwang, March 23, 2016, http://news.cngold.com.cn/20160323d1903n66167864.html

145. Willy Lam, "Will 'Core of the Leadership' Xi Jinping Rule for 15 Years or More?" *China Brief* 16, no. 5 (2016): 5, https://jamestown.org/program/will-core-of-the-leadership-xi-jinping-rule-for-15-years-or-more; Alice Miller, "Projecting the Next Politburo Standing Committee," *China Leadership Monitor* 49 (Winter 2016): 1–17, http://www.hoover.org/sites/default/files/research/docs/clm49am.pdf; Zhengxu Wang and Anastas Vangeli, "The Rules and Norms of Leadership Succession in China: From Deng Xiaoping to Xi Jinping and Beyond," *China Journal* 76, no. 1 (2016): 24–40, http://www.journals.uchicago.edu/doi/full/10.1086/686141.

146. "The Ideal Chinese Husband: Xi Dada and the Cult of Personality Growing around China's President," *South China Morning Post*, February 29, 2016, http://www.scmp.com/news/china/policies-politics/article/1918443/ideal-chinese-husband-xi-dada-and-cult-personality.

147. Minxin Pei, "China's Rule of Fear," *Project Syndicate*, February 8, 2015, https://www.project-syndicate.org/commentary/china-fear-bureaucratic-paralysis-by-minxin-pei-2016-02.

148. Max Weber, "The Pure Type of Legitimate Authority," in *Max Weber on Charisma and Institution Building*, ed. S. N. Eisenstadt (Chicago: Chicago University Press, 1968), 46–47, 51–52.

149. Hannah Beech, "China's Chairman Builds a Cult of Personality," *Time*, March 31, 2016, http://time.com/4277504/chinas-chairman/.

150. Emily Fang, "China Blocks Economist and Time Websites, Apparently over Xi Jinping Articles," *New York Times*, April 8, 2016, http://www.nytimes.com/2016/04/09/world/asia/china-blocks-economist-time.html.

151. As of this writing (2017), Hong Kong still remains the only part of the People's Republic of China where public commemoration of the 1989 Tiananmen massacre not only takes place every summer, but draws tens of thousands of participants.

152. Austin Ramzy, "Firebombs Thrown at Jimmy Lai's Home and Company in Hong Kong," *New York Times*, January 12, 2015, http://sinosphere.blogs.nytimes.com/2015/01/12/firebombs-thrown-at-jimmy-lais-home-and-company-in-hong-kong/; Te-Ping Chen, "Former Hong Kong Paper Editor Stabbed," *Wall Street Journal*, February 26, 2014, http://blogs.wsj.com/chinarealtime/2014/02/26/former-hong-kong-paper-editor-stabbed/; Freedom House, *Freedom in the World Report: Hong Kong 2016*, accessed October 30, 2016, https://freedomhouse.org/report/freedom-world/2016/hong-kong.

153. "Hong Kong Arrests after Protests against Mainland Tourists," *BBC News*, March 2, 2015, http://www.bbc.com/news/world-asia-china-31689188.

154. Shirley Zhao, Tony Cheung, and Gary Cheung, "Five Things to Know about Arthur Li's Appointment as HKU Council Chairman," *South China Morning Post*, December 31, 2015, http://www.scmp.com/news/

hong-kong/politics/article/1896777/five-things-know-about-arthur-lis-appointment-hku-council; Suzanne Sataline, "Hong Kong Academic Freedom under Fire," *Boston Globe*, August 14, 2015, https://www.bostonglobe.com/ideas/2015/08/13/hong-kong-academic-freedom-under-fire/hJ6upYtbMalJgE9EzoMmWI/story.html.

155. Carole Petersen and Alvin Cheung, "Academic Freedom and Critical Speech in Hong Kong: China's Response to Occupy Central and the Future of 'One Country, Two Systems,'" *North Carolina Journal of International Law* 42 (2017): 665.

156. Kris Cheng, "Internal Rules Restricted Corruption Investigation Involving Chief Exec., Lawmaker Claims," *Hong Kong Free Press*, July 13, 2016, https://www.hongkongfp.com/2016/07/13/internal-rules-restricted-corruption-investigation-involving-chief-exec-lawmaker-claims.

157. "Hong Kong's Short Squeeze," *Wall Street Journal*, May 5, 2016, http://www.wsj.com/articles/hong-kongs-short-squeeze-1462488294. Some also detected suggestions that such political sensitivities were spreading more broadly, pointing to the 2016 decision by securities regulators to impose a $1.4 million U.S. fine on a credit-rating agency that had "red-flagged" risks in mainland Chinese companies listed in Hong Kong. Eduard Gismatullin, "Moody's Fined $1.4 Million as Hong Kong Tribunal Sides with SFC," *Bloomberg*, March 31, 2016, http://www.bloomberg.com/news/articles/2016-03-31/hong-kong-s-sfc-sees-first-credit-ratings-win-in-moody-s-case.

158. Emily Rauhala, "Hong Kong Bookseller's Televised 'Confession' Was Absurd and Incoherent—And That's the Point," *Washington Post*, January 18, 2016, https://www.washingtonpost.com/news/worldviews/wp/2016/01/18/hong-kong-booksellers-televised-confession-was-absurd-and-incoherent-and-thats-the-point/; Pila Siu and Tony Cheung, "Outrage Expressed in Hong Kong over Missing Bookseller, but No Answers Forthcoming," *South China Morning Post*, June 17, 2016, http://www.scmp.com/news/hong-kong/law-crime/article/1977002/outrage-expressed-hong-kong-over-missing-bookseller-no.

159. Ng Kang-chung and Owen Fung, "Hong Kong National Party Is Born: Will Push for Independence, Will Not Recognise the Basic Law," *South China Morning Post*, March 28, 2016, http://www.scmp.com/news/hong-kong/politics/article/1931384/hong-kong-national-party-born-will-push-independence-will.

160. As Chan noted, "We will soon launch a series of actions to subvert the elections which will largely undermine the legitimacy of the polls." Jeffie Lam, "Banned Hong Kong Independence Candidate Vows to 'Subvert' Elections," *South China Morning Post*, July 31, 2016, http://www.scmp.com/news/hong-kong/politics/article/1997341/banned-hong-kong-independence-candidate-vows-subvert.

Chapter 4

1. "Religious Composition by Country, in Numbers," Pew Research Center, Religion and Life Survey, December 18, 2012, http://www.pewforum.org/2012/12/18/table-religious-composition-by-country-in-numbers/.

2. Evan Osnos, *Age of Ambition* (New York: Farrar, Straus and Giroux, 2014); Ian Johnson, *The Souls of China: The Return of Religion after Mao* (New York: Pantheon, 2017).

3. David Aikman, *Jesus in Beijing* (Washington, DC: Regnery, 2003), 193–204; Back to Jerusalem, accessed June 12, 2017, https://backtojerusalem.com/home/about/.

4. David Palmer, *Qigong Fever: Body, Science, and Utopia in China* (New York: Columbia University Press, 2007).

5. Xiyun Yang, "China's Censors Rein in 'Vulgar' Reality TV Show," *New York Times*, July 18, 2010, http://www.nytimes.com/2010/07/19/world/asia/19chinatv.html. For a clip of the infamous segment, see http://www.shinychinese.com/i-would-rather-cry-in-a-bmw-than-smile-on-a-bicycle/.

6. Jessica Misener, "Chinese Girl, 21, Wears Dress Made of Money," *Huffington Post*, November 21, 2012, www.huffingtonpost.com/2012/11/21/chinese-girl-money-dress-banknotes_n_2171029.html

7. Chris Buckley, "Mao's Birth Commemorated in Gold and Gem-Encrusted Statue," *New York Times*, December 13, 2013, accessed August 22, 2014, http://sinosphere.blogs.nytimes.com/2013/12/13/maos-birth-commemorated-in-gold-and-gem-encrusted-statue/.

8. Words of Abdul-Baha from Diary of Mirza Ahmad Sohrab, "China Is the Country of the Future," *Star of the West* 8, no. 3 (1917): 37.

9. However, "modern scholars believe that these tales of death and destruction were exaggerated by later [Confucian] scholars . . . to vilify the Qin." Michael Schuman, *Confucius and the World He Created* (New York: Basic Books, 2015), 44. See also Mark Edward Lewis, *The Early Chinese Empires, Qin and Han* (Cambridge, MA: Belknap Press of Harvard University Press, 2007), 53–54.

10. Stanley Weinstein, *Buddhism under the T'ang* (Cambridge: Cambridge University Press, 1987), 114–36.

11. Kenneth K. S. Ch'en, *Buddhism in China: A Historical Survey* (Princeton, NJ: Princeton University Press, 1964), 389–98, 452–54.

12. Joseph W. Esherick, *Origins of the Boxer Uprising* (Berkeley: University of California Press, 1987), 68–95.

13. Vincent Goossaert and David A. Palmer, *The Religious Question in Modern China* (Chicago and London: University of Chicago Press, 2011), 152–61.

14. Central Committee of the Chinese Communist Party, "Guanyu woguo shehui zhuyi shiqi zongjiao wenti de jiben guandian he jiben zhengce"

[The Basic Viewpoint and Policies Regarding the Question of Religion during China's Socialist Period], issued March 31, 1982.

15. Even leaders in the state religious bureaucracy express this sentiment. Ye Xiaowen, former director of the State Administration of Religious Affairs, noted that in 2009 that "religion continues to concern us" as a latent threat to Party control. Robert Kuhn, *How Chinese Leaders Think* (Singapore: John Wiley and Sons, 2011), 364.

16. The red-black-gray division adopted in this chapter is set out in Fenggang Yang, *Religion in China: Survival and Revival under Communist Rule* (New York: Oxford University Press, 2012), 85–122.

17. Shun-hing Chan, "Changing Church and State Relations in Contemporary China: The Case of Mindong Diocese, Fujian Province," *The China Quarterly* 212 (2012): 982–99.

18. "Government Collaboration," Badi Foundation, accessed August 22, 2014, http://www.badi-foundation.org/en/collaboration/government-collaboration/.

19. "Zhongguo shehui kexueyuan shijie zongjiao yanjiusuo Bahayijiao yanjiu zhongxin" [Chinese Academy of Social Sciences, Institute of World Religions, Baha'i Research Center], accessed August 22, 2014, http://iwr.cass.cn/jg/200912/t20091230_1145.htm.

20. Palmer, *Qigong Fever*, 141; David Ownby, *Falun Gong and the Future of China* (New York: Oxford University Press, 2008), 58–77.

21. Benjamin Penny, *The Religion of Falun Gong* (Chicago and London: University of Chicago Press, 2012), 77–88.

22. Ownby, *Falun Gong*, 165–71.

23. James W. Tong, *Revenge of the Forbidden City: The Suppression of the Falun Gong in China, 1995–2005* (New York: Oxford University Press, 2009), 5–6.

24. Ibid., 52–129; Andrew Jacobs, "China Still Presses Crusade against Falun Gong," *New York Times*, April 27, 2009, http://www.nytimes.com/2009/04/28/world/asia/28china.html?_r=0.

25. Dan Zak, "A World away from China, Geng He Seeks Justice for Her Dissident Husband," *Washington Post*, February 16, 2012, accessed August 22, 2014, http://www.washingtonpost.com/lifestyle/style/a-world-away-from-china-geng-he-seeks-justice-for-her-dissident-husband/2012/02/08/gIQA2EGjIR_story.html; David W. Chen, "How the Family of a Dissident Fled China," *New York Times*, May 9, 2009, accessed August 22, 2014, http://www.nytimes.com/2009/05/10/world/asia/10dissident.html.

26. Penny, *The Religion of Falun Gong*, 75. See also The Epoch Times, *Nine Commentaries on the Communist Party* (Taiwan: Yih Chyun, 2004). The title *Nine Commentaries* is an explicit reference to the Chinese Communist Party's own letter issued at the height of the 1963–1964 Sino-Soviet split, criticizing Moscow's "revisionist" ideological line.

27. Ownby's work details this evolution through 2005. Ownby, *Falun Gong*, 200–227.

28. "Our Story," Shen Yun Performing Arts, accessed August 23, 2014, http://www.shenyunperformingarts.org/our-story.

29. David Holm, *Art and Ideology in Revolutionary China* (New York: Oxford University Press, 1991).

30. Fenggang Yang and Dedong Wei, "The Balin Buddhist Temple: Thriving under Communism," in *State, Market, and Religions in Chinese Societies*, eds. Fenggang Yang and Joseph Tamney (Leiden and Boston: Brill Academic, 2005), 63–86.

31. For a comprehensive look at the activities of the Bailin temple, see their website, at http://www.bailinsi.net.

32. As with the other officially recognized beliefs, the modern state-run Daoist association was built on the foundations of religious institutions established during the Nationalist period. See the organization's website at http://www.taoist.org.cn/.

33. See The Amity Foundation, http://www.amityfoundation.org.

34. Bob Fu, *God's Double Agent* (Grand Rapids, MI: Baker Books, 2013), 171–75.

35. Karrie J. Koesel, "The Rise of a Chinese House Church: The Organizational Weapon," *The China Quarterly* 215 (2013): 572–89.

36. See David Ownby, "Chinese Millenarian Traditions: The Formative Age," *American Historical Review* 104 (1999): 1525, noting that "China fashioned a Buddhist apocalyptic, rather than the other way around."

37. Matthew Bowman, *The Mormon People* (New York: Random House, 2012), 121.

38. Ibid., 149–253. See also Thomas Alexander, *Mormonism in Transition, A History of the Latter-Day Saints 1890–1930* (Urbana: University of Illinois Press, 1986).

39. Goossaert and Palmer, *Religious Question in Modern China*, 136.

40. Ibid., 146–52.

41. Yunfeng Lu and Graeme Lang, "Impact of the State on the Evolution of a Sect," *Sociology of Religion* 67, no. 3 (2006): 259.

42. Emily Dunn, "'Cult,' Church, and the CCP: Introducing Eastern Lightning," *Modern China* 35, no. 1 (2009): 96–119.

43. Chai Huiqun, Gu Jia, Li Yifan, Quannengshen de "xintu" [A "Believer" in the Church of the Almighty God], Nanfang Zhoumo [Southern Weekend], June 5, 2014, available at http://www.infzm.com/content/101194.

44. Aikman, *Jesus in Beijing*, 90–93.

45. Jonathan D. Spence, *God's Chinese Son* (New York: W. W. Norton and Company, 1997).

46. Barbara Demick, "China Imposes Intrusive Rules on Uighurs in Xinjiang," *Los Angeles Times*, August 5, 2014, http://www.latimes.com/world/asia/la-fg-china-privacy-20140805-story.html.

47. Agence France-Presse, "Chinese City Bans Islamic Beards, Headwear, and Clothing on Buses," *Guardian*, August 6, 2014, https://www.theguardian.com/world/2014/aug/06/chinese-city-bans-islamic-beards-headwear-and-clothing-on-buses.

48. "China's Far West: A Chechnya in the Making," *Economist*, August 9, 2014, http://www.economist.com/news/leaders/21611067-iron-fist-xinjiang-fuelling-insurrection-chinas-leadership-must-switch-tactics.

49. Xinhua, Xi Jinping: Zai jinian kongzi danchen 2565 nian yantaohui de jianghua [Xi Jinping's Speech at the Discussion Seminar on the 2565 Anniversary of Confucius' Birth], September 24, 2014, available at http://news.xinhuanet.com/politics/2014-09/24/c_1112612018.htm.

50. Ian Johnson, "Church-State Conflict in China Coalesces around a Toppled Spire," *New York Times*, May 29, 2014, http://www.nytimes.com/2014/05/30/world/asia/church-state-clash-in-china-coalesces-around-a-toppled-spire.html.

51. Ian Johnson, "Decapitated Churches in China's Christian Heartland," *New York Times*, May 21, 2016, http://www.nytimes.com/2016/05/22/world/asia/china-christians-zhejiang.html; Edward Wong, "Pastor in China Who Resisted Cross Removal Gets 14 Years in Prison," *New York Times*, February 26, 2016, http://www.nytimes.com/2016/02/27/world/asia/china-zhejiang-christians-pastor-crosses.html.

52. Xinhua, Xi Jinping: Quanmian tigao xin xingshi xia zongjiao gongzuo shuiping [Xi Jinping: Comprehensively Improve the Quality of Religious Work under the New Circumstances Facing Us], April 23, 2016, available at http://news.xinhuanet.com/politics/2016-04/23/c_1118716540.htm. The central guidelines appear to have given a central stamp of approval to a policy line circulating within the State Administration of Religious Affairs (SARA) in recent years. See, for example, the comments of SARA director Wang Zuo'an, that China should construct a Christian theology guided by the Bible, respecting basic Christian beliefs, but appropriate for China's national character, fused with Chinese culture, and according with Party tenets. Xinhua,中国基督教信徒人数在2300万至4000万之间 [Chinese Christians Number between 23 and 40 Million], August 6, 2014, http://news.xinhuanet.com/yzyd/local/20140806/c_1111950471.htm.

53. Daren Byler, "Uyghur Names as Signal and Noise," *Milestones*, June 2, 2017, https://www.milestonesjournal.net/articles/2017/6/2/uyghur-names-as-signal-and-noise; Kavitha Surana, "China Tell Citizens to Inform in Parents Who 'Lure' Kids into Religion," *Foreign Policy*, October 12, 2016, http://foreignpolicy.com/2016/10/12/china-tells-citizens-to-inform-on-parents-who-lure-kids-into-religion/.

54. Chris Buckley, "Chinese Jews of Ancient Lineage Huddle Under Pressure," *New York Times*, September 24, 2016, http://www.nytimes.com/2016/09/25/world/asia/china-kaifeng-jews.html.

Chapter 5

1. Samuel Huntington, *Political Order in Changing Societies* (New Haven: Yale University Press, 1968).

2. Such a shift even shows up in Fukuyama's work, as he has attempted to grapple with the failure of many post-colonial and other societies to build stable states, much less establish liberal democracies. Francis Fukuyama, *The Origins of Political Order: From Prehuman Times to the French Revolution* (New York: Farrar, Straus and Giroux,2011), ix–xiv.

3. Randall Peerenboom, *China Modernizes* (New York: Oxford University Press, 2007), 31–33, 280.

4. Xinhua, "中共党代会报告首次提出2020年人均GDP比2000年翻两番" [For First Time, Party Plenum Communique Proposes Tripling Per-Capita GDP by 2020, Compared with 2000 Levels], *Xinhua*, October 16, 2007, accessed (October 14, 2016),, http://news.xinhuanet.com/politics/2007-10/16/content_6888218.htm.

5. Fareed Zakaria, *The Future of Freedom* (New York: W. W. Norton & Co., 2003); Francis Fukuyama, "Is There a Proper Sequence in Democratic Transitions," *Current History* (November 2011): 310. For a trenchant criticism of such sequentialist views, see Thomas Carrothers, "How Democracies Emerge: The Sequencing Fallacy," *Journal of Democracy* 18 (2007).

6. Zakaria, *The Future of Freedom*, 70.

7. Data taken from the ERS International Macroeconomic Data Set, available on the U.S. Department of Agriculture's website, at https://www.ers.usda.gov/data-products/international-macroeconomic-data-set/international-macroeconomic-data-set/#Historical.

8. Peerenboom, *China Modernizes*, 64–5.

9. Jan Teorell, "Statistical Evidence," in *Pathways to Freedom: Political and Economic Lessons from Democratic Transitions*, eds. Isobel Coleman and Terra Lawson-Remer (New York: Council on Foreign Relations, 2013), 24.

10. See, for example, Adam Przeworski and Fernando Limongi, "Modernization: Theories and Facts," *World Politics* 49, no. 2 (1997): 177–79.

11. For a general narrative of Taiwan's political transitions, see Murray A. Rubinstein, "Political Taiwanization and Pragmatic Diplomacy," in *Taiwan: A New History*, ed. Murray Rubinstein (Armonk: M. E. Sharpe, 2007), 436–81. For a gripping first-hand narrative by one of the key participants, see Lu Hsiu-lien and Ashley Esarey, *My Fight for a New Taiwan: One Woman's Journey from Prison to Power* (Seattle: University of Washington Press, 2014).

12. Shelley Rigger, *From Opposition to Power: Taiwan's Democratic Progressive Party* (Boulder, CO: Lynne Rienner Publishers, 2001): 18-19.

13. Hsin-Huang Michael Hsiao, "Social Movements in Taiwan: A Typological Analysis," in *East Asian Social Movements: Power, Protest, and*

Change in a Dynamic Region, eds. Jeffrey Broadbent and Vicky Brockman (New York: Springer, 2011), 237–40.

14. Ming Yue Kan, "Taiwan's Democratic Transition: A Critical Examination of Its [Origins]" (M.A. thesis, City University of Hong Kong, March 1999), 86, http://lbms03.cityu.edu.hk/theses/c_ftt/mphil-sa-b14923993f.pdf.

15. Bruce J. Dickson, "Taiwan's Democratization: What Lessons for China," in *Taiwan's Presidential Politics: Democratization and Cross-strait Relations in the Twenty-First Century*, ed. Muthiah Alagappa (Armonk, NY: M. E. Sharpe, 2001), 125.

16. For an outstanding look at protest dynamics in South Korea during the 1970s, see Paul Chang, *Protest Dialectics: State Repression and South Korea's Democracy Movement, 1970–79* (Stanford: Stanford University Press, 2015).

17. Two excellent sources on Korean political developments are Don Oberdorfer and Robert Carlin, *The Two Koreas: A Contemporary History* (New York: Basic Books, 2014), and *Korean Society: Civil Society, Democracy, and the State*, ed. Charles Armstrong (London: Routledge, 2002).

18. Gi-Wook Shin, Paul Y. Chang, Jung-eun Lee, and Sookyung Kim, "South Korea's Democracy Movement (1970–1993): Stanford Korea Democracy Project Report," *The Freeman Spageli Institute for International Studies*, December 2007, 6–11, accessed October 14, 2016, https://aparc.fsi.stanford.edu/sites/default/files/KDP_Report_(final)-1.pdf.

19. Norman Davies, *God's Playground: A History of Poland*, vol. 2 (New York: Oxford University Press, 2005), 413–508; Nancy L. Clark and William Worger, *South Africa: The Rise and Fall of Apartheid* (New York: Routledge, 2004); Maye Kassem, *Egyptian Politics: The Dynamics of Authoritarian Rule* (Boulder, CO: Lynne Rienner Publishers, 2004).

20. Shannon O'Neil, *Two Nations Indivisible: Mexico, the United States, and the Road Ahead* (New York: Oxford University Press, 2013), 59–89, Julia Preston and Samuel Dillon, *Opening Mexico: The Making of a Democracy* (New York: Farrar, Straus and Giroux, 2004).

21. Overview histories of the Indian experience include Barbara Metcalf and Thomas Metcalf, *A Concise History of Modern India*, 3rd ed. (New York: Cambridge University Press, 2012), and Burton Stein, *A History of India* (Malden, MA: Wiley-Blackwell, 2010). For a closer examination of twentieth-century Indian politics, see Stuart Corbridge and John Harriss, *Reinventing India* (Cambridge: Polity Press, 2000).

22. The 1919 Rowlatt Acts, for example, indefinitely extended sweeping emergency measures that entitled imperial authorities to suppress political dissent and imprison suspects without trial.

23. Metcalf and Metcalf, *A Concise History*, 201.

24. Ian Bremmer, *The J Curve* (New York: Simon and Schuster, 2006), 3–25.

25. Toyin Falola and Matthew Heaton, *A History of Nigeria* (Cambridge: Cambridge University Press, 2008): 136–80.

26. Such a conclusion is also supported by the works of others who have looked at broad cross-national economic comparisons. See Angus Maddison, *Contours of the World Economy, 1–2030 ad: Essays in Macro-Economic History* (New York: Oxford University Press, 2007) and related data at The Maddison-Project, http://www.ggdc.net/maddison/maddison-project/home.htm, 2013 version.

27. Murray Scot Tanner, "China Rethinks Unrest," *The Washington Quarterly* 27, no. 3 (2004): 138–40; Edward Cody, "China Grows More Wary over Rash of Protests," *Washington Post*, August 10, 2005, http://www.washingtonpost.com/wp-dyn/content/article/2005/08/09/AR2005080901323.html.

28. This section is directly adapted from the author's earlier article. Carl Minzner, "China at the Tipping Point? The Turn against Legal Reform," *Journal of Democracy* 24, no. 1 (2013): 65–72.

29. Richard Pipes, *Russia under the Old Regime* (New York: Charles Scribner's Sons, 1974): 295.

30. As one historian has noted, "If there is a single, repetitive theme in the history of Russia during the last decades of the old regime, it is that of the need for reform and the failure of successive governments to achieve it in the face of the Tsar's opposition." Orlando Figes, *Revolutionary Russia, 1891–1991: A History* (New York: Henry Holt & Co., 2014), 28.

Chapter 6

1. Orville Schell and John Delury, *Wealth and Power: China's Long March to the 21st Century* (New York: Random House, 2013), 384.

2. Federal News Service, "Full Text of Clinton's Speech on China Trade Bill," *New York Times*, March 9, 2000, https://partners.nytimes.com/library/world/asia/030900clinton-china-text.html.

3. See, e.g., "The Chinese people are not likely to rise up and fight for democracy any time soon. But they are looking for change, and agitating (mostly in small ways) for some of the freedoms that go with democracy. . . . [I]n the longer term [the Chinese Communist Party] will find it hard to contain these forces." "The New Class War," *Economist*, July 9, 2016, http://www.economist.com/news/special-report/21701653-chinas-middle-class-larger-richer-and-more-vocal-ever-threatens.

4. Ning Hui, David Wertime, "Is This the New Face of China's Silent Majority," *Foreign Policy*, October 22, 2014, http://foreignpolicy.com/2014/10/22/is-this-the-new-face-of-chinas-silent-majority/.

5. David Shambaugh, *China's Future* (Malden, MA: Polity Press, 2016), 1–6, 132–33, 136.

6. Ibid., 125–26.

7. Ibid., 112.
8. Ibid., 98–99, 132.
9. Ibid., 130.
10. Ibid., 4.
11. Neil Connor, "China to Curb News Reports That Promote 'Western Lifestyles'," *Telegraph*, September 1, 2016, http://www.telegraph.co.uk/news/2016/09/01/china-to-curb-news-that-promotes-western-lifestyles/.
12. Naturally, this also has the advantage of eliding the inevitable analytical and normative morass of Hitler/Stalin analogies that inevitably arise whenever the "totalitarian" label is thrown around.
13. Scholars have flagged China's rapidly aging population as likely to lead to rising domestic tensions over social benefits, even as it reduces its propensity for military adventurism abroad. Mark Haas, "A Geriatric Peace? The Future of U.S. Power in a World of Aging Populations," *International Security* 32, no. 1 (Summer 2007): 123–4, 131.
14. Stein Ringen, *The Perfect Dictatorship: China in the 21st Century* (Hong Kong: Hong Kong University Press, 2016), 178.
15. Jessica Chen Weiss, *Powerful Patriots: National Protest in China's Foreign Relations* (New York: Oxford University Press, 2014), 247–48.
16. See, e.g., Samuel Huntington, "Political Development and Political Decay," *World Politics* 17, no. 3 (1965): 386; Stathis N. Kalyvas, "The Decay and Breakdown of Communist One-Party Systems," *Annual Review of Political Science* 2 (1999), 323; Ellen Lust, "Institutes and Governance," in *The Middle East*, ed. Ellen Lust (Thousand Oaks, CA: Congressional Quarterly Press, 2017), 186. Naturally, specific paths differ. The arteries of once-revolutionary parties can harden as they become bureaucratic and staid (such as the USSR in the 1970s and 1980s). Or they can sink into progressively corrupt, personalized dictatorships (as with Arab regimes in Libya and Egypt). Or they can experience an internal seizure of power by a ruthless leader, who purges rivals and hollows out existing political institutions in a quest to expand his own influence (as with the USSR under Stalin).
17. Think, for example, of one version of Parkinson's law—the tendency of any bureaucracy toward expansion, creating additional work for itself (additional meetings, more administrators)—in a self-replicating cycle. This is familiar to anyone who works in a large institution (say, hypothetically, an American law school). But it also finds resonance in the historic growth of the Chinese bureaucracy, with the regularly increasing numbers of officials per capita. Yuen Yuen Ang, "Counting Cadres: A Comparative View of the Size of China's Public Employment," *China Quarterly* 211 (2012): 676, 690–94.
18. During the mid-nineteenth century, such intervention in Shanghai took the form of loosely organized foreign mercenaries (the Ever-Victorious

Army) operating under the authority of the Qing to suppress Taiping rebel forces. In the early twentieth century: extraterritorial concession zones run and administered by foreigners, with their own tax and police forces. What might their hypothetical twenty-first-century versions look like? A ponderously named multinational peacekeeping force stationed on the Bund? Or might international military contractors such as Blackwater, which sold their services to U.S. authorities in Iraq and Chinese state-owned firms in Africa (and whose former head is currently opening facilities in Xinjiang and Yunnan) be retained by domestic Chinese companies or foreign multinational firms to provide security in Shanghai?

19. Ian Black, "Report on Syria Conflict Finds 11.5% of Population Killed or Injured," *Guardian*, February 10, 2016, https://www.theguardian.com/world/2016/feb/11/report-on-syria-conflict-finds-115-of-population-killed-or-injured.

20. These are intended only as rough ballpark figures. Fairbank and Goldman place the population of the last Ming at 160 million. John Fairbank and Merle Goldman, *China: A New History* (Cambridge, MA: Belknap Press, 2006). Comparable figures for the late Qing are roughly 400 million. Death tolls vary dramatically depending on what is included for the period in question. Perhaps some 15–20 million Chinese perished during the Sino-Japanese war, 5–6 million in the civil war between Nationalists and Communists, and 3 million in the 1928–1930 famine. Note that even these could *underestimate* the overall impact of previous dynastic transitions. For example, historian Jonathan Spence estimates that between 1573 and 1685, China's population dropped by a third, from 150 to 100 million. Jonathan Spence, *Search for Modern China* (New York: W. W. Norton & Co., 1999), 79.

21. For the Qing, China's population at large (particularly the Han ethnic majority) was just as much a potential threat to their control as any foreign adversary. China's population at large (i.e., the Han ethnic majority) was not only a target to be mobilized in service of regime interests (for example, by co-opting Han intellectuals into government service via the examination system), but also a potential internal threat to be guarded against (such as by barring Han migration into both Xinjiang and their own heartland of Manchuria).

22. Jens Kastner, "KMT's Assets Come under Fresh Scrutiny," *Nikkei Asia Review*, January 26, 2016, http://asia.nikkei.com/Politics-Economy/Policy-Politics/KMT-s-assets-come-under-fresh-scrutiny.

23. Didi Kirsten Tatlow, "Hoping to Work in China? If You're a Class C Foreigner, It May Be Tough," *New York Times*, September 21, 2016, http://www.nytimes.com/2016/09/22/world/asia/china-work-permit-visa.html.

24. Associated Press, "Beware of 'Dangerous Love' with Foreign Spies, China Tells Its Women," *Guardian*, April 19, 2016, https://www.theguardian.com/world/2016/apr/20/beware-of-dangerous-love-with-foreign-spies-china-tells-its-women.

25. These are far from hypothetical questions. Beijing is currently aggressively pushing to penetrate and control Chinese-language media overseas. In both Australia and Canada, it has deployed the advertising budgets of mainland banks and state-owned enterprises to pressure local Chinese-language newspapers to silence critical voices. Dan Levin, "Chinese-Canadians Fear China's Rising Clout iIs Muzzling Them," *New York Times*, August 27, 2016, http://www.nytimes.com/2016/08/28/world/americas/chinese-canadians-china-speech.html. And it has begun to speak up in defending the interests of ethnic Chinese in other countries. *Economist*, "Big Motherland," October 10, 2015, http://www.economist.com/news/asia/21672357-chinas-principle-non-interference-may-not-apply-when-ethnic-chinese-are-concerned-big-motherland.

26. Jeffrey Bader, "A Framework for U.S. Policy toward China," Brookings Institution, October 10, 2016, https://www.brookings.edu/research/a-framework-for-u-s-policy-toward-china-2/; Kurt Campbell, *The Pivot: The Future of American Statecraft in Asia* (New York: Twelve, 2016); Henry Kissinger, *On China* (New York: Penguin Press, 2011); Susan Shirk, *China: Fragile Superpower* (New York: Oxford University Press, 2007).

27. World Bank National Accounts Data and OECD National Accounts data files, "Trade (% of GDP)," World Bank website, http://data.worldbank.org/indicator/NE.TRD.GNFS.ZS.

28. Chris Rasmussen, "Jobs Supported by Exports 2015: An Update," Office of Trade and Economic Analysis, International Trade Administration, Department of Commerce, April 8, 2016, http://www.trade.gov/mas/ian/build/groups/public/@tg_ian/documents/webcontent/tg_ian_005500.pdf.

Conclusion

1. I am indebted to Richard C. Bush of the Brookings Institution for the Dujiangyan analogy.

2. W. E. Willmott, "Dujiangyan: Irrigation and Society in Sichuan, China," *The Australian Journal of Chinese Affairs* 22 (1989) 143–53.

3. "Mount Qingcheng and the Dujiangyan Irrigation System," UNESCO World Heritage website, http://whc.unesco.org/en/list/1001.

Epilogue

1. Up until 2017, Party leaders had followed a clear progression in how they commemorated ideological contributions of past leaders. Each received mention in the Party charter. But while Mao and Deng were referred to by name, the pet theories of Jiang Zemin and Hu Jintao were not—reflecting their less influential status. Thus: "The Communist Party of

China takes Marxism-Leninism, Mao Zedong Thought, Deng Xiaoping Theory, the important thought of Three Represents and the Scientific Outlook on Development as its guide to action…" Note also the declining level of exaltation applied to each subsequent contribution. As of 2017, one could argue that reflected that China was steadily moving away from an era dominated the thoughts of an individual leader. Not now. Adding Xi's banner phrase breaks that in a very visible manner. It refers to him by name. And it does so with explicit phrasing recalling that reserved for Mao.

2. This epilogue is partially adapted from two of the author's recent works—"The End of China's Reform Era," 13(4) *Asia Policy* 83 (2018); and remarks made at a September 2018 conference held at the Bush School of Government and Public Service at UT Austin, and subsequently published on the website of the Scowcroft Institute of International Affairs as a white paper.

3. Perhaps not coincidentally, Beijing's ongoing campaign targeting corruption and enforcing political loyalty among film celebrities claimed its most prominent target at almost exactly the same time. Fan Bingbing, China's most famous actress, emerged from a three-month long disappearance on October 2, 2018. Facing charges of $131 million in unpaid back taxes, she not only issued an abject public confession to her tens of millions of followers on social media, concluding with a striking declaration of fealty, "Without the party and the state's good policies, without the love from the people, there would have been no Fan Bingbing."

4. Released in January 2019, and reportedly developed by an arm of Alibaba, *Xuexi Qiangguo* (capable of being alternatively translated as "Study and Make the Nation Great" or "Study Xi and Make the Nation Great") rapidly soared to become the most popular smartphone app in China—not the least because authorities mandated usage for Party members and state employees, tying it to a range of career incentives.

5. For example, until recently, Party leaders have regularly held annual plenum meetings every fall. They did not do so in fall 2018. Of course, they did, unusually, hold one in spring 2018 to confirm scrapping term limits on Xi's role as state president. So this *could* just be an exercise in bureaucratic rescheduling. But watch this space. With long-held norms toppling like dominoes, this is precisely the kind of thing that should set off warning bells.

6. Based on China's current trajectory, I would tend expect this to take the form of a more virulent strand of ethno-nationalism (i.e., with parallels among what one sees taking place on the far-right political movements in the West). But as Chapter 6 suggests, I could also imagine a left-wing version of this as well—with some in Beijing seeking to return to the Party's revolutionary roots in the midst of an economic crisis, and reviving concepts that have lain dormant for decades, such as class struggle (*jieji douzheng*). Of course, those two are not mutually exclusive.

INDEX

World Trade Organization, 22, 161

Xia Junfeng, 55
Xi Jinping
anti-corruption campaigns, 28–29
Chinese Dream promotion, 59–60
and Confucianism, 138
consolidation of power, 11–12, 28–30
economic forecasts, 61
economic reform, 12
and Hard Authoritarianism, 164
loss of bureaucratic cohesion under, 102–9
Meng Jianzhu and, 227n
and one-Party system, 12
reform of state-owned enterprises, 63–64
suppression of ideological nonconformity in the arts, 140
and "traditional faiths," 6–7
and unwinding of reform, 33–34
and Zhou Xiaoping, 163
Xinfang (letters and visits) bureaus, 89
Xingwei yishu (performance art), 96

Xinjiang, 25, 137–39
Xuequfang (apartments in desirable school districts), 58
Xu Yuyuan, 57
Xu Zhiyong, 13–14, 24, 76, 96

Yang Jia, 54
Yangmei (strawberries), 126
Yangtze River, 1, 194
Yellow River, 2–3
Yifa zhiguo yigui zhidang (use law to govern the country, use internal regulations to govern the Party), 104
Yiguandao, 134–35
Yipiao fojue (priority target with veto power), 92
Yirenping, 96
Yong qian lai mai wending (buying stability with cash), 95
Yuan dynasty, 39, 171
Yu guoji jiegui (linking up with the outside world), 22
Yu Jianrong, 56, 101–2
Yulun jiandu (public opinion supervision), 75
Yu the Great, 2

Zakaria, Fareed, 146
Zasulich, Vera, 158–59
Zen (Chan) Buddhism, 127–28
Zeng Qinghong, 165

"Zhang, Mr." (Baha'i adherent), 114–17, 120, 121
Zhang Yimou, 40
Zhao Ziyang, 20, 21
Zhejiang province, 31, 97, 126, 139
Zhengnengliang (positive energy), 85
Zhengzhi guiju (political rules), 107
Zhongguo meng. See Chinese Dream
Zhongnanhai complex, 123
Zhou Enlai, 180–81
Zhou Xiaoping, 163, 164
Zhou Yongkang, 241n
and court system, 104
imprisonment on corruption charges, 11–12
public security spending, 98
purge of, 28, 106, 107, 163
quasi-independent fiefdom of, 10, 26
Xi and, 29
Zhuan Falun, 122
Zhuanke (junior college) students, 219n
Zhu Rongji, 75, 79–81, 161–64
Zhu Suli, 39, 40
Zuzhihua, zhengzhihua, jietouhua (organized, politicized, pushed towards street action), 96

Ingram Content Group UK Ltd.
Milton Keynes UK
UKHW021823040523
421146UK00019B/627